Taste *of* Home.

Make-Ahead
Comfort Foods

TASTE OF HOME BOOKS • RDA ENTHUSIAST BRANDS, LLC • MILWAUKEE, WI

Taste of Home
Make-Ahead
Comfort Foods

250+
PREP-NOW
EAT-LATER
RECIPES

©2023 RDA Enthusiast Brands, LLC.
1610 N. 2nd St., Suite 102
Milwaukee, WI 53212-3906

Visit us at tasteofhome.com for other
Taste of Home books and products.

ISBN: 978-1-62145-887-6

Chief Content Officer, Home & Garden:
Jeanne Sidner
Content Director: Mark Hagen
Associate Creative Director:
Raeann Thompson
Senior Editor: Christine Rukavena
Editor: Hazel Wheaton
Senior Art Director: Courtney Lovetere
Senior Designer: Jazmin Delgado
Deputy Editor, Copy Desk: Dulcie Shoener
Copy Editor: Sara Strauss

COVER
Photographer: Dan Roberts
Food Stylist: Josh Rink
Set Stylist: Stacey Genaw

Pictured on front cover:
All-American Turkey Potpie, p. 155

Pictured on spine:
Slow-Cooker Pizza Dip, p. 62

Pictured on back cover:
Three-Cheese Meatball Mostaccioli, p. 231
Freezer Breakfast Sandwiches, p. 32
Banana Split Icebox Cake, p. 214

Printed in China

1 3 5 7 9 10 8 6 4 2

PAGE 55

MAKE TIME FOR REAL COMFORT FOOD!

Comfort food means sumptuous and satisfying dishes. Rich flavors that come from hours of cooking. Decadent desserts and hearty favorites. With today's hectic lifestyles, who has time for all that? You do!

With **Make-Ahead Comfort Foods**, the best way to beat the clock is by cooking smarter, not racing to the finish line. A bit of advance planning lets you create the meals your family loves on your own schedule.

Inside you'll find:

- 252 fabulous recipes—each one offering scheduling flexibility so you can plan ahead.

- A special section sharing the secrets of make-ahead success—stocking your freezer, making the most of your slow cooker, basic meal prep and more.

- Full nutritional information with every recipe.

Also, throughout the book three at-a-glance icons immediately identify recipes that will fit your particular timeline:

❄ Freezer Friendly

🅟🅜 Refrigerate Overnight

🍲 Slow Cooker

Every recipe in this volume can be adapted to your schedule so you can enjoy time with your family at the table instead of spending it in the kitchen.

Casseroles and soups to fill your freezer, savory stews that taste even better the next day, desserts and sweet treats that chill in the fridge until you're ready to serve them—you'll find all these and much more in the new **Make-Ahead Comfort Foods** from **Taste of Home**!

PAGE 93

CONTENTS

MORE WAYS TO CONNECT WITH US:

THE SECRETS TO MAKE-AHEAD SUCCESS

From prepping in advance and using your freezer space wisely to getting the most out of your slow cooker, here's how to keep ahead of the curve when getting meals on the table!

MAKE YOUR OWN PANCAKE MIX!

Pancakes are an amazing make-ahead option, whether you're prepping the batter the night before for Overnight Pancakes (p. 14) or freezing already-made pancakes for easy reheating (see Fluffy Banana Pancakes, p. 27). But there's still another option—*making your own homemade dry pancake mix*, which you can keep in an airtight container in the refrigerator for up to 6 months.

- **To make the mix:** *Whisk together 8 cups **all-purpose flour**, 2 cups **buttermilk blend powder**, ½ cup **sugar**, 8 tsp. **baking powder**, 4 tsp. **baking soda** and 2 tsp. **salt**.*

- **To make pancakes**: *Beat 1 large **egg**, 1 cup **water**, and 2 Tbsp. **canola oil**. Whisk in 1½ cups pancake mix. Let stand for 5 minutes. Pour batter by ⅓ cupfuls onto a lightly greased hot griddle; turn when bubbles form on top of pancakes. Cook until the second side is golden brown. Makes about 6 pancakes per batch.*

- **To make waffles:** *Separate 3 large **eggs**. Beat the egg yolks with 2 cups **water** and ¼ cup **canola oil**. Stir in 2½ cups pancake/waffle mix just until moistened. Beat the egg whites until stiff peaks form; fold into the batter. Bake in a preheated waffle iron according to the manufacturer's directions until golden brown. Makes 13 waffles per batch.*

THE VEGGIE ADVANTAGE

Cutting vegetables in advance always saves time when you're ready to cook—and unlike most fruits, they won't brown and ferment when exposed to air. So think about slicing, dicing and chopping your veggies a few days ahead of time. This makes nights when you're serving stir-fry or fajitas super efficient. Just make sure the container in which you keep your cut ingredients is airtight, especially if onions are involved. You can meal prep even further in advance by keeping cut vegetables in the freezer too.

For vegetable fajitas, *thinly slice 1 small **zucchini**, 1 medium **yellow summer squash**, ½ lb. **fresh mushrooms** and 1 small **onion**; julienne one medium **carrot**. Combine vegetables and place in an airtight container in the refrigerator. To make the fajitas, saute the vegetables with **salt** and **pepper** until crisp-tender, 5-7 minutes, then fill up **flour tortillas** and top with **shredded cheddar cheese**, **sour cream** and **salsa**.*

CASSEROLES—THE PERFECT MAKE-FIRST/BAKE-LATER DISH

A casserole is every home cook's best friend, whether you refrigerate it to bake the next day or freeze it to bake the next month. You can easily stash the leftovers for later, too, especially when you know these simple tips for how to freeze casseroles.

1 Line the baking dish with parchment

To avoid tying up your baking dishes in the freezer, line your dish with parchment before filling it. Place it in the freezer until the casserole is solid, then pop out the parchment and load it in a separate container for long-term freezing. When it's time to bake, transfer the frozen casserole back to the original dish. You could also use foil baking pans, especially if your recipe yields two casseroles (see our 2-for-1 Meals, starting on p. 250).

2 Freeze crunchy toppings separately

Toppings add texture but will get soggy in the freezer. Freeze them separately in an airtight container. Sprinkle them on after defrosting your main dish.

3 Separate into portions

If there are only one or two people in the house, or you want to save the leftovers for work/school lunches, cut a casserole into smaller portions instead of freezing it whole.

4 Thaw before baking

Before you pop your casserole into the oven, don't forget to thaw it. The safest way is to let it thaw overnight in the fridge, so make sure to plan ahead.

5 Avoid freezing dairy-heavy casseroles

Cottage cheese, sour cream or creme fraiche won't hold up in the freezer, so if your recipe contains a significant amount of these ingredients, avoid freezing. You can usually still assemble it a day or so ahead of time and keep the casserole in the refrigerator until ready to bake; store leftovers in the refrigerator in an airtight container for two to three days.

RICE: THE MAKE-AHEAD MVP

Rice is a perfect base for many different meals, so having cooked rice in the fridge is a huge timesaver. Rice does dry out when cold, but it's easy to restore to soft, fluffy goodness. One note—rice can contain a particular type of bacteria that isn't always killed during cooking. So, cool down cooked rice as quickly as possible, and store it in the refrigerator for four days at most. To freeze, let it cool completely in the fridge first and then freeze it in an airtight container (we like scooping single servings into individual containers). To use, try one of the reheating methods below. Be sure to reheat it to at least 165°F.

Microwave: Place rice in a microwave-safe container; add 1 Tbsp. broth or water per cup of rice and break up any clumps using a fork. Cover with a lid or a damp kitchen towel to trap the steam, keeping the rice moist. Cook on full power for 1-2 minutes, stirring to make sure it's heated all the way to the center.

Stovetop: Place rice in a small saucepan; add 1 Tbsp. broth or water per cup of rice. (You can also add a pat of butter for more richness.) Break up clumps using a fork; cover with a tight-fitting lid. Cook 3-5 minutes over low heat, stirring occasionally, until heated through.

Wok: To make fried rice, heat 1 Tbsp. oil in a wok or skillet over high heat. Add rice, breaking up any clumps and moving the rice around the pan so the oil coats each granule. Cook, uncovered, until rice is plump and heated through, about 3 minutes. Add your favorite ingredients to make a filling meal.

TIPS FOR SLOW-COOKING

A slow cooker simmers food at a low temperature over a long period of time. The gadget's ability to evenly cook foods unattended frees home cooks to do other things around the house, run errands or go to work for the day. Plus, slow cookers are straightforward to use and require no more setup than plugging it in. For best results:

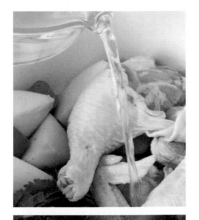

Fill your slow cooker to ⅔–¾ capacity. Overfilling the cooker can lead to spills and undercooked food. Underfilling can cause overcooking. Consult your appliance's manual for maximum volume capacity before using.

Make sure there's a bit of liquid at the base of your slow cooker. Because the lid captures steam, slow-cooker recipes need less liquid than stovetop recipes, but they do need some. Liquid at the bottom keeps the ingredients from getting too hot, sticking to the pot and burning. Good options are broth, water and even barbecue sauce.

Cut up large pieces of meat. Whether it's a whole chicken or a roast, cutting meat into pieces lessens the cook time and makes it easier to fit more ingredients into the cooker.

Don't peek! Opening the lid and checking on your food releases heat and can extend your cooking time by up to 15 minutes per peek.

SLOW-COOKER SAFETY FAQ

As with all electric cookware, there are a few safety concerns to be aware of when you're using a slow cooker.

Is the food safe? Temperature plays a big role in food safety. Dangerous bacteria spreads when perishable food is anywhere between 40° and 140°F. Slow cookers are designed to heat food up to temps between 165° and 200°F, which kills bad bacteria and results in tender, flavorful foods.

Is it safe to cook frozen food in the slow cooker? According to the FDA, it's much safer to let frozen meat thaw before you cook it. If using a prepared frozen package, follow its specific thawing instructions.

Is it safe to leave it on overnight? Slow cookers are designed for cooking over long periods of time. While you might not step away from an oven or stovetop while it's in use, it's okay to leave a slow cooker. Most modern slow cookers have an automatic shut-off after 24 hours. If you're leaving the house, make sure the appliance is set to low, placed away from walls and set on a heatproof surface. Fire departments recommend keeping appliances unplugged when not in use, so when you're done with your slow cooker, unplug it and store it.

Is my vintage slow cooker safe to use? If you're still using your sturdy old Crock-Pot from the '70s, just check and make sure the cords are in good condition. If the cord is frayed or not perfectly intact the full distance from the appliance to the plug, do not use the Crock-Pot. And if the appliance starts to emit a weird smell, definitely just get rid of it. When in doubt, we recommend treating yourself to an upgrade!

FREEZER BASICS

Start with fresh food. Any food past its prime will not improve upon freezing. Season sparingly before freezing and add more seasoning later; spices change flavor during freezer storage.

Keep things cold. Use a thermometer to ensure your freezer temperature is at or below 0°. Depending on the make of your freezer, this setting could be labeled "Cold," "Low" or an actual temperature.

Don't freeze hot food. Placing warm or hot food in the freezer brings the temperature of the freezer up almost as fast as it brings the temperature of the food down, and other foods close to it can thaw. Chill food in the fridge to at least room temperature before moving it to the freezer. To cool something quickly, place it in an ice bath while it's still in its container.

Label everything. Record the date and contents on each container, even if you can see what's inside, so

you won't have to guess how long it's been frozen. If you're freezing something before it's been cooked, include baking instructions on the label.

Wrap it up. Tightly wrap meats in heavy-duty foil or freezer paper, using freezer tape to seal if necessary. For other foods, use durable, leakproof containers. If you're using bags, be sure you have freezer bags instead of storage bags (those use a thinner plastic and aren't designed for the freezer). Press to remove all air. Lay bags flat while freezing—that way, you can stack several packages after they're frozen, saving space. If you're using food storage containers, make sure you've left enough headspace for liquid to expand as it freezes.

Make single servings. A pound of bacon or an entire batch of cookie dough can be too much to thaw at once. Pack small amounts separately, then store the smaller packages together in a larger container.

Don't overfill—or underfill—your freezer. Already-frozen food acts like ice in a cooler and helps chill other food. But an overstuffed freezer prevents the even circulation of cold air, creating warmer pockets and creating freezer burn. Ideally,

your freezer should be ⅔ full. When possible, use freezer shelves to allow air circulation.

Organize your inventory. Keep foods with a higher risk of foodborne illnesses, such as raw meats, near the back of the freezer where the temperature is more consistent and on the bottom shelf to minimize the potential for contamination. Reserve the door (the warmest place in your freezer) for alcohol, nuts, flour, juice or freezer packs.

Do monthly checkups. Take a few minutes each month to take inventory. Reshuffle items and throw out food that's been frozen too long. Regular checks let you remember what you have and how to find it quickly without a lot of open-door time.

"First in, first out," or FIFO, is a simple practice used in restaurants and other food-service industries. It means using the oldest foods in the freezer first to ensure timely usage and less waste.

HOW TO THAW FOOD SAFELY

Defrosting in the refrigerator is safe and fuss free, but it's the slowest method, so plan ahead. Small items, like a pound of ground beef, defrost overnight. Most items take one or two days. For small beef and pork roasts, allow three to five hours per pound of meat; for larger cuts, allow five to seven hours. A whole turkey will take 24 hours for every 4-5 pounds of weight.

Cold water defrosting requires less time than the refrigerator but more attention. Place food in a watertight plastic storage bag; place the bag in cold water. Change the water every 30 minutes until food is thawed.

Microwave defrosting is suitable for last-minute thawing of small items. Unwrap the food and place it in a microwave-safe dish. Cook the food immediately after defrosting.

ABOUT FREEZER BURN

We associate freezer burn with ice on the surface of food, but that's only a symptom. The ice crystals come from the food itself; if there's warmer air next to the food, moisture escapes from the food—drying it out— and freezes at the surface.

To prevent freezer burn, prevent the moisture from escaping in the first place. To do that, keep temperatures consistently cold and keep the air out.

Follow the basics (opposite page) for eliminating as much air as possible and keeping the freezer cold. If you're freezing a large quantity of food, add it to the freezer a few items at a time— filling the freezer all at once will bring up the temperature and it'll take much longer to get the temp down below the freezing point.

WHICH FOODS FREEZE WELL?

While you can freeze almost anything, some foods freeze better than others. The top food groups for freezing are:
- Fruit
- Blanched vegetables
- Raw and cooked meat
- Butter
- Cookies

FREEZER CONTAINERS— DO'S & DON'TS

Freeze foods in:
- Rigid containers or glass freezer containers
- Heavy-duty foil or freezer paper
- Vacuum-sealed packages
- Freezer bags
- Wide-mouth freezer or canning jars

Avoid freezing foods in:
- Glass jars from food products
- Margarine or cottage cheese tubs
- Milk cartons
- Food storage bags

FREEZING IN JARS

You can freeze food in Mason jars, but they require special care since glass can crack.

Pick the right jar: Choose a clean, thick-walled glass jar with straight sides. Do not use repurposed jars, such as pickle or relish jars, or jars with walls that are rounded at the top—the curves limit the space food has to expand.

Leave headspace: While some jars have a freeze line etched into them, err on the side of caution and leave at least 1 in. headspace. If you're freezing a particular food for the first time, leave 1½–2 in. to see how much it expands.

Fridge first: Don't place glass jars directly in the freezer; glass can shatter if its temperature changes too much too quickly. Place jarred food in the refrigerator overnight before transferring it to the freezer.

PAGE 38

PAGE 37

Time-Saving Breakfasts

Whether it's a hot, delicious breakfast on the go or a sumptuous spread
for a weekend brunch, make-ahead is magic for any morning meal.
Go ahead and sleep in—these recipes have you covered!

PAGE 39

PAGE 42

OVERNIGHT
PANCAKES

SLOW-COOKER BACON & SWISS BREAKFAST

When we have overnight guests, I like to prepare things ahead of time so we can enjoy the company. It often gets crazy when everyone first wakes up, and I like to have food available whenever people are ready to eat. I devised this slow-cooker breakfast recipe when I was feeding 22 people at a destination wedding!
—Donna Gribbins, Shelbyville, KY

PREP: 15 min.
COOK: 4 hours + standing
MAKES: 12 servings

- 1 pkg. (28 oz.) frozen O'Brien potatoes, thawed
- 1 lb. bacon strips, cooked and crumbled
- 2 cups shredded Swiss cheese
- 12 large eggs
- 2 cups 2% milk
- 1 tsp. seasoned salt
- 1 tsp. pepper
  Minced chives, optional

1. In a greased 4- or 5-qt. slow cooker, layer potatoes, bacon and cheese. In a large bowl, whisk eggs, milk, seasoned salt and pepper; pour over top. Cook, covered, on low 4-5 hours or until eggs are set.
2. Turn off slow cooker. Remove crock insert to a wire rack; let stand, uncovered, 30 minutes before serving. Garnish with minced chives, if desired.
1 serving: 277 cal., 16g fat (7g sat. fat), 220mg chol., 507mg sod., 13g carb. (3g sugars, 2g fiber), 18g pro.

ⓅⓂ OVERNIGHT PANCAKES

Our kids love waking up to these golden, fluffy pancakes. The batter is refrigerated overnight, making them perfect for busy mornings.
—Lisa Sammons, Cut Bank, MT

PREP: 10 min. + chilling
COOK: 10 min.
MAKES: 30 pancakes

- 1 pkg. (¼ oz.) active dry yeast
- ¼ cup warm water (110° to 115°)
- 4 cups all-purpose flour
- 1 Tbsp. baking powder
- 2 tsp. baking soda
- 2 tsp. sugar
- 1 tsp. salt
- 6 large eggs, room temperature
- 4 cups buttermilk
- ¼ cup canola oil

1. Dissolve yeast in warm water; let stand 5 minutes. Meanwhile, in another bowl, combine the next 5 ingredients. Whisk eggs, buttermilk and oil; stir into flour mixture just until moistened. Stir in yeast mixture. Cover and refrigerate 8 hours or overnight.
2. To make the pancakes, lightly grease griddle and preheat over medium heat. Pour the batter by ¼ cupfuls onto griddle; cook until bubbles on top begin to pop and bottoms are golden brown. Turn; cook until the second side is golden brown.
3 pancakes: 319 cal., 10g fat (2g sat. fat), 116mg chol., 862mg sod., 44g carb. (6g sugars, 2g fiber), 12g pro.

SLOW-COOKER BACON &
SWISS BREAKFAST

🍲 CHEESY SAUSAGE GRAVY

I appreciate the make-ahead convenience of this breakfast dish shared by a friend many years ago. I've served it to overnight guests, and they never fail to ask for the recipe.
—*P.J. Prusia, Raymore, MO*

PREP: 15 min. • **COOK:** 7 hours
MAKES: 8 servings

- 1 lb. bulk pork sausage
- ¼ cup butter, cubed
- ¼ cup all-purpose flour
- ¼ tsp. pepper
- 2½ cups whole milk
- 2 cans (10¾ oz. each) condensed cheddar cheese soup, undiluted
- 6 hard-boiled large eggs, chopped
- 1 jar (4½ oz.) sliced mushrooms, drained
  Warm biscuits

1. In a large skillet, cook and crumble sausage over medium heat until no longer pink; drain and remove sausage.
2. In same skillet, melt butter. Stir in flour and pepper until smooth. Gradually whisk in milk. Bring to a boil; cook and stir for 2 minutes or until thickened and bubbly. Stir in soup until blended. Stir in eggs, mushrooms and sausage.
3. Transfer to a 3-qt. slow cooker. Cover; cook on low for 7-8 hours. Stir; serve over biscuits.

¾ cup: 318 cal., 25g fat (11g sat. fat), 210mg chol., 761mg sod., 12g carb. (6g sugars, 1g fiber), 13g pro.

CHEESY
SAUSAGE GRAVY

CHOCOLATE-HAZELNUT ESPRESSO CINNAMON ROLLS

These jumbo cinnamon rolls will stand out at your next brunch. Bursting with chocolate, hazelnut, espresso and cinnamon, they will please any palate and bring to mind your favorite coffee shop bakery.

—Pam Ivbuls, Elkhorn, NE

PREP: 45 min. + chilling
BAKE: 25 min. • **MAKES:** 8 servings

- 2 pkg. (¼ oz. each) active dry yeast
- ½ cup warm water (110° to 115°)
- ½ cup half-and-half cream (110° to 115°)
- ½ cup 2% milk (110° to 115°)
- 2 Tbsp. sugar
- 2 Tbsp. butter, softened
- 2 Tbsp. Nutella
- 1 Tbsp. hazelnut flavoring syrup
- 1 tsp. salt
- 1 tsp. instant espresso powder
- 3¾ to 4¼ cups bread flour

FILLING
- 1 cup Nutella
- ¼ cup butter, melted
- 1 Tbsp. all-purpose flour
- 1 Tbsp. ground cinnamon
- 1 tsp. hazelnut flavoring syrup
- ½ tsp. instant espresso powder

GLAZE
- ½ cup confectioners' sugar
- 2 tsp. butter, softened
- 2 tsp. buttermilk
- 2 tsp. hazelnut flavoring syrup
  Chopped hazelnuts, optional

1. In a large bowl, dissolve the yeast in warm water. Add the cream, milk, sugar, butter, Nutella, hazelnut syrup, salt, espresso powder and 2 cups flour; beat on medium speed until smooth. Stir in enough remaining flour to form a soft dough (dough will be sticky).

2. Turn dough onto a floured surface; knead until smooth and elastic, 6-8 minutes. Place in a greased bowl, turning once to grease the top. Cover and let rise in a warm place until doubled, about 45 minutes.

3. Punch dough down. Turn onto a lightly floured surface. Roll into a 20x16-in. rectangle. Combine filling ingredients until smooth. Spread over dough to within ½ in. of edges. Roll up jelly-roll style, starting with a short side; pinch seam to seal. Cut into 8 slices. Place slices in a greased or parchment-lined 13x9-in. baking pan. Cover and refrigerate overnight.

4. Remove from refrigerator; cover and let rise in a warm place until almost doubled, about 45 minutes.

5. Preheat oven to 350°. Bake until rolls are golden brown, 25-30 minutes. Meanwhile, combine the confectioners' sugar, butter, buttermilk and hazelnut syrup until smooth. Drizzle over the warm rolls. Sprinkle with hazelnuts if desired. Serve warm.

1 roll: 616 cal., 25g fat (9g sat. fat), 35mg chol., 407mg sod., 89g carb. (37g sugars, 4g fiber), 12g pro.

CHOCOLATE-HAZELNUT ESPRESSO CINNAMON ROLLS

🅿🅼 CHOCOLATE PEANUT BUTTER OVERNIGHT OATS

Soon after I learned about overnight oats I decided to create a recipe with my favorite sugary combination: chocolate and peanut butter. It's a perfect breakfast for busy mornings.
—Anna Bentley, Swanzey, NH

TAKES: 10 min. + chilling
MAKES: 1 serving

- ½   cup old-fashioned oats
- ⅓   cup chocolate or plain almond milk
- 1   Tbsp. baking cocoa
- 1   Tbsp. creamy peanut butter, warmed
- 1   Tbsp. maple syrup
       Miniature dairy-free semisweet chocolate chips, optional

In a small container or Mason jar, combine oats, milk, cocoa, peanut butter and maple syrup. Seal; refrigerate overnight. If desired, top with additional peanut butter and miniature chocolate chips.
½ cup: 346 cal., 13g fat (2g sat. fat), 0 chol., 121mg sod., 53g carb. (21g sugars, 6g fiber), 10g pro.

BREAKFAST BISCUIT CUPS

❄ BREAKFAST BISCUIT CUPS

The first time I made these cups, my husband and his assistant coach came into the kitchen just as I was pulling the pan from the oven. They devoured the biscuits!
—Debra Carlson, Columbus Junction, IA

PREP: 30 min. • **BAKE:** 20 min.
MAKES: 8 servings

- ⅓ lb. bulk pork sausage
- 1 Tbsp. all-purpose flour
- ⅛ tsp. salt
- ½ tsp. pepper, divided
- ¾ cup plus 1 Tbsp. 2% milk, divided
- ½ cup frozen cubed hash brown potatoes, thawed
- 1 Tbsp. butter
- 2 large eggs
- ⅛ tsp. garlic salt
- 1 can (16.3 oz.) large refrigerated flaky biscuits
- ½ cup shredded Colby-Monterey Jack cheese

FREEZE & STORE
Freeze cooled biscuit cups in a freezer container, separating layers with waxed paper. To use, microwave 1 frozen biscuit cup on high until heated through, 50-60 seconds.

1. In a large skillet, cook sausage over medium heat until no longer pink, breaking into crumbles; drain. Stir in the flour, salt and ¼ tsp. pepper until blended; gradually add ¾ cup milk. Bring to a boil; cook and stir mixture until thickened, about 2 minutes. Remove from heat and set aside.

2. In another large skillet over medium heat, cook potatoes in butter until tender. Whisk together eggs, garlic salt, and remaining 1 Tbsp. milk and ¼ tsp. pepper; add to skillet. Cook and stir until almost set.

3. Press biscuits onto the bottom and up the sides of 8 ungreased muffin cups. Spoon the egg mixture, half the cheese, and the sausage into cups; sprinkle with remaining cheese.

4. Bake at 375° until golden brown, 18-22 minutes. Cool for 5 minutes before removing from pan.

1 biscuit cup: 303 cal., 18g fat (6g sat. fat), 72mg chol., 774mg sod., 26g carb. (7g sugars, 1g fiber), 9g pro.

TEST KITCHEN TIP
Shredded hash browns instead of cubed would work just fine for this recipe. A bit of maple syrup added to the sausage (or poured over the top) makes for a marvelous sweet and savory treat.

STRAWBERRY
OVERNIGHT OATS

✳ DELUXE HASH BROWN CASSEROLE

My son-in-law gave me the recipe for this casserole, which my kids say is addictive. It's also an amazing make-ahead dish.
—Amy Oswalt, Burr, NE

PREP: 10 min. • **BAKE:** 50 min.
MAKES: 12 servings

- 1½ cups sour cream onion dip
- 1 can (10¾ oz.) condensed cream of chicken soup, undiluted
- 1 envelope ranch salad dressing mix
- 1 tsp. onion powder
- 1 tsp. garlic powder
- ½ tsp. pepper
- 1 pkg. (30 oz.) frozen shredded hash brown potatoes, thawed
- 2 cups shredded cheddar cheese
- ½ cup crumbled cooked bacon

Preheat oven to 375°. In a large bowl, mix the first 6 ingredients; stir in the potatoes, cheese and bacon. Transfer to a greased 13x9-in. baking dish. Bake until golden brown, 50-60 minutes.
⅔ cup: 273 cal., 17g fat (6g sat. fat), 36mg chol., 838mg sod., 20g carb. (2g sugars, 2g fiber), 10g pro.

┌─ **FREEZE OPTION** ─────────

Cover and freeze unbaked casserole. To use, partially thaw in refrigerator overnight. Remove from refrigerator 30 minutes before baking. Preheat oven to 375°. Bake casserole as directed until top is golden brown and a thermometer inserted in the center reads 165°, increasing time to 1¼-1½ hours.

🅿 STRAWBERRY OVERNIGHT OATS

This easy gluten-free and dairy-free breakfast will be ready and waiting for you in the morning. Use more or less sugar depending on the sweetness of your strawberries.
—Jolene Martinelli, Fremont, NH

PREP: 1¼ hours + chilling
MAKES: 1 serving

- 1 cup sliced fresh strawberries
- ½ tsp. sugar
- ¾ cup old-fashioned oats
- 3 Tbsp. powdered peanut butter
- 1½ tsp. chia seeds
- 1 cup unsweetened almond milk

In a small bowl, combine the strawberries and sugar. Let stand 1 hour; mash if desired. In a pint jar, layer ¼ cup oats, 1 Tbsp. powdered peanut butter, ½ tsp. chia seeds and ⅓ cup strawberry mixture. Repeat layers twice. Pour almond milk over top; seal and refrigerate overnight.
1 serving: 352 cal., 10g fat (1g sat. fat), 0 chol., 183mg sod., 60g carb. (12g sugars, 12g fiber), 10g pro.

DELUXE HASH BROWN
CASSEROLE

OVERNIGHT FRUIT SALAD

OVERNIGHT FRUIT SALAD

I first tasted this rich fruit salad at my wedding reception many years ago. The ladies who did the cooking wouldn't share the recipe at the time, but eventually I got it. I've made it for many meals, and our daughters copied the recipe when they married.
—Eileen Duffeck, Lena, WI

PREP: 30 min. + chilling
MAKES: 16 servings

- 3 large eggs, beaten
- ¼ cup sugar
- ¼ cup white vinegar
- 2 Tbsp. butter
- 2 cups green grapes
- 2 cups miniature marshmallows
- 1 can (20 oz.) pineapple chunks, drained
- 1 can (15 oz.) mandarin oranges, drained
- 2 medium firm bananas, sliced
- 2 cups heavy whipping cream, whipped
- ½ cup chopped pecans

1. In a double boiler over medium heat, cook and stir eggs, sugar and vinegar until mixture is thickened and reaches 160°. Remove from the heat; stir in butter. Cool.
2. In a large serving bowl, combine grapes, marshmallows, pineapple, oranges and bananas; add cooled dressing and stir to coat. Refrigerate for 4 hours or overnight. Just before serving, fold in whipped cream and chopped pecans.
½ cup: 244 cal., 16g fat (8g sat. fat), 84mg chol., 44mg sod., 24g carb. (21g sugars, 1g fiber), 3g pro.

EASY BREAKFAST STRATA

EASY BREAKFAST STRATA

We start this breakfast casserole the night before so it's ready for the oven the next day. That way, we don't have to deal with the prep and dirty dishes first thing in the morning!
—Debbie Johnson, Centertown, MO

PREP: 25 min. + chilling
BAKE: 30 min. • **MAKES:** 12 servings

- 1 loaf (1 lb.) herb or cheese bakery bread, cubed
- 1 lb. bulk pork sausage
- 1 medium green pepper, chopped
- 1 medium onion, chopped
- 1 cup shredded cheddar cheese
- 6 large eggs
- 1 tsp. ground mustard
- 2 cups 2% milk

1. Place the bread cubes in a greased 13x9-in. baking dish. In a large skillet, cook and crumble sausage with pepper and onion over medium-high heat until no longer pink, 5-7 minutes. With a slotted spoon, place sausage mixture over bread. Sprinkle with cheese.
2. In a large bowl, whisk together the eggs, mustard and milk; pour egg mixture over top. Refrigerate, covered, overnight.
3. Remove strata from the refrigerator while oven heats. Bake, uncovered, at 350° until a knife inserted in center comes out clean, 30-35 minutes. Let stand 5 minutes before cutting.
1 piece: 295 cal., 16g fat (6g sat. fat), 126mg chol., 555mg sod., 23g carb. (4g sugars, 2g fiber), 14g pro.

AMISH APPLE SCRAPPLE

🍲 📱 CINNAMON BLUEBERRY FRENCH TOAST

I like to prep this breakfast in the evening, let it chill, then turn on the slow cooker when we wake up in the morning. It's done just right.
—Angela Lively, Conroe, TX

PREP: 15 min. + chilling
COOK: 3 hours • **MAKES:** 6 servings

- 3 large eggs
- 2 cups 2% milk
- ¼ cup sugar
- 1 tsp. ground cinnamon
- 1 tsp. vanilla extract
- ¼ tsp. salt
- 9 cups cubed French bread (about 9 oz.)
- 1 cup fresh or frozen blueberries, thawed
  Maple syrup

1. Whisk the first 6 ingredients. Place half the bread in a greased 5-qt. slow cooker; top with ½ cup blueberries and half the milk mixture. Repeat layers. Refrigerate, covered, 4 hours or overnight.
2. Cook, covered, on low until a knife inserted in the center comes out clean, 3-4 hours. Serve warm with syrup.
1 cup: 265 cal., 6g fat (2g sat. fat), 100mg chol., 430mg sod., 42g carb. (18g sugars, 2g fiber), 11g pro.

TEST KITCHEN TIP
Substitute whole wheat French bread for white to increase fiber. If you can't find it, cube 100% whole wheat buns.

📱 AMISH APPLE SCRAPPLE

Just the aroma of this cooking takes me back to my days growing up in Pennsylvania. The recipe was a favorite at home and at church breakfasts.
—Marion Lowery, Medford, OR

PREP: 1 hour 20 min. + chilling
COOK: 10 min. • **MAKES:** 8 servings

- ¾ lb. bulk pork sausage
- ½ cup finely chopped onion
- 4 Tbsp. butter, divided
- ½ cup diced apple, unpeeled
- ¾ tsp. dried thyme
- ½ tsp. ground sage
- ¼ tsp. pepper
- 3 cups water, divided
- ¾ cup cornmeal
- 1 tsp. salt
- 2 Tbsp. all-purpose flour
  Maple syrup

1. In a large skillet, cook sausage and onion over medium-high heat until sausage is no longer pink and onion is tender. Remove from skillet; set aside.
2. Discard all but 2 Tbsp. of the drippings. Add 2 Tbsp. butter, apple, thyme, sage and pepper to the drippings; cook over low heat until the apple is tender, about 5 minutes. Remove from heat; stir in sausage mixture. Set aside.
3. In a large heavy saucepan, bring 2 cups water to a boil. Combine cornmeal, salt and remaining 1 cup water; slowly pour into boiling water, stirring constantly. Return to a boil. Reduce heat; simmer, covered, for 1 hour, stirring occasionally. Stir in sausage mixture. Pour into a greased 8x4-in. loaf pan. Refrigerate, covered, 8 hours or overnight.
4. Slice ½ in. thick. Sprinkle flour over both sides of each slice. In a large skillet, heat remaining 2 Tbsp. butter over medium heat. Add slices; cook until both sides are browned. Serve with syrup.
1 piece: 251 cal., 18g fat (7g sat. fat), 44mg chol., 667mg sod., 16g carb. (1g sugars, 1g fiber), 7g pro.

HEARTY BREAKFAST
EGG BAKE

PM HEARTY BREAKFAST EGG BAKE

I always fix this casserole ahead of time when overnight guests are visiting. Then I simply add some toast or biscuits and fresh fruit for a complete meal that everyone loves. This dish also reheats well.
—Pamela Norris, Fenton, MO

PREP: 10 min. + chilling
BAKE: 45 min. + standing
MAKES: 8 servings

- 1½ lbs. bulk pork sausage
- 3 cups frozen shredded hash brown potatoes, thawed
- 2 cups shredded cheddar cheese
- 8 large eggs, lightly beaten
- 1 can (10¾ oz.) condensed cream of mushroom soup, undiluted
- ¾ cup evaporated milk

1. Crumble the sausage into a large skillet. Cook over medium heat until no longer pink; drain. Transfer to a greased 13x9-in. baking dish. Sprinkle with hash browns and cheese.
2. In a large bowl, whisk the remaining ingredients; pour over the top. Cover and refrigerate overnight.
3. Remove from refrigerator 30 minutes before baking; preheat oven to 350°. Bake, uncovered, for 45-50 minutes or until a knife inserted in the center comes out clean. Let stand 10 minutes before cutting.
1 piece: 427 cal., 32g fat (15g sat. fat), 281mg chol., 887mg sod., 12g carb. (4g sugars, 1g fiber), 21g pro.

**FLUFFY
BANANA PANCAKES**

FREEZE & STORE
Freeze cooled pancakes between layers of waxed paper in a freezer container. To use, place pancakes on an ungreased baking sheet, cover with foil and reheat in a preheated 375° oven for 5-10 minutes. Or place 2 pancakes on a microwave-safe plate and microwave on high until heated through, 40-50 seconds.

❄ FLUFFY BANANA PANCAKES

I love to make pancakes for my family on Saturday mornings. Since we often have ripe bananas, I decided to add them to a batch of pancake batter. The results were delicious!
—Lori Stevens, Riverton, UT

TAKES: 30 min.
MAKES: 7 servings

- 1   cup all-purpose flour
- 1   cup whole wheat flour
- 3   Tbsp. brown sugar
- 1   tsp. baking powder
- 1   tsp. baking soda
- 1   tsp. ground cinnamon
- ½   tsp. salt
- 2   large eggs, room temperature
- 2   cups buttermilk
- 2   Tbsp. canola oil
- 1   tsp. vanilla extract
- 1   ripe medium banana, finely chopped
- ⅓   cup finely chopped walnuts

1. In a large bowl, combine the first 7 ingredients. In another bowl, whisk eggs, buttermilk, oil and vanilla until blended. Add to the dry ingredients, stirring just until moistened. Fold in banana and walnuts.

2. Pour batter by ¼ cupfuls onto a hot griddle coated with cooking spray. Cook until bubbles begin to form on top and bottoms are golden brown. Turn; cook until second side is golden brown.

2 pancakes: 283 cal., 10g fat (2g sat. fat), 63mg chol., 503mg sod., 40g carb. (12g sugars, 4g fiber), 9g pro. **Diabetic exchanges:** 2½ starch, 1½ fat.

FLUFFY STRAWBERRY PANCAKES: Replace chopped banana with ¾ cup chopped strawberries (fresh); proceed as directed.

MOUNTAIN HAM SUPREME

ⓅⓂ MOUNTAIN HAM SUPREME

Little kids think it's really neat how the bread makes mountains in the pan. And it's very tasty, too.
—Keri Cotton, Eagan, MN

PREP: 20 min. + chilling
BAKE: 45 min. • **MAKES:** 12 servings

- 12   slices bread
- 1   lb. ground fully cooked ham
- 2   cups shredded cheddar cheese
- ½   cup mayonnaise
- 1   tsp. ground mustard
- 6   large eggs
- 2¼   cups 2% milk
- ¼   tsp. salt
- ¼   tsp. pepper

1. Toast bread. Mix the ham, cheese, mayonnaise and ground mustard. Spread mixture over 6 slices of bread; top with the remaining bread slices to make 6 sandwiches.
Cut sandwiches into triangles.

2. In a greased 13x9-in. baking dish, arrange the sandwich triangles cut side down, with points facing up, pressing together as needed to fit in 2 rows. Whisk eggs, milk, salt and pepper until well blended. Pour over sandwich triangles. Refrigerate, covered, overnight.

3. Remove the casserole from refrigerator 30 minutes before baking. Preheat oven to 300°. Bake, uncovered, until a knife inserted in center comes out clean, 45-50 minutes.

1 serving: 366 cal., 24g fat (9g sat. fat), 137mg chol., 903mg sod., 17g carb. (4g sugars, 1g fiber), 19g pro.

❄ HOMEMADE PORK SAUSAGE

These country-style patties are so simple to prepare. You'll never again settle for store-bought versions that are loaded with preservatives and not nearly as good.
—Bertha Bench, Mineral Wells, TX

TAKES: 20 min.
MAKES: 8 servings

- 2 lbs. ground pork
- 2 tsp. ground sage
- 1½ tsp. salt
- 1½ tsp. pepper
- ½ tsp. cayenne pepper
- ½ tsp. brown sugar

1. Combine all the ingredients; mix well. Shape mixture into eight 4-in. patties.
2. In a large skillet over medium heat, cook the patties until a thermometer reads 160°, 3-4 minutes on each side. Remove to paper towels to drain.
1 patty: 242 cal., 17g fat (6g sat. fat), 76mg chol., 502mg sod., 1g carb. (0 sugars, 0 fiber), 21g pro.

┌─ **FREEZE OPTION** ──────────┐

Place uncooked patties on a foil-lined baking sheet; freeze, covered, until firm. Transfer the patties to a freezer container; return to the freezer. To use, cook frozen patties as directed, increasing cooking time as necessary for a thermometer to read 160°.

└──────────────────────────────┘

OVERNIGHT YEAST WAFFLES

PM OVERNIGHT YEAST WAFFLES

Starting the day with an appealing, hearty breakfast is certainly a step in the right direction when you're trying to follow a healthy eating plan. These waffles are so good that I freeze them to have some handy for busy mornings.
—Mary Balcomb, Florence, OR

PREP: 15 min. + chilling
COOK: 5 min./batch
MAKES: 10 servings

- 1 pkg. (¼ oz.) active dry yeast
- ½ cup warm water
   (110° to 115°)
- 1 tsp. sugar
- 2 cups warm 2% milk
   (110° to 115°)
- ½ cup butter, melted
- 2 large eggs, room
   temperature, lightly beaten
- 2¾ cups all-purpose flour
- 1 tsp. salt
- ½ tsp. baking soda

1. In a large bowl, dissolve yeast in warm water. Add sugar; let stand for 5 minutes. Add the milk, butter and eggs; mix well. Combine flour and salt; stir into the milk mixture. Refrigerate, covered, overnight.
2. Stir batter; add baking soda and stir well. Bake waffles in a preheated waffle iron according to manufacturer's directions until golden brown.
2 waffles: 220 cal., 12g fat (7g sat. fat), 74mg chol., 366mg sod., 22g carb. (3g sugars, 1g fiber), 6g pro.

❄ BREAKFAST SAUSAGE BREAD

Any time we take this savory, satisfying bread to a potluck, it goes over very well. We never bring any home. My husband usually makes it. He prides himself on the beautiful golden loaves.
—Shirley Caldwell, Northwood, OH

PREP: 25 min. + rising
BAKE: 25 min.
MAKES: 2 loaves (16 pieces each)

- 2 loaves (1 lb. each) frozen white bread dough, thawed
- ½ lb. mild pork sausage
- ½ lb. bulk spicy pork sausage
- 1½ cups diced fresh mushrooms
- ½ cup chopped onion
- 3 large eggs, divided use
- 2½ cups shredded mozzarella cheese
- 1 tsp. dried basil
- 1 tsp. dried parsley flakes
- 1 tsp. dried rosemary, crushed
- 1 tsp. garlic powder

1. Cover dough and let rise in a warm place until doubled, about 2 hours.

2. Preheat oven to 350°. In a large skillet, cook sausage, mushrooms and onion over medium-high heat until sausage is no longer pink, breaking up the sausage into crumbles, 6-8 minutes. Drain. Transfer to a bowl; cool.

3. Stir in 2 eggs, cheese and seasonings. Roll each loaf of dough into a 16x12-in. rectangle. Spread half the sausage mixture over each rectangle to within 1 in. of edges. Roll up jelly-roll style, starting with a short side; pinch seams to seal. Place on a greased baking sheet.

4. In a small bowl, whisk the remaining egg. Brush over the tops. Bake until golden brown, 25-30 minutes. Serve warm.

1 piece: 102 cal., 6g fat (2g sat. fat), 32mg chol., 176mg sod., 8g carb. (1g sugars, 1g fiber), 5g pro.

FREEZE OPTION

Securely wrap cooled loaves in foil and then freeze. To use, place a foil-wrapped loaf on a baking sheet and reheat in a 450° oven until heated through, 10-15 minutes. Carefully remove foil; return to oven a few minutes longer until crust is crisp.

BREAKFAST SAUSAGE BREAD

ⓟⓜ SWEET ORANGE CROISSANT PUDDING

Time-crunched cooks are sure to appreciate the make-ahead convenience of this delightful dish. Feel free to replace the orange marmalade with any jam or jelly that suits your taste.
—Mary Gabriel, Las Vegas, NV

PREP: 15 min. + chilling
BAKE: 40 min. + cooling
MAKES: 8 servings

- 4 croissants, split
- 1 cup orange marmalade, divided
- 3 large eggs
- 1¼ cups whole milk
- 1 cup heavy whipping cream
- ½ cup sugar
- 1 tsp. grated orange zest, optional
- ½ tsp. almond extract

1. Spread croissant bottoms with 3 Tbsp. marmalade; replace tops. Cut each croissant into 5 slices; place in a greased 11x7-in. baking dish.
2. Whisk together the next 4 ingredients, orange zest if desired, and extract. Pour the mixture over the croissants. Refrigerate, covered, overnight.
3. Remove from refrigerator 30 minutes before baking; preheat oven to 350°. Place dish in a larger baking dish. Fill larger dish with 1 in. boiling water.
4. Bake, uncovered, until a knife inserted in center comes out clean, 40-45 minutes. Remove pan from water bath; cool on a wire rack 10 minutes. Brush remaining marmalade over top. Cut and serve warm.
1 piece: 416 cal., 20g fat (11g sat. fat), 143mg chol., 287mg sod., 55g carb. (42g sugars, 1g fiber), 7g pro.

SWEET ORANGE CROISSANT PUDDING

❄ PM MAKE-AHEAD EGGS BENEDICT TOAST CUPS

When I was growing up, we had a family tradition of having eggs Benedict with champagne and orange juice for Christmas breakfast. But now that I'm cooking, a fussy breakfast isn't my style. I wanted to come up with a dish I could make ahead, that would mimic the flavors of traditional eggs Benedict and would also freeze well. All I can say is, this one fits the bill!
—Lyndsay Wells, Ladysmith, BC

PREP: 30 min. • **BAKE:** 10 min.
MAKES: 1 dozen

6 **English muffins, split**
1 **envelope hollandaise sauce mix**
12 **slices Canadian bacon, quartered**
1 **tsp. pepper**
1 **Tbsp. olive oil**
6 **large eggs**
1 **Tbsp. butter**

1. Preheat oven to 375°. Flatten muffin halves with a rolling pin; press into greased muffin cups. Bake until lightly browned, about 10 minutes.

2. Prepare the hollandaise sauce according to package directions; cool slightly. Sprinkle bacon with pepper. In a large skillet, cook bacon in oil over medium heat until partially cooked but not crisp. Remove to paper towels to drain. Divide bacon among muffin cups. Wipe skillet clean.

3. Whisk eggs and ½ cup cooled hollandaise sauce until blended. In the same skillet, heat butter over medium heat. Pour in egg mixture; cook and stir until eggs are thickened and no liquid egg remains. Divide the egg mixture among muffin cups; top with the remaining hollandaise sauce.

4. Bake until heated through, 8-10 minutes. Serve warm.

Overnight option: Refrigerate the unbaked cups, covered, overnight. Bake until golden brown, 10-12 minutes.

1 toast cup: 199 cal., 11g fat (5g sat. fat), 114mg chol., 495mg sod., 15g carb. (2g sugars, 1g fiber), 9g pro.

FREEZE OPTION

Cover and freeze unbaked cups in the muffin tin until firm. Remove from the tin and transfer to an airtight container; return to freezer. To use, bake in muffin tin as directed, increasing time to 25-30 minutes. Cover loosely with foil if needed to prevent overbrowning.

MAKE-AHEAD EGGS
BENEDICT TOAST CUPS

❄ FREEZER BREAKFAST SANDWICHES

On a busy morning, these grab-and-go sandwiches save the day. A hearty combo of eggs, Canadian bacon and cheese will keep you fueled through lunchtime and beyond.

—Christine Rukavena, Milwaukee, WI

PREP: 25 min. • **COOK:** 15 min.
MAKES: 12 sandwiches

- 12 large eggs
- ⅔ cup 2% milk
- ½ tsp. salt
- ¼ tsp. pepper

SANDWICHES

- 12 English muffins, split
- 4 Tbsp. butter, softened
- 12 slices Colby-Monterey Jack cheese
- 12 slices Canadian bacon

1. Preheat oven to 325°. In a large bowl, whisk the eggs, milk, salt and pepper until blended. Pour into a 13x9-in. baking pan coated with cooking spray. Bake until set, 15-18 minutes. Cool on a wire rack.

2. Meanwhile, toast English muffins (or bake at 325° until lightly browned, 12-15 minutes). Spread 1 tsp. butter on each muffin bottom.

3. Cut eggs into 12 portions. Layer muffin bottoms with an egg portion, a cheese slice (tearing cheese to fit) and a Canadian bacon slice. Replace muffin tops. Wrap sandwiches in waxed paper and then in foil; freeze in a freezer container.

4. To use frozen sandwiches, remove foil. Microwave a waxed paper-wrapped sandwich at 50% power until thawed, 1-2 minutes. Turn sandwich over; microwave at 100% power until hot and a thermometer reads at least 160°, 30-60 seconds. Let stand 2 minutes before serving.

1 sandwich: 334 cal., 17g fat (9g sat. fat), 219mg chol., 759mg sod., 26g carb. (3g sugars, 2g fiber), 19g pro.

WHY YOU'LL LOVE IT...

"This is good...better than store-bought sandwiches. It's easy to make, too. You could easily substitute a different cheese and meat. This recipe is a keeper."
—MUDDYFROGWATER, TASTEOFHOME.COM

FREEZE & STORE

Wrap the individual sandwiches in waxed paper, and then in foil before freezing. The foil protects them from freezer burn; the wax paper allows for mess-free reheating and eating on the go.

FREEZER BREAKFAST SANDWICHES

PM PEANUT BUTTER BANANA OVERNIGHT OATS

Talk about wholesome and quick! You'll be satisfied right up to your next meal with these easy, creamy overnight oats.
—Taste of Home *Test Kitchen*

PREP: 10 min. + chilling
MAKES: 1 serving

- 1 Tbsp. creamy peanut butter, warmed
- 1 Tbsp. honey
- 3 Tbsp. fat-free milk
- ⅓ cup old-fashioned oats
- ¼ cup mashed ripe banana
  Optional: Sliced ripe banana and honey

In a small container, combine the peanut butter, honey, milk, oats and mashed banana until smooth. Seal; refrigerate overnight. If desired, top with banana and drizzle with honey.
1 serving: 325 cal., 10g fat (2g sat. fat), 1mg chol., 89mg sod., 54g carb. (29g sugars, 5g fiber), 9g pro.

❄ PEANUT BUTTER & BANANA WAFFLES

These are a refreshing change from everyday waffles. I make big batches so I can freeze the leftovers and reheat them later for a quick breakfast.
—Christina Addison, Blanchester, OH

PREP: 10 min. • **COOK:** 5 min./batch
MAKES: 16 waffles

- 1¾ cups all-purpose flour
- 2 Tbsp. sugar
- 3 tsp. baking powder
- ¼ tsp. salt
- ¾ cup creamy peanut butter
- ½ cup canola oil
- 2 large eggs, room temperature
- 1¾ cups 2% milk
- 1 cup mashed ripe bananas (about 2 medium)
  Maple syrup, optional

1. In a large bowl, whisk flour, sugar, baking powder and salt. Place peanut butter in another bowl; gradually whisk in oil. Whisk in eggs and milk. Add to dry ingredients; stir just until moistened. Stir in bananas.
2. In preheated waffle maker according to manufacturer's directions, bake until golden. Serve with syrup if desired.
2 waffles: 299 cal., 19g fat (3g sat. fat), 34mg chol., 266mg sod., 26g carb. (8g sugars, 2g fiber), 8g pro.

┌ FREEZE OPTION ─

Cool waffles on wire racks. Freeze between layers of waxed paper in freezer containers. Reheat in a toaster on medium setting. Or microwave each waffle on high until heated through, 30-60 seconds. If desired, serve with maple syrup.

ITALIAN SAUSAGE EGG BAKE

🅟 ITALIAN SAUSAGE EGG BAKE

This hearty entree warms up any breakfast or brunch menu with its herb-seasoned flavor.
—Darlene Markham, Rochester, NY

PREP: 20 min. + chilling
BAKE: 50 min. • **MAKES:** 12 servings

- 8 slices white bread, cubed
- 1 lb. Italian sausage links, casings removed, sliced
- 2 cups shredded sharp cheddar cheese
- 2 cups shredded part-skim mozzarella cheese
- 9 large eggs, lightly beaten
- 3 cups 2% milk
- 1 tsp. dried basil
- 1 tsp. dried oregano
- 1 tsp. fennel seed, crushed

1. Place bread cubes in a greased 13x9-in. baking dish; set aside. In a large skillet, cook sausage over medium heat until no longer pink; drain. Spoon sausage over bread; sprinkle with cheeses.
2. In a large bowl, whisk the eggs, milk and seasonings; pour over the casserole. Refrigerate, covered, overnight.
3. Remove from refrigerator 30 minutes before baking; preheat oven to 350°. Bake, uncovered, until a knife inserted in the center comes out clean, 50-55 minutes. Let stand for 5 minutes before cutting.
1 piece: 316 cal., 20g fat (10g sat. fat), 214mg chol., 546mg sod., 13g carb. (5g sugars, 1g fiber), 21g pro.

ⓟ CHRISTMAS MORNING SWEET ROLLS

These make-ahead rolls have been a holiday tradition in our house for years. The eggnog in the frosting makes them extra special on Christmas morning.
—Kimberly Williams, Brownsburg, IN

PREP: 45 min. + chilling
BAKE: 20 min. • **MAKES:** 1 dozen

- 1 pkg. (¼ oz.) active dry yeast
- 1 cup warm water (110° to 115°)
- ½ cup sugar
- 1 tsp. salt
- 4 to 4½ cups all-purpose flour
- ¼ cup canola oil
- 1 large egg, room temperature

FILLING
- ⅓ cup sugar
- 1½ tsp. ground cinnamon
- ¼ tsp. ground nutmeg
- 3 Tbsp. butter, softened

FROSTING
- 2½ cups confectioners' sugar
- 5 Tbsp. butter, softened
- ½ tsp. ground cinnamon
- ½ tsp. vanilla extract
- 2 to 3 Tbsp. eggnog

1. Dissolve yeast in warm water. In a large bowl, combine sugar, salt, 1 cup flour, oil, egg and the yeast mixture; beat on medium speed until smooth. Stir in enough remaining flour to form a soft dough (dough will be sticky).

2. Place the dough in a greased bowl, turning once to grease the top (do not knead). Refrigerate, covered, overnight.

3. For filling, in a small bowl, mix the sugar, cinnamon and nutmeg. Punch down dough; turn onto a lightly floured surface. Roll into a 18x8-in. rectangle. Spread with butter to within ½ in. of edges; sprinkle with sugar mixture. Roll up jelly-roll style, starting with a long side; pinch seam to seal. Cut into 12 slices.

4. Place slices in a greased 13x9-in. baking pan, cut side down. Cover with a kitchen towel, let rise in a warm place until doubled, about 45 minutes.

5. Bake at 350° until golden brown, 20-25 minutes. Place on a wire rack to cool slightly. Beat the confectioners' sugar, butter, cinnamon, vanilla and enough eggnog to reach the desired consistency; spread over warm rolls.

1 roll: 424 cal., 13g fat (5g sat. fat), 37mg chol., 267mg sod., 72g carb. (39g sugars, 2g fiber), 5g pro.

TEST KITCHEN TIP
Give the frosting a little holiday cheer by adding ½ tsp. rum extract. The dough can be held in the refrigerator 8 to 24 hours before assembling. You can even prepare the rolls and store them in the refrigerator overnight before baking. In the morning, let them sit at room temperature for 30 minutes before baking

CHRISTMAS MORNING
SWEET ROLLS

MAPLE BACON
FRENCH TOAST BAKE

🅟 MAPLE BACON FRENCH TOAST BAKE

Our family loves Sunday brunch. Each season I try to bring a little different flavor to the table. This French toast bake reminds us of fall. Whole or 2% milk works best, but I use regular almond milk because I can't have dairy and it works, too!
—Peggie Brott, Milford, KS

PREP: 35 min. + chilling
BAKE: 50 min. • **MAKES:** 12 servings

- 8 cups cubed bread
- 8 large eggs
- 2 cups 2% milk
- ½ cup packed brown sugar
- ⅓ cup maple syrup
- ½ tsp. ground cinnamon
- 1 lb. bacon strips, cooked and crumbled

1. Place bread in a greased 13x9-in. baking dish. In a large bowl, whisk eggs, milk, brown sugar, syrup and cinnamon. Pour over bread. Sprinkle with bacon. Refrigerate, covered, 4 hours or overnight.
2. Remove casserole from the refrigerator 30 minutes before baking; preheat oven to 350°. Bake, uncovered, until a knife inserted in center comes out clean, 50-60 minutes. Let stand 5-10 minutes before serving.
1 piece: 256 cal., 10g fat (3g sat. fat), 141mg chol., 426mg sod., 29g carb. (18g sugars, 1g fiber), 12g pro.

OVERNIGHT SAUSAGE & GRITS

🅟 OVERNIGHT SAUSAGE & GRITS

This recipe is so appealing because you can make it the night before and then pop it into the oven an hour before you want to eat. It works well as a side with pancakes or waffles, but you can also make it the main course for brunch events.
—Susan Ham, Cleveland, TN

PREP: 10 min. + chilling
BAKE: 1 hour • **MAKES:** 12 servings

- 3 cups hot cooked grits
- 2½ cups shredded cheddar cheese
- 1 lb. bulk pork sausage, cooked and crumbled
- 3 large eggs
- 1½ cups 2% milk
- 3 Tbsp. butter, melted
- ¼ tsp. garlic powder

1. Mix grits, cheese and sausage. In a separate bowl, beat eggs and milk; stir into grits. Add the butter and garlic powder. Transfer to a greased 13x9-in. baking dish. Refrigerate, covered, for 8 hours or overnight.
2. Remove from refrigerator 30 minutes before baking; preheat oven to 350°. Bake, uncovered, until a knife inserted in center comes out clean, about 1 hour. Let stand for 5 minutes before cutting.
1 piece: 259 cal., 19g fat (10g sat. fat), 104mg chol., 491mg sod., 11g carb. (2g sugars, 0 fiber), 11g pro.

FREEZE & STORE
Wrap cooled egg wrap in foil or parchment and freeze in a freezer container. To use, thaw in refrigerator overnight. Remove from foil or parchment; wrap the tortilla in a moist paper towel. Microwave on high until heated through, 30-60 seconds.

BREAKFAST WRAPS

❄ BREAKFAST WRAPS

We like quick and simple morning meals during the week, and these wraps can be prepped ahead of time. Just a minute in the microwave, and breakfast is ready to go.
—Betty Kleberger, Florissant, MO

TAKES: 15 min. • **MAKES:** 4 servings

- 6 **large eggs**
- 2 **Tbsp. 2% milk**
- ¼ **tsp. pepper**
- 1 **Tbsp. canola oil**
- 1 **cup shredded cheddar cheese**
- ¾ **cup diced fully cooked ham**
- 4 **flour tortillas (8 in.), warmed**

1. In a small bowl, whisk the eggs, milk and pepper. In a large skillet, heat oil. Add egg mixture; cook and stir over medium heat until the eggs are completely set. Stir in cheese and ham.

2. Spoon egg mixture down the center of each tortilla; roll up.

1 serving: 436 cal., 24g fat (10g sat. fat), 364mg chol., 853mg sod., 28g carb. (1g sugars, 0 fiber), 25g pro.

PIZZA BREAKFAST WRAPS: Prepare recipe as directed, replacing cheddar cheese and ham with mozzarella cheese and cooked sausage. Serve with warm marinara sauce on the side.

PULLED PORK BREAKFAST WRAPS: Prepare recipe as directed, replacing cheddar cheese and ham with smoked Gouda cheese and precooked pulled pork. Serve with warm barbecue sauce on the side.

**APPLE-CINNAMON
BAKED FRENCH TOAST**

🅿🅼 APPLE-CINNAMON BAKED FRENCH TOAST

When my wife and I hosted a breakfast for our church group, we wanted to avoid the last-minute rush of cooking. So we made this make-ahead French toast. Everyone loved it and requested the recipe.
—John Cashen, Moline, IL

PREP: 20 min. + chilling
BAKE: 45 min. • **MAKES:** 6 servings

- 12 slices day-old French bread (¾ in. thick), divided
- 6 large eggs, lightly beaten
- 2¾ cups 2% milk
- ⅔ cup sugar, divided
- 1 Tbsp. vanilla extract
- 4 medium apples, peeled and thinly sliced
- 2 tsp. ground cinnamon
- ¾ tsp. ground nutmeg
- 1 Tbsp. butter
  Optional: Whipped cream and maple syrup

1. Arrange 6 bread slices in a greased 13x9-in. baking dish. Combine eggs, milk, ⅓ cup sugar and vanilla; pour half over the bread. Top with apples. Combine cinnamon, nutmeg and remaining ⅓ cup sugar; sprinkle over the apples. Top with remaining bread slices; pour the remaining egg mixture over bread. Dot with butter. Refrigerate, covered, 8 hours or overnight.
2. Remove from refrigerator 30 minutes before baking; preheat the oven to 350°. Bake, uncovered, 45-50 minutes or until a knife inserted in center comes out clean. Let stand 5 minutes before serving. If desired, serve with whipped cream and syrup.
1 piece: 378 cal., 10g fat (5g sat. fat), 200mg chol., 352mg sod., 58g carb. (37g sugars, 3g fiber), 13g pro.

🅟 BREAKFAST PRALINE BREAD PUDDING

Baked French toast inspired this simple make-ahead dish that's perfect for a large holiday meal in the morning. It also travels well.

—Erin Furby, Anchorage, AK

PREP: 20 min. + chilling
BAKE: 40 min. • **MAKES:** 12 servings

- 8 large eggs, lightly beaten
- 2 cups half-and-half cream
- 1 cup 2% milk
- 2 Tbsp. brown sugar
- 3 tsp. vanilla extract
- 1 tsp. ground cinnamon
- ¾ tsp. ground nutmeg
- ½ tsp. salt
- 1 loaf (1 lb.) French bread, cut into 1-in. cubes
- 1 cup chopped pecans
- ½ cup packed brown sugar
- ½ cup butter, melted

1. In a large bowl, whisk the first 8 ingredients until blended. Stir in bread. Transfer mixture to a greased 13x9-in. baking dish. Sprinkle with pecans and brown sugar; drizzle with butter. Refrigerate, covered, several hours or overnight.

2. Preheat oven to 350°. Remove bread pudding from refrigerator; uncover and let stand while oven heats. Bake until puffed, golden and a knife inserted in the center comes out clean, 40-50 minutes. Serve warm.

1 serving: 403 cal., 23g fat (10g sat. fat), 183mg chol., 479mg sod., 37g carb. (15g sugars, 2g fiber), 12g pro.

BROCCOLI & CHICKEN CHEESE STRATA

🅟 BROCCOLI & CHICKEN CHEESE STRATA

On our dairy farm, chores often delay mealtime. That's when this strata comes in handy. I'll prepare it beforehand and later pop it in the oven for a quick and easy meal—it works for breakfast or dinner.

—Margery Moore, Richfield Springs, NY

PREP: 15 min. + chilling
BAKE: 1 hour + standing
MAKES: 8 servings

- 12 slices bread
- 2¼ cups shredded cheddar cheese, divided
- 3 cups frozen chopped broccoli, thawed and drained
- 2 cups diced cooked chicken
- 1 Tbsp. butter, melted
- 6 large eggs
- 3 cups 2% milk
- 2 Tbsp. finely chopped onion
- ¾ tsp. salt
- ½ tsp. ground mustard
- ¼ tsp. pepper

1. Using a doughnut cutter, cut 12 rings and holes in bread; set aside. Tear the remaining bread scraps and place in a greased 13x9-in. baking dish. Sprinkle with 2 cups cheese, broccoli and chicken. Arrange bread rings and holes on top; brush with melted butter.

2. Beat the next 6 ingredients; pour over the top. Refrigerate, covered, 8 hours or overnight.

3. Remove the strata from refrigerator 30 minutes before baking; preheat oven to 325°. Bake, uncovered, 55-60 minutes. Sprinkle with the remaining ¼ cup cheese; bake until a knife inserted in the center comes out clean, about 5 minutes longer. Let stand 5-10 minutes before cutting.

1 piece: 440 cal., 22g fat (10g sat. fat), 213mg chol., 794mg sod., 30g carb. (8g sugars, 3g fiber), 31g pro.

(PM) OVERNIGHT BAKED EGGS BRUSCHETTA

I like to spend as much time as I can with my guests when they stay with me, so I rely on make-ahead recipes to help that happen. Most overnight brunch casseroles are similar, so I came up with a breakfast bruschetta for a fun change of pace.
—Judi Berman-Yamada, Portland, OR

PREP: 45 min. + chilling
BAKE: 10 min. • **MAKES:** 9 servings

- 1 tube (13.8 oz.) refrigerated pizza crust
- 1 Tbsp. cornmeal
- 3 Tbsp. olive oil, divided
- 1½ cups shredded part-skim mozzarella cheese, divided
- ¾ lb. sliced baby portobello mushrooms
- ¾ tsp. garlic powder
- ¾ tsp. dried rosemary, crushed
- ½ tsp. pepper
- ¼ tsp. salt
- 2 cups pizza sauce
- 1 Tbsp. white vinegar
- 9 large eggs
- 2 oz. fresh goat cheese, crumbled
- ½ cup french-fried onions
  Fresh basil leaves

1. Preheat oven to 400°. Unroll pizza crust and press onto bottom of a greased 15x10x1-in. baking pan that's been sprinkled with cornmeal. Brush crust with 1 Tbsp. oil; sprinkle with ¾ cup mozzarella cheese. Bake for 8 minutes.

2. Meanwhile, in a large skillet, heat remaining 2 Tbsp. oil over medium-high heat. Add mushrooms; cook and stir until tender. Stir in garlic powder, rosemary, pepper and salt. Stir in pizza sauce; spread mushroom mixture over crust.

3. In a large skillet with high sides, bring vinegar and 2-3 in. water to a boil. Reduce heat to maintain a gentle simmer. Break cold eggs, 1 at a time, into a small bowl. Holding bowl close to surface of water, slip eggs into water.

4. Cook eggs, uncovered, until whites are completely set and yolks begin to thicken but are not hard, 3-5 minutes. Using a slotted spoon, remove eggs; place over mushroom mixture in baking pan. Sprinkle goat cheese and remaining ¾ cup mozzarella over the eggs and mushrooms. Refrigerate, covered, overnight.

5. Remove pan from refrigerator 30 minutes before baking; preheat oven to 400°. Sprinkle onions over top. Bake, uncovered, until golden brown and heated through, 10-15 minutes. Top with basil just before serving.

1 piece: 345 cal., 17g fat (5g sat. fat), 227mg chol., 798mg sod., 29g carb. (6g sugars, 2g fiber), 17g pro.

OVERNIGHT BAKED EGGS BRUSCHETTA

GREEN CHILE
BRUNCH BAKE

❄ BLUEBERRY OATMEAL PANCAKES

Wonderful blueberry flavor abounds in these thick and moist pancakes. My kids adore them, and I love that they're so easy to make or reheat.
—Amy Spainhoward, Bowling Green, KY

PREP: 20 min. • **COOK:** 5 min./batch
MAKES: 7 servings (1¼ cups syrup)

- 2 cups all-purpose flour
- 2 packets (1.51 oz. each) instant maple and brown sugar oatmeal mix
- 2 Tbsp. sugar
- 2 tsp. baking powder
- ⅛ tsp. salt
- 2 large egg whites
- 1 large egg
- 1½ cups fat-free milk
- ½ cup reduced-fat sour cream
- 2 cups fresh or frozen blueberries

BLUEBERRY SYRUP
- 1½ cups fresh or frozen blueberries
- ½ cup sugar

1. In a large bowl, combine the first 5 ingredients. In another bowl, whisk the egg whites, egg, milk and sour cream. Stir into dry ingredients just until moistened. Fold in blueberries.
2. Spoon batter by ¼ cupfuls onto a hot griddle coated with cooking spray. Turn when bubbles form on top of pancake; cook until second side is golden brown.
3. In a microwave-safe bowl, combine the syrup ingredients. Microwave, uncovered, on high for 1 minute; stir. Microwave until hot and bubbly, 1-2 minutes longer. Serve the syrup warm with pancakes.
2 pancakes with about 2 Tbsp. syrup: 336 cal., 3g fat (1g sat. fat), 29mg chol., 302mg sod., 68g carb. (32g sugars, 4g fiber), 10g pro.

🅟🅜 GREEN CHILE BRUNCH BAKE

It's easy to make this ahead of time in a 13x9-in. pan. It is filling, is perfect for a crowd and helps out busy parents.
—Trista Thinnes, Fort Worth, TX

PREP: 30 min. + chilling
BAKE: 45 min. • **MAKES:** 8 servings

- 1 lb. bulk pork sausage
- 10 cups cubed day-old French bread
- 2 cups shredded sharp cheddar cheese
- 1 can (4 oz.) mushroom stems and pieces, drained
- 5 green onions, chopped
- 6 large eggs
- 2¾ cups half-and-half cream
- 1 can (4 oz.) chopped green chiles, drained
- 1½ tsp. Worcestershire sauce
- ½ tsp. salt
- ¼ tsp. ground mustard
- ¼ tsp. paprika
- ¼ tsp. pepper
- ⅛ to ¼ tsp. hot pepper sauce

1. In a large skillet, cook sausage over medium heat until no longer pink, 5-7 minutes, breaking into crumbles; drain and set aside. Place bread cubes in a greased 13x9-in. baking dish. Top with cheese, mushrooms, green onions and cooked sausage.
2. In a large bowl, whisk the remaining ingredients. Pour over the layers. Refrigerate, covered, overnight.
3. Preheat oven to 350°; remove strata from refrigerator while oven heats. Bake, uncovered, until a knife inserted near center comes out clean, 45-50 minutes. Let bake stand 5-10 minutes before cutting.
1 piece: 503 cal., 34g fat (16g sat. fat), 239mg chol., 1052mg sod., 22g carb. (5g sugars, 1g fiber), 24g pro.

TEST KITCHEN TIP

Make this strata in muffin cups for individual servings perfect for a buffet. The centers bake up tender and moist while the tops get perfectly toasted.

BLUEBERRY
OATMEAL PANCAKES

FREEZE & STORE
See p. 26 for
instructions for freezing
& reheating pancakes.

SAUSAGE & PANCAKE BAKE

Trial and error made this recipe one that my family asks for time and time again. It's so easy and very good.
—Ethel Sanders, Oklahoma City, OK

PREP: 15 min. • **BAKE:** 30 min.
MAKES: 8 servings

- 1 lb. bulk pork sausage
- 2 cups biscuit/baking mix
- 1⅓ cups 2% milk
- 2 large eggs
- ¼ cup canola oil
- 2 medium apples, peeled and thinly sliced
- 2 Tbsp. cinnamon sugar
  Maple syrup

Preheat oven to 350°. In a large skillet over medium heat, cook and crumble sausage until no longer pink, 5-7 minutes; drain. Mix biscuit mix, milk, eggs and oil until blended; stir in sausage. Transfer mixture to a greased 13x9-in. baking dish. Top with apples; sprinkle with cinnamon sugar. Bake 30-45 minutes, until set. Serve with syrup.

1 piece: 379 cal., 24g fat (6g sat. fat), 80mg chol., 692mg sod., 30g carb. (9g sugars, 1g fiber), 11g pro.

TO MAKE AHEAD
Refrigerate prepared recipe, covered, several hours or overnight. To use, preheat oven to 350°. Remove the casserole from refrigerator; uncover and let stand while oven heats. Bake as directed, increasing time as necessary until a knife inserted in the center comes out clean.

SAUSAGE & PANCAKE BAKE

🅿🅼 SPICY BREAKFAST LASAGNA

It's fun to cook up something new for family and friends—especially when it gets rave reviews. When I took this dish to our breakfast club at work, people said it really woke up their taste buds!
—Guthrie Torp Jr., Highland Ranch, CO

PREP: 20 min. + chilling
BAKE: 35 min. • **MAKES:** 16 servings

- 3 cups 4% cottage cheese
- ½ cup minced chives
- ¼ cup sliced green onions
- 18 large eggs
- ⅓ cup 2% milk
- ½ tsp. salt
- ¼ tsp. pepper
- 1 Tbsp. butter
- 8 lasagna noodles, cooked and drained
- 4 cups frozen shredded hash browns, thawed
- 1 lb. bulk pork sausage, cooked and crumbled
- 8 oz. sliced Monterey Jack cheese with jalapeno peppers
- 8 oz. sliced Muenster cheese

1. In a bowl, combine cottage cheese, chives and onions. In another bowl, whisk eggs, milk, salt and pepper until blended. In a large skillet, heat butter over medium heat. Pour in egg mixture; cook and stir until eggs are thickened and no liquid egg remains. Remove from heat.
2. Place 4 lasagna noodles in a greased 13x9-in. baking dish. Layer with 2 cups hash browns, scrambled eggs, sausage and half the cottage cheese mixture. Cover with the Monterey Jack cheese. Top with the remaining 4 lasagna noodles, hash browns and cottage cheese mixture. Cover with Muenster cheese. Refrigerate, covered, 8 hours or overnight.

3. Remove dish from refrigerator 30 minutes before baking; preheat oven to 350°. Bake, uncovered, until a knife inserted in the center comes out clean, 35-40 minutes. Let stand for 5 minutes before cutting.
1 piece: 366 cal., 23g fat (11g sat. fat), 256mg chol., 640mg sod., 16g carb. (3g sugars, 1g fiber), 23g pro.

SPICY BREAKFAST LASAGNA

WHY YOU'LL LOVE IT...

"This was a perfect recipe to prepare the night before, refrigerate and cook the next morning. My 5-year-old and 16-year-old picky eaters even asked me to make this again."
—CHERWITT, TASTEOFHOME.COM

PAGE 54

PAGE 53

PAGE 52

Snacks & Appetizers

Whether you're hankering for an afternoon snack or prepping
for a party spread, these recipes are ready and waiting
for just when you need them.

PAGE 57

PAGE 58

MINI SHEPHERD'S PIES

TACO JOE DIP

❄ MINI SHEPHERD'S PIES

I'm as confident serving these little pies to company as to family. If I have enough time, I'll use homemade biscuits and mashed potatoes.
—Ellen Osborne, Clarksville, TN

PREP: 30 min. • **BAKE:** 20 min.
MAKES: 5 servings

- 1   lb. ground beef
- ¼   cup chopped onion
- 1   garlic clove, minced
- ⅓   cup chili sauce or ketchup
- 1   Tbsp. cider vinegar
- 1¼ cups water
- 3   oz. cream cheese, cubed
- 3   Tbsp. butter
- 1¼ cups mashed potato flakes
- 2   tubes (6 oz. each) small refrigerated buttermilk biscuits
- ½   cup crushed potato chips
      Paprika, optional

1. In a large skillet, cook and crumble beef with onion and garlic over medium heat until no longer pink, 5-7 minutes; drain. Stir in chili sauce and vinegar.
2. In a small saucepan, combine water, cream cheese and butter; bring to a boil. Remove from heat; stir in potato flakes.
3. Press each biscuit onto bottom and up side of a greased muffin cup. Fill with beef mixture; top with mashed potatoes. Sprinkle with potato chips.
4. Bake at 375° until topping is golden brown, 20-25 minutes. If desired, sprinkle with paprika.

2 mini shepherd's pies: 612 cal., 36g fat (15g sat. fat), 92mg chol., 1094mg sod., 49g carb. (11g sugars, 2g fiber), 24g pro.

FREEZE OPTION

Freeze cooled pies in a single layer in freezer containers. To use, partially thaw in the refrigerator overnight. Reheat on a baking sheet in a preheated 375° oven until heated through, 15-18 minutes.

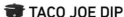 **TACO JOE DIP**

My daughter was the first in our family to try this recipe. She thought it was delicious so she passed it on to me. My husband and I think it's terrific. Because it's made in a slow cooker, it's perfect for parties or busy days.
—Lang Secrest, Sierra Vista, AZ

PREP: 5 min. • **COOK:** 5 hours
MAKES: about 7 cups

- 1   can (16 oz.) kidney beans, rinsed and drained
- 1   can (15¼ oz.) whole kernel corn, drained
- 1   can (15 oz.) black beans, rinsed and drained
- 1   can (14½ oz.) stewed tomatoes, undrained
- 1   can (8 oz.) tomato sauce
- 1   can (4 oz.) chopped green chiles, drained
- 1   envelope taco seasoning
- ½   cup chopped onion
     Thinly sliced green onions, optional
     Tortilla chips and fresh mini bell peppers

In a 5-qt. slow cooker, combine the first 8 ingredients. Cover and cook on low for 5-6 hours. If desired, sprinkle with green onions. Serve dip with tortilla chips and mini peppers.
¼ cup: 49 cal., 0 fat (0 sat. fat), 0 chol., 291mg sod., 9g carb. (2g sugars, 2g fiber), 2g pro.

TEST KITCHEN TIP

To make this into a soup, add a 29-oz. can of tomato sauce to the slow cooker with the other ingredients. It will serve 6-8.

🍲 SLAW-TOPPED BEEF SLIDERS

When I was working full time, I relied on these delicious, fast-to-fix beef sliders for simple meals. Bagged coleslaw mix and bottled dressing save on both prep time and cleanup.
—Jane Whittaker, Pensacola, FL

PREP: 20 min. • **COOK:** 6 hours
MAKES: 1 dozen

- 3 cups coleslaw mix
- ½ medium red onion, chopped (about ⅔ cup)
- ⅛ tsp. celery seed
- ¼ tsp. pepper
- ⅓ cup coleslaw salad dressing

SANDWICHES
- 1 boneless beef chuck roast (2 lbs.)
- 1 tsp. salt
- ½ tsp. pepper
- 1 can (6 oz.) tomato paste
- ¼ cup water
- 1 tsp. Worcestershire sauce
- 1 small onion, diced
- 1 cup barbecue sauce
- 12 slider buns or dinner rolls, split

1. Combine coleslaw, onion, celery seed and pepper. Add salad dressing; toss to coat. Refrigerate until serving.
2. Sprinkle roast with salt and pepper; transfer roast to a 5-qt. slow cooker. Mix tomato paste, water and Worcestershire sauce; pour over roast. Top with onion. Cook, covered, on low 6-8 hours or until meat is tender.
3. Shred meat with 2 forks; return to slow cooker. Stir in barbecue sauce; heat through. Place beef on buns; top with coleslaw. Add bun tops.
1 slider: 322 cal., 12g fat (4g sat. fat), 67mg chol., 726mg sod., 34g carb. (13g sugars, 3g fiber), 20g pro.

SLAW-TOPPED BEEF SLIDERS

❄ CHICKEN BACON TRIANGLES

We host an annual Christmas party, and I whip up a new menu item every year. These golden hors d'oeuvres were an absolute hit.
—Annette Fecht, Sorrento, BC

PREP: 60 min. + chilling
BAKE: 15 min. • **MAKES:** 4 dozen

- ½ lb. bacon strips, chopped
- ¾ lb. boneless skinless chicken breasts, cubed
- ½ cup condensed cream of mushroom soup, undiluted
- 4 oz. cream cheese, cubed
- 2 garlic cloves, minced
- 1½ tsp. dried minced onion
- ⅛ tsp. pepper
- 1 cup shredded part-skim mozzarella cheese
- ½ cup shredded Parmesan cheese
- 24 sheets phyllo dough, 14x9 in.
- ¼ cup butter, melted
  Ranch dip, optional

1. In a large skillet, cook bacon over medium heat until crisp. Remove to paper towels with a slotted spoon; drain, reserving drippings in pan. Saute chicken in the drippings until no longer pink; drain.

2. Add the soup, cream cheese, garlic, onion, pepper and bacon to the skillet; cook and stir until blended. Remove from the heat. Stir in mozzarella and Parmesan cheeses; cool slightly. Cover and refrigerate for at least 2 hours.

3. Lightly brush 1 sheet of phyllo dough with butter; place another sheet of phyllo on top and brush with butter. (Keep the remaining phyllo covered with a damp towel to prevent it from drying out.) Cut into four 14x2¼-in. strips.

4. Place 1 scant Tbsp. of filling on lower corner of each strip. Fold dough over the filling, forming a triangle. Fold the triangle up, then fold triangle over, forming another triangle. Continue folding, like a flag, until you come to the end of the strip. Brush the end of dough with butter and press onto triangle to seal. Repeat with the remaining strips of dough and with remaining sheets of phyllo.

5. Place triangles on a greased baking sheet. Bake at 375° until golden brown, 15-17 minutes. If desired, serve with ranch dip.

1 appetizer: 70 cal., 5g fat (2g sat. fat), 13mg chol., 121mg sod., 4g carb. (0 sugars, 0 fiber), 3g pro.

FREEZE OPTION

Freeze unbaked triangles on baking sheets; when frozen, transfer to resealable freezer containers. Bake frozen triangles until golden brown, 18-22 minutes.

CHICKEN BACON TRIANGLES

BLACK FOREST HAM PINWHEELS

Dried cherries are the sweet surprise in these delightfully different spirals. I roll up the tortillas and pop them in the fridge well before party time, and then just slice and serve.
—Kate Dampier, Quail Valley, CA

PREP: 20 min. + chilling
MAKES: about 3½ dozen

- 1 pkg. (8 oz.) cream cheese, softened
- 4 tsp. minced fresh dill
- 1 Tbsp. lemon juice
- 2 tsp. Dijon mustard
  Dash each salt and pepper
- ½ cup dried cherries, chopped
- ¼ cup chopped green onions
- 5 flour tortillas (10 in.), room temperature
- ½ lb. sliced deli Black Forest ham
- ½ lb. sliced Swiss cheese

1. Beat cream cheese, dill, lemon juice, mustard, salt and pepper until blended. Stir in cherries and onions. Spread over each tortilla; layer with ham and cheese.

2. Roll up tightly; securely wrap in waxed paper. Refrigerate at least 2 hours. Cut into ½-in. slices.

1 piece: 78 cal., 4g fat (2g sat. fat), 13mg chol., 151mg sod., 6g carb. (2g sugars, 0 fiber), 4g pro.

APPETIZER PINWHEELS: Omit dill, lemon juice, mustard, salt, pepper, cherries, onion, ham and cheese. Beat cream cheese with 1 cup sour cream, 1 can (4¼ oz.) drained chopped ripe olives, 1 can (4 oz.) well-drained chopped green chiles, 1 cup shredded cheddar cheese, ½ cup chopped green onions, dash garlic powder and dash salt until blended. Spread over tortillas and proceed as recipe directs.

CARAMELIZED
HAM & SWISS BUNS

BLACK FOREST HAM
PINWHEELS

Ⓟ CARAMELIZED HAM & SWISS BUNS

My next-door neighbor shared this recipe with me, and I simply cannot improve it! You can make it ahead and cook it quickly when company arrives. The combo of flavors makes these sandwiches so delicious.
—Iris Weihemuller, Baxter, MN

PREP: 25 min. + chilling
BAKE: 30 min. • **MAKES:** 1 dozen

- 1 pkg. (12 oz.) Hawaiian sweet rolls
- ½ cup horseradish sauce
- ¾ lb. sliced deli ham
- 6 slices Swiss cheese, halved
- ½ cup butter, cubed
- 2 Tbsp. finely chopped onion
- 2 Tbsp. brown sugar
- 1 Tbsp. spicy brown mustard
- 2 tsp. poppy seeds
- 1½ tsp. Worcestershire sauce
- ¼ tsp. garlic powder

1. Without separating rolls, cut rolls in half horizontally; arrange bottom halves in a greased 9x9-in. square baking pan. Spread cut side of roll bottoms with horseradish sauce. Layer with ham and cheese; replace the roll tops.

2. In a small skillet, heat butter over medium-high heat. Add onion; cook and stir until tender, 1-2 minutes. Stir in remaining ingredients. Pour over the rolls. Refrigerate, covered, several hours or overnight.

3. Preheat oven to 350°. Bake, covered, 25 minutes. Uncover; bake until golden brown, 5-10 minutes longer.

1 sandwich: 315 cal., 17g fat (9g sat. fat), 61mg chol., 555mg sod., 29g carb. (13g sugars, 2g fiber), 13g pro

TEST KITCHEN TIP

You can make a Reuben version of this recipe by using corned beef or pastrami instead of ham. Add a layer of sauerkraut, and use caraway seeds instead of the poppy.

SAUSAGE
BACON BITES

PM SAUSAGE BACON BITES

These tasty morsels are perfect with almost any egg dish or as finger foods party guests can just pick up and pop into their mouths.

—Pat Waymire, Yellow Springs, OH

PREP: 20 min. + chilling
BAKE: 35 min.
MAKES: about 3½ dozen

- ¾ lb. sliced bacon
- 2 pkg. (8 oz. each) frozen fully cooked breakfast sausage links, thawed
- ½ cup plus 2 Tbsp. packed brown sugar, divided

1. Cut bacon strips widthwise in half; cut sausage links in half. Wrap a piece of bacon around each piece of sausage. Place ½ cup brown sugar in a shallow bowl; roll the wrapped sausages in sugar. Secure each sausage with a toothpick. Place in a foil-lined 15x10x1-in. baking pan. Cover and refrigerate for 4 hours or overnight.
2. Preheat oven to 350°. Sprinkle wrapped sausages with 1 Tbsp. brown sugar. Bake until bacon is crisp, 35-40 minutes, turning once. Sprinkle with remaining brown sugar.
1 wrapped sausage: 51 cal., 4g fat (1g sat. fat), 6mg chol., 100mg sod., 4g carb. (4g sugars, 0 fiber), 2g pro.

SAVORY PARTY BREAD

SAVORY PARTY BREAD

It's impossible to stop nibbling on warm pieces of this cheesy, onion-y loaf. The bread fans out for a fun presentation.

—Kay Daly, Raleigh, NC

PREP: 10 min. • **BAKE:** 25 min.
MAKES: 8 servings

- 1 unsliced round loaf sourdough bread (1 lb.)
- 1 lb. Monterey Jack cheese
- ½ cup butter, melted
- ½ cup chopped green onions
- 2 to 3 tsp. poppy seeds

1. Preheat oven to 350°. Cut bread widthwise into 1-in. slices to within ½ in. of bottom of loaf. Repeat cuts in opposite direction. Cut cheese into ¼-in. slices; cut slices into small pieces. Place cheese in cuts in bread.
2. In a small bowl, mix butter, green onions and poppy seeds; drizzle over bread. Wrap in foil; place on a baking sheet. Bake 15 minutes. Unwrap; bake until the cheese is melted, about 10 minutes longer.
1 serving: 481 cal., 31g fat (17g sat. fat), 91mg chol., 782mg sod., 32g carb. (1g sugars, 2g fiber), 17g pro.
MUSHROOM SWISS BREAD: Use Swiss cheese and a drained 4½-oz. jar of sliced mushrooms instead of the Monterey Jack and green onions. Use ¼ tsp. garlic powder instead of the poppy seeds.

TO MAKE AHEAD
To save time, slice the bread and fill it with cheese a day ahead. Before company arrives, melt the butter and add it to the green onions and poppy seeds, drizzle it over the bread, and bake.

🅿🅜 BEST EVER FRIED CHICKEN WINGS

For game days, I shake up these saucy wings. When I run out, friends hover by the snack table until I bring out more. When they ask me how I do it, they never believe it's so easy!
—Nick Iverson, Denver, CO

PREP: 10 min. + chilling
COOK: 20 min.
MAKES: about 4 dozen

- 4 lbs. chicken wings
- 2 tsp. kosher salt
   Oil for deep-fat frying

BUFFALO WING SAUCE
- ¾ cup Louisiana-style hot sauce
- ¼ cup unsalted butter, cubed
- 2 Tbsp. molasses
- ¼ tsp. cayenne pepper

SPICY THAI SAUCE
- 1 Tbsp. canola oil
- 1 tsp. grated fresh gingerroot
- 1 garlic clove, minced
- 1 minced Thai chile pepper or ¼ tsp. crushed red pepper flakes
- ¼ cup packed dark brown sugar
- 2 Tbsp. lime juice
- 2 Tbsp. minced fresh cilantro
- 1 Tbsp. fish sauce

SPICY BARBECUE SAUCE
- ¾ cup barbecue sauce
- 2 chipotle peppers in adobo sauce, finely chopped
- 2 Tbsp. honey
- 1 Tbsp. cider vinegar
   Thinly sliced green onions, optional

1. With a sharp knife, cut through the 2 wing joints; discard wing tips. Pat chicken dry with paper towels. Toss wings with kosher salt and place on a wire rack in a 15x10x1-in. baking pan. Refrigerate at least 1 hour or overnight.

2. In an electric skillet or deep-fat fryer, heat oil to 375°. Fry wings in batches until skin is crisp and meat is tender, 8-10 minutes. Drain on paper towels.

3. For **Buffalo Wing Sauce**, bring hot sauce just to a boil in a small saucepan. Remove from heat; whisk in the butter 1 cube at a time. Stir in molasses and cayenne pepper.

4. For **Spicy Thai Sauce**, heat oil in a small saucepan over medium heat. Add the ginger, garlic and chile pepper; cook and stir until fragrant, about 2 minutes. Stir in brown sugar and lime juice. Bring to a boil; cook until just thickened, about 5 minutes. Stir in cilantro and fish sauce.

5. For **Spicy Barbecue Sauce**, heat prepared barbecue sauce in a small saucepan over medium heat. Stir in chipotle peppers, honey and vinegar. Bring to a boil; cook and stir until slightly thickened, about 5 minutes.

6. Toss wings with 1 of the sauces. If desired, sprinkle with green onion slices.

1 piece: 87 cal., 8g fat (2g sat. fat), 15mg chol., 218mg sod., 1g carb. (1g sugars, 0 fiber), 4g pro.

BEST EVER FRIED CHICKEN WINGS

DILL DIP

Be prepared—you'll likely need to make a double batch of this delightful dip. One is never enough when we have a get-together. It tastes fantastic with just about any vegetable, so use whatever you have on hand as a dipper.
—Kathy Beldorth, Three Oaks, MI

PREP: 10 min. + chilling
MAKES: 2 cups

- 1 cup mayonnaise
- 1 cup sour cream
- 2 Tbsp. dried parsley flakes
- 1 Tbsp. dried minced onion
- 2 tsp. dill weed
- 1½ tsp. seasoned salt
- 1 tsp. sugar
  Fresh vegetables or potato chips

In a small bowl, combine first 7 ingredients. Chill for at least 1 hour. Serve with vegetables or potato chips.
2 Tbsp.: 123 cal., 13g fat (3g sat. fat), 5mg chol., 219mg sod., 1g carb. (1g sugars, 0 fiber), 1g pro.

TEST KITCHEN TIP

Dairy-based dips like this one will last 3-4 days in the refrigerator; store in an airtight container. To make the dip a little lighter, use reduced-fat mayonnaise and sour cream.

DILL DIP

MINI CHEESE BALLS

PIZZA PUFFS

Ⓟ MINI CHEESE BALLS

These mini cheese balls are the perfect quick appetizer for any party. Roll them in toasted sesame seeds, fresh rosemary and/or paprika to add even more flavor.
—Judy Spivey, Ennice, NC

PREP: 30 min. + chilling
MAKES: 36 cheese balls

1   pkg. (8 oz.) cream cheese, softened
2   cups shredded sharp cheddar cheese
    Optional toppings: Toasted sesame seeds, minced fresh rosemary and paprika
    Optional garnishes: Halved rye crisps and rolled tortilla chips

1. In a large bowl, combine cheeses. Shape into 36 balls; roll balls in toppings as desired. Cover and refrigerate 8 hours or overnight.
2. To serve, if desired, press a rye crisp or rolled tortilla chip into the top of each cheese ball.
1 cheese ball: 47 cal., 4g fat (2g sat. fat), 13mg chol., 61mg sod., 1g carb. (0 sugars, 0 fiber), 2g pro.

FREEZE & STORE
Cover and freeze unbaked pizza puffs on waxed paper-lined baking sheets until firm. Transfer to a freezer container; seal and return to freezer. To use, preheat oven to 400°; bake pizza puffs on greased baking sheets as directed, increasing time as necessary until puffs are golden brown.

❄ PIZZA PUFFS

What's more fun than a pizza puff?
Skip the kind sold in the frozen aisle
and try this homemade version. You
can substitute any meat or vegetable
for the pepperoni and any cheese for
the mozzarella.
—Vivi Taylor, Middleburg, FL

TAKES: 30 min.
MAKES: 20 servings

- 1 loaf (1 lb.) frozen pizza dough, thawed
- 20 slices pepperoni
- 8 oz. part-skim mozzarella cheese, cut into 20 cubes
- ¼ cup butter
- 2 small garlic cloves, minced
  Dash salt
  Marinara sauce, warmed
  Optional: Crushed red pepper flakes and grated Parmesan cheese

1. Preheat oven to 400°. Shape dough into 1½-in. balls; flatten into ⅛-in.-thick circles. Place 1 pepperoni slice and 1 cheese cube in center of each circle; wrap dough around pepperoni and cheese. Pinch edges to seal; reshape into a ball. Repeat with remaining dough, cheese and pepperoni. Place seam side down on greased baking sheets; bake until light golden brown, 10-15 minutes. Cool slightly.
2. Meanwhile, in a small saucepan, melt butter over low heat. Add garlic and salt, taking care not to brown butter or garlic; brush over puffs. Serve with the marinara sauce; if desired, top with red pepper flakes and grated Parmesan.
1 pizza puff: 120 cal., 6g fat (3g sat. fat), 15mg chol., 189mg sod., 11g carb. (1g sugars, 0 fiber), 5g pro.

FAVORITE MARINATED MUSHROOMS

EASY PIMIENTO CHEESE

Every good Southerner has a version of pimiento cheese. It's wonderful in a sandwich with a fresh summer tomato, inside a grilled cheese sandwich or served plain with some crackers.
—Josh Carter, Birmingham, AL

PREP: 15 min. + chilling
MAKES: 16 servings

- 1⅓ cups mayonnaise
- 2 jars (4 oz. each) pimiento strips, chopped
- 1½ tsp. Worcestershire sauce
- ¼ tsp. cayenne pepper
- ¼ tsp. pepper
- 1 block (8 oz.) sharp cheddar cheese, shredded
- 1 block (8 oz.) extra-sharp cheddar cheese, shredded

In a large bowl, combine the first 5 ingredients. Add cheeses and stir to combine. Refrigerate, covered, at least 1 hour.
¼ cup: 238 cal., 23g fat (7g sat. fat), 29mg chol., 286mg sod., 2g carb. (1g sugars, 0 fiber), 7g pro.

🅿ⓂFAVORITE MARINATED MUSHROOMS

These mushrooms make a great appetizer. Sometimes I'll add them to salads for tangy flavor or even serve them as a side dish.
—Brenda Snyder, Hesston, PA

PREP: 15 min. + marinating
MAKES: 4 cups

- 2 lbs. fresh mushrooms
- 1 envelope (0.7 oz.) Italian salad dressing mix
- 1 cup water
- ½ cup olive oil
- ⅓ cup cider vinegar
- 2 Tbsp. lemon juice
- 1 Tbsp. sugar
- 1 Tbsp. minced fresh parsley
- 1 Tbsp. reduced-sodium soy sauce
- 2 tsp. crushed red pepper flakes
- 3 garlic cloves, minced
- ½ tsp. salt
- ⅛ tsp. pepper

1. Remove mushroom stems (discard or save for another use). Place caps in a large saucepan and cover with water. Bring to a boil. Reduce heat; cook for 3 minutes, stirring occasionally. Drain and cool.
2. In a small bowl, whisk the salad dressing mix and the next 11 ingredients. Place mushrooms in a large bowl; add dressing and stir to coat. Refrigerate, covered, 8 hours or overnight.
½ cup: 166 cal., 14g fat (2g sat. fat), 0 chol., 602mg sod., 9g carb. (5g sugars, 2g fiber), 4g pro.

TEST KITCHEN TIP

These mushrooms get better the longer they marinate. For the most robust flavor, let them marinate 8 hours or overnight; they'll last in an airtight container in the refrigerator for up to 10 days.

EASY PIMIENTO
CHEESE

❄ 🍲 SLOW-COOKER PIZZA DIP

I created this dip for my daughter's pizza-themed birthday party. It was an instant hit and I've continued to bring this along to other gatherings. Everyone loves it!
—Stephanie Gates, Waterloo, IA

PREP: 15 min. • **COOK:** 2 hours
MAKES: 20 servings

- ½ lb. ground beef
- ½ lb. bulk pork sausage
- 1 can (28 oz.) crushed tomatoes
- ½ cup diced green pepper
- ¼ cup grated Parmesan cheese
- 2 Tbsp. tomato paste
- 2 tsp. Italian seasoning
- 1 garlic clove, minced
- ¾ tsp. crushed red pepper flakes
- ¼ tsp. salt
- ¼ tsp. pepper
- Hot garlic bread

1. In a large skillet, cook and crumble beef and sausage over medium heat until no longer pink, 5-7 minutes. Using a slotted spoon, transfer meat to a 3-qt. slow cooker. Stir in all remaining ingredients except garlic bread.
2. Cook, covered, on low until heated through, 2-3 hours. Serve with garlic bread.

¼ cup dip: 68 cal., 4g fat (1g sat. fat), 14mg chol., 198mg sod., 4g carb. (2g sugars, 1g fiber), 4g pro.

┌ FREEZE OPTION ─────

Freeze cooled dip in freezer containers. To use, partially thaw in refrigerator overnight. Heat through in a saucepan, stirring occasionally.

SLOW-COOKER PIZZA DIP

CRAB AU GRATIN SPREAD

When the holidays roll around, I love to serve this warm, comforting appetizer. Canned crab makes it easy to whip up.
—Suzanne Zick, Maiden, NC

TAKES: 30 minutes
MAKES: about 2 cups

- 2 Tbsp. plus 1 tsp. butter, divided
- 3 Tbsp. all-purpose flour
- ½ tsp. salt
- ⅛ tsp. paprika
- ½ cup half-and-half cream
- ½ cup whole milk
- ¼ cup white wine or chicken broth
- 1 can (6 oz.) crabmeat, drained, flaked and cartilage removed or ⅔ cup chopped imitation crabmeat
- 1 can (4 oz.) mushroom stems and pieces, drained and chopped
- 1½ tsp. minced chives
- ½ cup shredded cheddar cheese
- 1 Tbsp. dry bread crumbs
  Assorted crackers and fresh vegetables

1. Preheat oven to 400°. In a large saucepan, melt 2 Tbsp. butter. Stir in the flour, salt and paprika until smooth. Gradually add the cream, milk and wine. Bring to a boil; cook and stir 1-2 minutes or until thickened. Stir in crab, mushrooms and chives; heat through. Stir in cheese just until melted. Transfer to a greased shallow 1-qt. baking dish.
2. Melt the remaining 1 tsp. butter; toss with bread crumbs. Sprinkle over crab mixture. Bake, uncovered, for 10-15 minutes or until bubbly.
3. Let stand 5 minutes. Serve with crackers and vegetables. If desired, sprinkle with additional minced chives.
2 Tbsp.: 64 cal., 4g fat (2g sat. fat), 22mg chol., 185mg sod., 2g carb. (1g sugars, 0 fiber), 4g pro.

CRAB
AU GRATIN
SPREAD

TO MAKE AHEAD

To make this recipe ahead of time, prepare the melted cheese mixture and transfer it to a 1-qt. baking dish. Cover dish and refrigerate for up to 2 days. Remove the dish from the refrigerator; let mixture come to room temperature. Then proceed with the recipe as directed.

❄ SAUSAGE CHEESE BALLS

These bite-sized meatballs are a favorite of mine. Try a different cheese instead of cheddar or serve with Dijon mustard instead of sauces.
—Anna Damon, Bozeman, MT

TAKES: 30 min.
MAKES: 20 servings

- ½ cup shredded cheddar cheese
- 3 Tbsp. biscuit/baking mix
- 1 Tbsp. finely chopped onion
- 1 Tbsp. finely chopped celery
- ⅛ tsp. garlic powder
- ⅛ tsp. pepper
- ¼ lb. bulk pork sausage
  Optional: Sweet-and-sour and barbecue sauces

1. In a small bowl, combine the first 6 ingredients. Crumble the sausage over the mixture and mix lightly but thoroughly. Shape into 1-in. balls.
2. Place in a shallow baking pan coated with cooking spray. Bake, uncovered, at 375° until balls are golden brown and no longer pink inside, 12-15 minutes. Drain on paper towels. Serve with sauces if desired.

1 ball: 30 cal., 2g fat (1g sat. fat), 6mg chol., 64mg sod., 1g carb . (0 sugars, 0 fiber), 1g pro.

FREEZE OPTION

Place the uncooked balls in a single layer on a sheet pan in the freezer. Once frozen, transfer to a freezer-safe container; keep in freezer. To use, take out as many as you need and bake at 375° from frozen until heated through, allowing a little extra time.

MUSHROOM CAPONATA

SAUSAGE CHEESE BALLS

MUSHROOM CAPONATA

This is a lovely appetizer with crostini, pita bread, bagel chips or crackers. I've also used it as a topping over a salad of mixed greens. It can be made up to two days in advance and refrigerated; just before serving, warm over low heat.
—Julia Cotton, Chalfont, PA

PREP: 40 min. • **COOK:** 10 min.
MAKES: 6 cups

- 2 large green peppers, chopped
- 1 large onion, chopped
- 2 Tbsp. butter, divided
- 2 Tbsp. olive oil, divided
- 2 lbs. fresh mushrooms, coarsely chopped
- ½ cup pitted Greek olives, chopped
- ¼ cup balsamic vinegar
- ¼ cup tomato paste
- 1 Tbsp. sugar
- 1 tsp. dried oregano
- ½ tsp. salt
- ¼ tsp. coarsely ground pepper
  Bagel chips or lightly toasted French bread baguette slices

1. In a large cast-iron or other heavy skillet, saute the green peppers and onion in 1 Tbsp. butter and 1 Tbsp. oil until golden brown, about 10 minutes.
2. Add half the mushrooms and remaining 1 Tbsp. butter and 1 Tbsp. oil; saute until tender. Remove the onion mixture and set aside. Saute the remaining mushrooms until tender. Return all to the pan. Cover and simmer mixture over medium-high heat for 2 minutes.
3. Add olives, vinegar, tomato paste, sugar, oregano, salt and pepper. Reduce heat; simmer, uncovered, until thickened, about 10 minutes.
4. Serve caponata warm or at room temperature with bagel chips or baguette slices.
¼ cup: 53 cal., 3g fat (1g sat. fat), 3mg chol., 107mg sod., 6g carb. (3g sugars, 1g fiber), 2g pro.
Diabetic Exchanges: ½ starch, ½ fat.

MARINATED
CHEESE

ⓟⓜ MARINATED CHEESE

This special appetizer always makes it to our neighborhood parties and is the first to disappear from the buffet table. It's attractive, delicious—and so easy!
—Laurie Casper, Coraopolis, PA

PREP: 30 min. + marinating
MAKES: about 2 lbs.

- 2 blocks (8 oz. each) white cheddar cheese
- 2 pkg. (8 oz. each) cream cheese
- ¾ cup chopped roasted sweet red peppers
- ½ cup olive oil
- ¼ cup white wine vinegar
- ¼ cup balsamic vinegar
- 3 Tbsp. chopped green onions
- 3 Tbsp. minced fresh parsley
- 2 Tbsp. minced fresh basil
- 1 Tbsp. sugar
- 3 garlic cloves, minced
- ½ tsp. salt
- ½ tsp. pepper
  Assorted crackers or toasted sliced French bread

1. Slice each block of cheddar cheese into twenty ¼-in. slices. Cut each block of cream cheese into 18 slices. Construct four 6-in.-long blocks of stacked cheeses, sandwiching 9 cream cheese slices between the 10 cheddar slices for each stack. Place in a 13x9-in. dish.
2. In a small bowl, combine the roasted peppers, oil, vinegars, onions, herbs, sugar, garlic, salt and pepper; pour over the cheese stacks.
3. Cover and refrigerate stacks overnight, turning cheese blocks once. Drain excess marinade. Serve cheese with crackers or toasted bread.
1 oz. cheese: 121 cal., 11g fat (6g sat. fat), 30mg chol., 153mg sod., 1g carb. (0 sugars, 0 fiber), 5g pro.

TOMATO APPLE CHUTNEY

🍲 TOMATO APPLE CHUTNEY

During the fall and winter, I love to make different kinds of chutney to give as hostess gifts. Cook this chutney in a slow cooker, and you don't have to fuss with it until you are ready to serve.
—Nancy Heishman, Las Vegas, NV

PREP: 15 min. • **COOK:** 5 hours
MAKES: 30 servings

- 3 cans (14½ oz. each) fire-roasted diced tomatoes with garlic, undrained
- 2 medium red onions, chopped
- 1 large apple, peeled and chopped
- 1 cup golden raisins
- ¾ cup cider vinegar
- ½ cup packed brown sugar
- 1 Tbsp. chopped seeded jalapeno pepper
- 1 Tbsp. minced fresh cilantro
- 2 tsp. curry powder
- ½ tsp. salt
- ¼ tsp. ground allspice
  Baked pita chips

Combine first 11 ingredients in a greased 3-qt. slow cooker. Cook, uncovered, on high 5-6 hours or until thickened. Serve warm with pita chips.
¼ cup: 48 cal., 0 fat (0 sat. fat), 0 chol., 152mg sod., 11g carb. (8g sugars, 1g fiber), 1g pro.

TEST KITCHEN TIP

It's unusual to cook food uncovered in the slow cooker, but it is essential for this chutney. Keeping the cover off allows the liquid to evaporate during cooking.

MUSTARD PRETZEL DIP

This flavorful dip is addictive, so be careful! It's also delicious with veggies.
—Iola Egle, Bella Vista, AR

PREP: 10 min. + chilling
MAKES: 3½ cups

- 1 cup sour cream
- 1 cup mayonnaise
- 1 cup prepared mustard
- ½ cup sugar
- ¼ cup dried minced onion
- 1 envelope (1 oz.) ranch salad dressing mix
- 1 Tbsp. prepared horseradish
  Sourdough pretzels or pretzel nuggets

In a large bowl, combine the first 7 ingredients. Cover and refrigerate at least 30 minutes. Serve with pretzels. Refrigerate any leftovers.

2 Tbsp.: 95 cal., 8g fat (2g sat. fat), 2mg chol., 342mg sod., 6g carb. (4g sugars, 0 fiber), 1g pro.

TO MAKE AHEAD
This dip needs to be refrigerated for at least 30 minutes before serving, but that's a minimum—you could prepare it a day or two in advance. Simply store it in the refrigerator in an airtight container until you're ready to serve.

MUSTARD
PRETZEL DIP

❅ SOFT BEER PRETZELS

What goes together better than beer and pretzels? Not much that I can think of. That's why I put them together into one delicious recipe.

—Alyssa Wilhite, Whitehouse, TX

PREP: 1 hour + rising • **BAKE:** 10 min.
MAKES: 8 pretzels

- 1   bottle (12 oz.) amber beer or nonalcoholic beer
- 1   pkg. (¼ oz.) active dry yeast
- 2   Tbsp. unsalted butter, melted
- 2   Tbsp. sugar
- 1½ tsp. salt
- 4   to 4½ cups all-purpose flour
- 10 cups water
- ⅔   cup baking soda

TOPPING
- 1   large egg yolk
- 1   Tbsp. water
     Coarse salt, optional

1. In a small saucepan, heat beer to 110°-115°; remove from heat. Stir in yeast until dissolved. In a large bowl, combine butter, sugar, 1½ tsp. salt, yeast mixture and 3 cups flour; beat on medium speed until the dough is smooth. Stir in enough remaining flour to form a soft dough (dough will be sticky).

2. Turn dough onto a floured surface; knead until smooth and elastic, 6-8 minutes. Place in a greased bowl, turning once to grease the top. Cover and let rise in a warm place until doubled, about 1 hour.

3. Punch dough down. Turn onto a lightly floured surface; divide and shape into 8 balls. Roll each ball into a 24-in. rope. Curve the ends of each rope to form a circle; twist ends once and lay over opposite side of circle, pinching ends to seal.

4. In a Dutch oven, bring water and baking soda to a boil. Drop pretzels, 2 at a time, into boiling water. Cook 30 seconds. Remove with a slotted spoon; drain well on paper towels.

5. Place 2 in. apart on greased baking sheets. In a small bowl, whisk egg yolk and water; brush over pretzels. Sprinkle with coarse salt if desired. Bake until golden brown, 10-12 minutes. Remove from pans to a wire rack to cool.

1 pretzel: 288 cal., 4g fat (2g sat. fat), 16mg chol., 604mg sod., 53g carb. (6g sugars, 2g fiber), 7g pro.

SOFT BEER PRETZELS

FREEZE & STORE
Freeze cooled pretzels in a freezer container, separating layers with waxed paper. To use, place frozen pretzels on a baking sheet in a preheated 400° oven until heated through.

BARBECUED MEATBALLS

Grape jelly and chili sauce are the secrets to these meatballs. If I'm having a party, I prepare them in advance and reheat them before guests arrive.
—Irma Schnuelle, Manitowoc, WI

PREP: 20 min. • **COOK:** 15 min.
MAKES: about 3 dozen

- ½ cup dry bread crumbs
- ⅓ cup finely chopped onion
- ¼ cup 2% milk
- 1 large egg, lightly beaten
- 1 Tbsp. minced fresh parsley
- 1 tsp. salt
- 1 tsp. Worcestershire sauce
- ½ tsp. pepper
- 1 lb. lean ground beef (90% lean)
- ¼ cup canola oil
- 1 bottle (12 oz.) chili sauce
- 1 jar (10 oz.) grape jelly

1. In a large bowl, combine the first 8 ingredients. Crumble beef over mixture and mix lightly but thoroughly. Shape into 1-in. balls. In a large skillet, brown meatballs in oil on all sides.
2. Remove meatballs and drain. In the same skillet, combine the chili sauce and jelly; cook and stir over medium heat until jelly has melted. Return meatballs to pan; heat through.
1 meatball: 71 cal., 3g fat (1g sat. fat), 13mg chol., 215mg sod., 9g carb. (7g sugars, 0 fiber), 3g pro.

HOT ARTICHOKE-SPINACH DIP

HOT ARTICHOKE-SPINACH DIP

One taste of this outrageously delicious dip and your guests will not stop until it's gone. The savory blend of spinach, artichokes and Parmesan cheese is irresistible. It tastes even better if you make it the night before and chill it in the fridge before baking.
—Michelle Krzmarzick, Torrance, CA

TAKES: 30 min. • **MAKES:** 3 cups

1 pkg. (8 oz.) cream cheese, softened
½ cup grated Parmesan cheese
¼ cup mayonnaise
1 garlic clove, minced
1 tsp. dried basil
¼ tsp. garlic salt
¼ tsp. pepper
1 can (14 oz.) water-packed artichoke hearts, rinsed, drained and chopped
½ cup frozen chopped spinach, thawed and squeezed dry
¼ cup shredded mozzarella cheese
   Assorted crackers

1. Preheat oven to 350°. In a large bowl, combine the cream cheese, Parmesan, mayonnaise, garlic, basil, garlic salt and pepper and mix well. Stir in the artichokes and spinach.
2. Transfer to a greased 9-in. pie plate. Sprinkle with mozzarella cheese. Bake, uncovered, until bubbly and edge is lightly browned, 20-25 minutes. Serve with crackers.
2 Tbsp.: 68 cal., 6g fat (3g sat. fat), 13mg chol., 139mg sod., 2g carb. (0 sugars, 0 fiber), 2g pro.

THE BEST HUMMUS

Hummus is my go-to appetizer when I need something quick, easy and impressive. Over the years I've picked up a number of tricks that make this the best hummus you'll ever have.
—James Schend, Pleasant Prairie, WI

PREP: 25 min. + chilling
COOK: 20 min. • **MAKES:** 1½ cups

- 1   can (15 oz.) garbanzo beans or chickpeas, rinsed and drained
- ½   tsp. baking soda
- ¼   cup fresh lemon juice
- 1   Tbsp. minced garlic
- ½   tsp. kosher salt
- ½   tsp. ground cumin
- ½   cup tahini
- 2   Tbsp. extra virgin olive oil
- ¼   cup cold water
  Optional: Olive oil, roasted garbanzo beans, toasted sesame seeds, ground sumac

1. Place garbanzo beans in a large saucepan; add water to cover by 1 in. Gently rub beans together to loosen outer skin. Pour off water and any floating skins. Repeat 2-3 times until no skins float to the surface; drain. Return to saucepan; add baking soda and enough water to cover by 1 in. Bring to a boil; reduce heat. Simmer, uncovered, until beans are very tender and just starting to fall apart, 20-25 minutes.
2. Meanwhile, in a blender, process lemon juice, garlic and salt until almost a paste. Let stand 10 minutes; strain and discard solids. Stir in cumin. In a small bowl, stir together tahini and olive oil.
3. Drain beans and add to the blender; add cold water. Loosely cover and process until completely smooth. Add lemon mixture and process. With the blender running, slowly add the tahini mixture, scraping the side as needed. Adjust the seasoning with additional salt and cumin if desired.
4. Transfer mixture to a serving bowl; cover and refrigerate for at least 30 minutes. If desired, top with additional olive oil and optional toppings.

¼ cup: 250 cal., 19g fat (3g sat. fat), 0 chol., 361mg sod., 15g carb. (2g sugars, 5g fiber), 7g pro.

THE BEST HUMMUS

FREEZE OPTION

Homemade hummus should last for up to 1 week in an airtight container in the refrigerator. You can also freeze hummus in an airtight container—just pour a thin layer of olive oil on top before freezing. To use, let it sit in the refrigerator for a day until thawed and then mix thoroughly before serving.

❋ BUFFALO-STYLE CHICKEN CHILI DIP

Longing for that Buffalo wing thing without the bones? This do-ahead dip freezes well, so you can pull it out whenever you have guests and want to spread a little cheer.
—Brenda Calandrillo, Mahwah, NJ

PREP: 30 min. • **COOK:** 30 min.
MAKES: 11 cups

- 3 celery ribs, finely chopped
- 1 large onion, chopped
- 1 large carrot, finely chopped
- 5 garlic cloves, minced
- 2 Tbsp. butter
- 2 lbs. ground chicken
- 1 Tbsp. olive oil
- 2 cups chicken broth
- 1 can (16 oz.) kidney beans, rinsed and drained
- 1 can (15 oz.) cannellini beans, rinsed and drained
- 1 can (15 oz.) crushed tomatoes
- 1 can (15 oz.) tomato sauce
- 1 can (6 oz.) tomato paste
- ¼ cup Louisiana-style hot sauce
- 3 tsp. smoked paprika
- 1 bay leaf
- ¾ tsp. salt
- ¼ tsp. pepper
  Crumbled blue cheese, optional
  Celery stalks and tortilla chips

**BUFFALO-STYLE
CHICKEN CHILI DIP**

1. In a Dutch oven, saute the celery, onion, carrot and garlic in butter until tender. Remove and set aside. In the same pan, cook chicken in oil until no longer pink; drain.

2. Stir in broth, beans, tomatoes, tomato sauce, tomato paste, hot sauce, paprika, bay leaf, salt, pepper and vegetable mixture. Bring to a boil; reduce heat. Simmer, uncovered, until slightly thickened, 12-15 minutes. Discard bay leaf.

3. Serve desired amount of dip; if desired, sprinkle with crumbled blue cheese. Serve with celery and chips.

¼ cup: 64 cal., 3g fat (1g sat. fat), 15mg chol., 192mg sod., 6g carb. (1g sugars, 1g fiber), 5g pro.

FREEZE OPTION

Cool any dip you don't plan to serve; transfer to freezer containers. Cover and freeze for up to 3 months. To use dip, thaw in the refrigerator overnight. Heat through in saucepan. If desired, sprinkle with cheese; serve with celery and chips.

SIMPLE SALMON DIP

This is my go-to dip recipe for summer barbecues. The secret is the green chiles—they add just enough heat.
—Susan Jordan, Denver, CO

PREP: 15 min. + chilling
MAKES: 1¼ cups

- 1 pkg. (8 oz.) reduced-fat cream cheese
- 2 Tbsp. canned chopped green chiles
- 1½ tsp. lemon juice
- 2 green onions, chopped, divided
- 2 oz. smoked salmon fillet
  Assorted crackers or toasted French bread baguette slices

1. In a small bowl, mix the cream cheese, green chiles, lemon juice and half of the green onions. Flake salmon into small pieces; stir into cream cheese mixture. Refrigerate, covered, at least 2 hours before serving.

2. Top dip with remaining green onion. Serve with crackers.

3 Tbsp.: 107 cal., 8g fat (5g sat. fat), 29mg chol., 246mg sod., 2g carb. (1g sugars, 0 fiber), 6g pro.

MINI ROSEMARY-
ROAST BEEF
SANDWICHES

ⓟⓜ MINI ROSEMARY-ROAST BEEF SANDWICHES

Roast beef sandwiches never last long at a party, especially if you dollop them with zesty toppings.
—Susan Hein, Burlington, WI

PREP: 25 min. + chilling
BAKE: 50 min. + chilling
MAKES: 2 dozen

- 1 beef top round roast (3 lbs.)
- 3 tsp. kosher salt
- 2 tsp. crushed dried rosemary
- 2 Tbsp. olive oil, divided
- 2 tsp. pepper
- 2 cups mild giardiniera, drained
- 1 cup reduced-fat mayonnaise
- 2 Tbsp. stone-ground mustard
- 1 to 2 Tbsp. prepared horseradish
- 24 Hawaiian sweet rolls, split

1. Sprinkle roast with salt and rosemary. Cover and refrigerate at least 8 hours or up to 24 hours.
2. Preheat oven to 325°. Uncover roast and pat dry. Rub roast with 1 Tbsp. oil; sprinkle with pepper. In a large cast-iron or other ovenproof skillet, heat remaining 1 Tbsp. oil over medium-high heat. Brown roast on both sides.
3. Transfer to oven; roast until a thermometer reads 135° for medium-rare, 50-60 minutes. (Temperature of the roast will continue to rise about 10° upon standing.) Remove the roast from skillet; let stand 1 hour. Refrigerate, covered, at least 2 hours, until cold.
4. Place giardiniera in a food processor; pulse until finely chopped. In a small bowl, mix the mayonnaise, mustard and horseradish.
5. To serve, thinly slice cold beef. Serve on rolls with mayonnaise mixture and giardiniera.
1 sandwich with about 2 tsp. mayonnaise mixture and 4 tsp. giardiniera: 220 cal., 9g fat (3g sat. fat), 50mg chol., 466mg sod., 18g carb. (7g sugars, 1g fiber), 17g pro.

CREAMY
DEVILED EGGS

❄ 🍲 CHEESY MEATBALLS

Can meatballs be lucky? My guys think so, and they want them for game time. My beef, sausage and cheese recipe has a big fan following.
—Jill Hill, Dixon, IL

PREP: 1 hour • **COOK:** 4 hours
MAKES: about 9 dozen

- 1 large egg
- ½ cup 2% milk
- 2 Tbsp. dried minced onion
- 4 Tbsp. chili powder, divided
- 1 tsp. salt
- 1 tsp. pepper
- 1½ cups crushed Ritz crackers (about 1 sleeve)
- 2 lbs. ground beef
- 1 lb. bulk pork sausage
- 2 cups shredded Velveeta
- 3 cans (10¾ oz. each) condensed tomato soup, undiluted
- 2½ cups water
- ½ cup packed brown sugar

1. Preheat oven to 400°. In a large bowl, whisk egg, milk, minced onion, 2 Tbsp. chili powder, and the salt and pepper; stir in crushed crackers. Add the beef, sausage and cheese and mix lightly but thoroughly.
2. Shape mixture into 1-in. balls. Place meatballs on greased racks in 15x10x1-in. baking pans. Bake until browned, 15-18 minutes.
3. Meanwhile, in a 5- or 6-qt. slow cooker, combine soup, water, brown sugar and the remaining 2 Tbsp. chili powder. Gently stir in meatballs. Cook, covered, on low until meatballs are cooked through, 4-5 hours.
1 meatball: 52 cal., 3g fat (1g sat. fat), 11mg chol., 134mg sod., 4g carb. (2g sugars, 0 fiber), 3g pro.

CREAMY DEVILED EGGS

These deviled eggs are nicely flavored with a tang of mustard and a spark of sweetness from pickle relish. We served them at my daughter's wedding reception.
—Barbara Towler, Derby, OH

PREP: 1 hour + chilling
MAKES: 6 dozen

- 36 hard-boiled large eggs
- 1 pkg. (8 oz.) cream cheese, softened
- 1½ cups mayonnaise
- ⅓ cup sweet pickle relish
- ⅓ cup Dijon mustard
- ¾ tsp. salt
- ¼ tsp. pepper
  Optional: Paprika and fresh parsley

1. Slice eggs in half lengthwise; remove yolks and set yolks and whites aside.
2. In a large bowl, beat cream cheese until smooth. Add the mayonnaise, relish, mustard, salt, pepper and yolks; mix well. Stuff or pipe into egg whites. If desired, garnish with paprika and parsley. Refrigerate until serving.
2 stuffed egg halves: 172 cal., 15g fat (4g sat. fat), 222mg chol., 254mg sod., 2g carb. (1g sugars, 0 fiber), 7g pro.

TEST KITCHEN TIP

For convenience, eggs can be cooked, peeled and chilled up to 2 days before serving.

CHEESY
MEATBALLS

❄ EASY EGG ROLLS

I've always loved egg rolls, but every recipe I saw seemed too complicated. So I decided to start with a packaged coleslaw mix. Now I can make these yummy treats at a moment's notice.
—Samantha Dunn, Leesville, LA

PREP: 30 min. • **COOK:** 30 min.
MAKES: 28 servings

- 1 lb. ground beef
- 1 pkg. (14 oz.) coleslaw mix
- 2 Tbsp. soy sauce
- ½ tsp. garlic powder
- ¼ tsp. ground ginger
- ⅛ tsp. onion powder
- 28 egg roll wrappers
- 1 Tbsp. all-purpose flour
  Vegetable oil for frying

1. In a large skillet, cook beef over medium heat until no longer pink, 5-7 minutes, breaking meat into crumbles; drain and cool slightly. Combine beef, coleslaw mix, soy sauce, garlic powder, ginger and onion powder. In a small bowl, combine flour and enough water to make a paste.

2. With 1 corner of an egg roll wrapper facing you, place ¼ cup filling just below the center of the wrapper. (Cover remaining wrappers with a damp paper towel until ready to use.) Fold the bottom corner over filling; moisten remaining wrapper edges with flour mixture. Fold side corners toward center over filling. Roll egg roll up tightly, pressing at tip to seal. Repeat.

3. In an electric skillet or deep-fat fryer, heat oil to 375°. Fry the egg rolls, a few at a time, until golden brown, 3-4 minutes, turning occasionally. Drain egg rolls on paper towels.

1 egg roll: 185 cal., 9g fat (1g sat. fat), 13mg chol., 261mg sod., 20g carb. (1g sugars, 1g fiber), 6g pro

---
FREEZE OPTION

You can freeze these egg rolls either before or after frying. Wrap them in aluminum foil and keep them in a freezer-safe container for up to 3 months. To use, thaw in the refrigerator. If already fried, re-fry egg rolls to crisp them or heat them in the oven. If not fried, fry as the recipe directs.

EASY
EGG ROLLS

**CREAMY
RED PEPPER
VEGGIE DIP**

❋ BUFFALO CHICKEN POCKETS

Here's my idea of pub food made easy: biscuits flavored with Buffalo wing sauce and blue cheese. They're my Friday night favorite.
—Maria Regakis, Saugus, MA

TAKES: 30 min.
MAKES: 8 servings

- ¾ lb. ground chicken
- ⅓ cup Buffalo wing sauce
- 1 tube (16.3 oz.) large refrigerated buttermilk biscuits
- ½ cup shredded cheddar cheese
  Blue cheese salad dressing, optional

1. Preheat oven to 375°. In a large skillet, cook the chicken over medium heat until meat is no longer pink, 5-7 minutes, breaking into crumbles; drain. Remove from heat; stir in the wing sauce.
2. On a lightly floured surface, roll each biscuit into a 6-in. circle and top each with ¼ cup chicken mixture and 2 Tbsp. cheese. Fold dough over filling; pinch the edge to seal.
3. Transfer to an ungreased baking sheet. Bake until golden brown, 12-14 minutes. If desired, serve with blue cheese dressing.
1 pocket: 258 cal., 12g fat (5g sat. fat), 35mg chol., 987mg sod., 25g carb. (3g sugars, 1g fiber), 12g pro.

┌─ **FREEZE OPTION** ─────────┐

Freeze cooled pockets in a freezer container. To use, reheat pockets on an ungreased baking sheet in a preheated 375° oven until heated through.

└─────────────────────────────┘

CREAMY RED PEPPER VEGGIE DIP

I received this, my go-to veggie dip recipe, from a college roommate. Thick and creamy with just a touch of sweetness, it's always a winner.
—Lynne German, Buford, GA

PREP: 15 min.
COOK: 5 min. + chilling
MAKES: 2 ½ cups

- 2 large eggs, slightly beaten
- 2 Tbsp. sugar
- 2 Tbsp. cider vinegar
- 1 Tbsp. butter, softened
- 1 Tbsp. all-purpose flour
- 1 pkg. (8 oz.) cream cheese, softened
- 1 small sweet red pepper, chopped
- 4 green onions (both white and green portions), chopped
  Fresh baby carrots
  Fresh broccoli florets

In a small saucepan over low heat, whisk together the first 5 ingredients. Increase heat to medium; whisk until thickened, 4-5 minutes. Remove from heat. Stir in cream cheese, pepper and onions; mix well. Refrigerate 2 hours; serve with baby carrots and broccoli florets.
¼ cup: 121 cal., 10g fat (6g sat. fat), 63mg chol., 96mg sod., 5g carb. (4g sugars, 0 fiber), 3g pro.

PAGE 103

PAGE 98

Side-Dish Staples

A delicious side dish makes a good meal great, but sides can get overlooked in the rush to get a meal on the table. Here are some first-rate sides that slot right into your schedule.

PAGE 106

PAGE 93

LEMON-SESAME
GREEN BEANS

🍲 PIZZA BEANS

This dish is wonderful for parties or as a main dish. It can even be made the day before and reheated.
—Taste of Home *Test Kitchen*

PREP: 20 min. • **COOK:** 6 hours
MAKES: 20 servings

- 1 lb. bulk Italian sausage
- 2 cups chopped celery
- 2 cups chopped onion
- 1 can (14½ oz.) cut green beans, drained
- 1 can (14½ oz.) cut wax beans, drained
- 1 can (16 oz.) kidney beans, rinsed and drained
- 1 can (16 oz.) butter beans, drained
- 1 can (15 oz.) pork and beans
- 3 cans (8 oz. each) pizza sauce
  Optional: Grated Parmesan cheese, minced fresh oregano and crushed red pepper flakes

In a large skillet, brown sausage over medium heat until no longer pink, breaking it into crumbles. Transfer to a 5-qt. slow cooker with a slotted spoon. Add celery and onion to skillet; cook until softened, about 5 minutes. Drain. Add vegetable mixture and the next 6 ingredients to slow cooker; mix well. Cook, covered, on low until bubbly, 6-8 hours. If desired, serve with toppings.
¾ cup: 142 cal., 6g fat (2g sat. fat), 12mg chol., 542mg sod., 17g carb. (4g sugars, 5g fiber), 7g pro.

LEMON-SESAME GREEN BEANS

There's a kabob shop in Charlottesville, Virginia, called Sticks, and it has wonderful sides, including sesame beans. I love them so much that I had to make my own version. You can use fresh or frozen green beans; haricots verts (French green beans) work well too. This salad only gets better as it sits, so it's a perfect (and convenient!) recipe to make a day or two in advance.
—Dyan Carlson, Kents Store, VA

TAKES: 20 min.
MAKES: 6 servings

- 1½ lbs. fresh green beans, trimmed and cut into 1-in. pieces
- 3 Tbsp. sesame oil
- 1 Tbsp. lemon juice
- 3 Tbsp. sesame seeds, toasted
- 3 tsp. grated lemon zest
- 2 garlic cloves, minced
- ½ tsp. salt
- ⅛ to ¼ tsp. crushed red pepper flakes
- ⅛ tsp. pepper

1. In a large saucepan, bring 4 cups water to a boil. Add green beans; cook, uncovered, for 3-4 minutes or just until crisp-tender. Remove green beans; drain well.
2. Whisk the remaining ingredients together until blended. Pour over the green beans; toss to coat. Serve hot or at room temperature.
⅔ cup: 124 cal., 9g fat (1g sat. fat), 0 chol., 204mg sod., 10g carb. (3g sugars, 5g fiber), 3g pro. **Diabetic exchanges:** 2 fat, 1 vegetable.

TEST KITCHEN TIP

To amp up the Italian flavor, saute 2-3 chopped sweet bell peppers along with the Italian sausage.

PIZZA
BEANS

DILL POTATOES ROMANOFF

These tangy potato cubes, topped with cheddar cheese, can be mixed ahead and refrigerated until you're ready to bake them. I like to serve them with steak and green beans.
—Rita Deere, Evansville, IN

PREP: 30 min. • **BAKE:** 25 min.
MAKES: 2 servings

- 2 cups cubed red potatoes
- ⅔ cup 1% cottage cheese
- ⅓ cup sour cream
- 1 Tbsp. all-purpose flour
- 1 Tbsp. dried minced onion
- ⅛ to ¼ tsp. dill weed
- ⅛ tsp. salt
- ¼ cup shredded cheddar cheese
  Snipped fresh dill, optional

1. Preheat oven to 350°. Place potatoes in a large saucepan and cover with water. Bring to a boil. Reduce heat; cover and cook 15 minutes or until tender. Drain and cool.
2. In a blender or food processor, puree the cottage cheese, sour cream and flour. Pour into a large bowl. Stir in the onion, dill and salt. Add potatoes; toss gently.
3. Transfer to a shallow 3-cup baking dish coated with cooking spray. Bake, uncovered, for 20 minutes. Sprinkle with shredded cheddar cheese; bake until the cheese is melted, about 5 minutes longer. If desired, garnish with fresh dill.
1 cup: 322 cal., 14g fat (8g sat. fat), 26mg chol., 566mg sod., 33g carb. (6g sugars, 3g fiber), 17g pro.

DILL POTATOES
ROMANOFF

❄ PORTOBELLO RISOTTO WITH MASCARPONE

Portobello mushrooms add a beefy flavor to this creamy classic. Each serving is topped with soft, buttery mascarpone cheese.

—Carmella Ryan, Rockville Centre, NY

PREP: 20 min. • **COOK:** 25 min.
MAKES: 6 servings

- 1½ cups water
- 1 can (14 oz.) reduced-sodium beef broth
- ½ cup chopped shallots
- 2 garlic cloves, minced
- 1 Tbsp. canola oil
- 1 cup uncooked arborio rice
- 1 Tbsp. minced fresh thyme or 1 tsp. dried thyme
- ½ tsp. salt
- ½ tsp. pepper
- ½ cup white wine or additional reduced-sodium beef broth
- 1 cup sliced baby portobello mushrooms, chopped
- ¼ cup grated Parmesan cheese
- ½ cup mascarpone cheese

1. In a large saucepan, heat water and broth and keep warm. In another large saucepan, saute shallots and garlic in oil until the shallots are tender, 2-3 minutes. Add the arborio rice, thyme, salt and pepper; cook and stir for 2-3 minutes. Reduce heat; stir in wine. Cook and stir until all of the liquid is absorbed.
2. Add heated broth, ½ cup at a time, stirring constantly. Allow the liquid to absorb between additions. Cook just until risotto is creamy and rice is almost tender, about 20 minutes.
3. Add mushrooms and Parmesan cheese; stir gently until the cheese is melted.

PORTOBELLO RISOTTO
WITH MASCARPONE

4. Serve immediately. Garnish each serving with 1 heaping Tbsp. of mascarpone cheese.
¾ cup risotto mixture with 1 heaping Tbsp. marscarpone cheese: 350 cal., 21g fat (10g sat. fat), 51mg chol., 393mg sod., 31g carb. (1g sugars, 1g fiber), 7g pro.

┌─ **FREEZE OPTION** ───

Before adding mascarpone cheese, freeze cooled risotto mixture in freezer containers. To use, partially thaw in refrigerator overnight. Heat through in a saucepan, stirring occasionally; add broth or water if necessary. Garnish as directed.

CORN & CUCUMBERS SALAD

This was one of my mother's recipes and I think of her whenever I make it. It's a nice change from a regular cucumber salad.
—Jean Moore, Pliny, WV

PREP: 10 min. + chilling
MAKES: 8 servings

 2 medium cucumbers, peeled and thinly sliced
 2 cups fresh corn, cooked
 ½ medium onion, thinly sliced
 ½ cup vinegar
 2 Tbsp. sugar
 2 Tbsp. water
 1 tsp. dill weed
 1 tsp. salt
 ¼ tsp. pepper
  Pinch cayenne pepper

In a large bowl, combine all ingredients. Chill, covered, for several hours.
¾ cup: 54 cal., 1g fat (0 sat. fat), 0 chol., 301mg sod., 12g carb. (6g sugars, 2g fiber), 2g pro.
Diabetic exchanges: 1 starch.

BEST EVER CRESCENT ROLLS

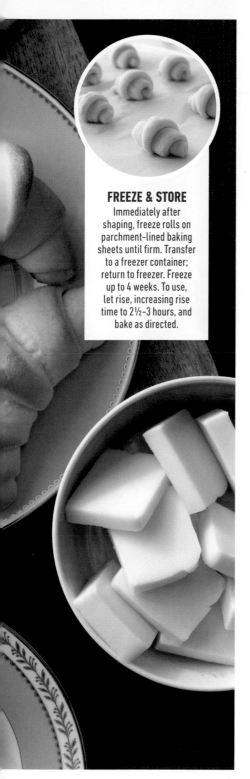

FREEZE & STORE

Immediately after shaping, freeze rolls on parchment-lined baking sheets until firm. Transfer to a freezer container; return to freezer. Freeze up to 4 weeks. To use, let rise, increasing rise time to 2½–3 hours, and bake as directed.

❄ ⓟ BEST EVER CRESCENT ROLLS

My daughter and I have cranked out dozens of these homemade crescent rolls. It's a real team effort. I cut the dough into pie-shaped wedges; she rolls them up.
—Irene Yeh, Mequon, WI

PREP: 40 min. + chilling
BAKE: 10 min./batch
MAKES: 32 rolls

- 3¾ to 4¼ cups all-purpose flour
- 2 pkg. (¼ oz. each) active dry yeast
- 1 tsp. salt
- 1 cup 2% milk
- ½ cup butter, cubed
- ¼ cup honey
- 3 large egg yolks. room temperature
- 2 Tbsp. butter, melted

1. Combine 1½ cups flour, yeast and salt. In a small saucepan, heat milk, cubed butter and honey to 120°-130°. Add to dry ingredients; beat on medium speed 2 minutes. Add egg yolks; beat on high 2 minutes. Stir in enough remaining flour to form a soft dough (dough will be sticky).
2. Turn dough onto a floured surface; knead until smooth and elastic, 6-8 minutes. Place in a greased bowl, turning once to grease the top. Cover and let rise in a warm place until doubled, about 45 minutes.
3. Punch down dough. Cover and refrigerate overnight.

4. Turn chilled dough onto a lightly floured surface; divide in half. Roll each portion into a 14-in. circle; cut each circle into 16 wedges. Lightly brush wedges with melted butter. Roll up from wide ends, pinching the pointed ends to seal. Place 2 in. apart on parchment-lined baking sheets, point side down. Curve ends to form crescents. Cover; let rise in a warm place until doubled, about 45 minutes.
5. Preheat oven to 375°. Bake until golden brown, 9-11 minutes. Remove from pans to wire racks; serve warm.

1 unfilled roll: 104 cal., 4g fat (3g sat. fat), 28mg chol., 107mg sod., 14g carb. (3g sugars, 1g fiber), 2g pro.

TO MAKE FILLED CRESCENT ROLLS: Sprinkle the dough with filling of choice immediately after brushing with butter; shape and bake as directed.

CHIVE CRESCENTS: Divide ⅔ cup minced fresh chives between the 2 circles of dough.

ORANGE-PECAN CRESCENTS: Toss 1 cup finely chopped pecans with ⅓ cup sugar and 4 tsp. grated orange zest; divide the mixture between the 2 circles.

CRANBERRY-THYME CRESCENTS: Toss 1 cup finely chopped dried cranberries with ⅔ cup finely chopped walnuts and 2 tsp. minced fresh thyme leaves; divide mixture between the 2 circles.

SLOW-COOKER
MASHED POTATOES

🍲 SLOW-COOKER MASHED POTATOES

Sour cream and cream cheese give richness to these smooth make-ahead potatoes. They are wonderful for Thanksgiving or Christmas dinner, as there is no last-minute mashing required.
—Trudy Vincent, Valles Mines, MO

PREP: 20 min. • **COOK:** 2 hours
MAKES: 10 servings

- 3 oz. cream cheese, softened
- ½ cup sour cream
- ¼ cup plus 1 Tbsp. softened butter, divided
- 1 envelope ranch salad dressing mix
- 1 Tbsp. minced fresh parsley
- 6 cups warm mashed potatoes (without added milk or butter)

In a large bowl, combine the cream cheese, sour cream, ¼ cup butter, salad dressing mix and parsley; stir in mashed potatoes. Transfer to a 3-qt. slow cooker. Cook, covered, on low for 2-3 hours. Top with remaining 1 Tbsp. butter.

¾ cup: 210 cal., 11g fat (7g sat. fat), 27mg chol., 670mg sod., 23g carb. (1g sugars, 4g fiber), 3g pro.
Note: This recipe was tested with fresh potatoes (not instant) in a slow cooker with heating elements surrounding the unit, not only in the base.

EASY PEASY BISCUITS

❄ EASY PEASY BISCUITS

I love that I can make these biscuits and have enough left over to freeze for another meal. They are wonderful with homemade peach preserves.
—Amanda West, Shelbyville, TN

PREP: 25 min. • **BAKE:** 10 min.
MAKES: 2 dozen

- 4 cups all-purpose flour
- 4 Tbsp. baking powder
- 1 Tbsp. sugar
- 1 Tbsp. ground flaxseed
- 1 tsp. sea salt
- 1 cup solid coconut oil
- 1½ cups 2% milk

1. Whisk flour, baking powder, sugar, flaxseed and salt. Add coconut oil; cut in with a pastry blender until mixture resembles coarse crumbs. Add milk; stir just until moistened.
2. Turn onto a lightly floured surface; knead gently 8-10 times. Pat or roll dough into a rectangle ½ in. thick; fold dough into thirds (as you would a letter). Pat or roll dough again into a rectangle ½ in. thick; cut with a pizza cutter or knife into 24 biscuits, each about 2½ in. square.
3. Place biscuits 1½ in. apart on ungreased baking sheets. Bake at 450° until light brown, 8-10 minutes. Serve warm.
1 biscuit: 167 cal., 10g fat (8g sat. fat), 1mg chol., 328mg sod., 17g carb. (1g sugars, 1g fiber), 3g pro.

┌ FREEZE OPTION ─

Freeze cut biscuit dough on waxed paper-lined baking sheets until firm. Transfer to airtight containers; return to freezer. To use, bake in a preheated 350° oven until light brown, 15-20 minutes. To freeze baked biscuits, let cool, then freeze in airtight containers. To use, heat in a 350° oven until warm, 5-10 minutes.

✳ SCALLOPED SWEET CORN CASSEROLE

I grew up enjoying my grandmother's sweet corn casserole. Now that I'm a grandmother myself, I still serve that comforting, delicious side dish.
—Lonnie Hartstack, Clarinda, IA

PREP: 25 min. • **BAKE:** 50 min.
MAKES: 8 servings

- 4 tsp. cornstarch
- ⅔ cup water
- ¼ cup butter, cubed
- 3 cups fresh or frozen corn
- 1 can (5 oz.) evaporated milk
- ¾ tsp. plus 1½ tsp. sugar, divided
- ½ tsp. plus ¾ tsp. salt, divided
- 3 large eggs
- ¾ cup 2% milk
- ¼ tsp. pepper
- 3 cups cubed bread
- 1 small onion, chopped
- 1 cup Rice Krispies, slightly crushed
- 3 Tbsp. butter, melted

1. Preheat oven to 350°. Mix cornstarch and water until smooth. In a large saucepan, heat butter over medium heat. Stir in corn, evaporated milk, ¾ tsp. sugar and ½ tsp. salt; bring just to a boil. Stir in the cornstarch mixture; return to a boil, stirring constantly. Cook and stir until thickened, 1-2 minutes; cool slightly.

2. Whisk eggs, milk, pepper and the remaining 1½ tsp. sugar and ¾ tsp. salt until blended. Stir in bread, onion and corn mixture. Transfer to a greased 8-in. square or 1½-qt. baking dish.

3. Bake, uncovered, 40 minutes. Toss Rice Krispies with melted butter; sprinkle over casserole. Bake until golden brown, 10-15 minutes longer.

⅔ cup: 258 cal., 15g fat (8g sat. fat), 104mg chol., 604mg sod., 26g carb. (9g sugars, 2g fiber), 8g pro.

FREEZE OPTION

Cool unbaked casserole, reserving Rice Krispies topping for baking; cover and freeze. To use, partially thaw in refrigerator overnight. Remove from refrigerator 30 minutes before baking. Preheat oven to 350°. Bake casserole as directed, increasing time as necessary to heat through and for a thermometer inserted in center to read 165°.

SCALLOPED SWEET CORN CASSEROLE

WINTER SQUASH WITH MAPLE GLAZE

You can use any type of winter squash in this simple vegetable bake, but I like to use at least two varieties. It can be assembled a day ahead, then baked just before serving.
—Teri Kreyche, Tustin, CA

PREP: 20 min. • **BAKE:** 50 min.
MAKES: 6 servings

- 2 cups chopped peeled parsnips
- 2 cups cubed peeled kabocha squash
- 2 cups cubed peeled butternut squash
- ⅓ cup butter, cubed
- ½ cup maple syrup
- 1 Tbsp. minced fresh rosemary or 1 tsp. dried rosemary, crushed
- 1 garlic clove, minced
- ½ tsp. salt
- ¼ tsp. pepper
- ¾ cup coarsely chopped almonds

1. Preheat oven to 375°. In a large bowl, combine parsnips and squashes. In a small saucepan, melt butter over medium heat; whisk in maple syrup, rosemary, garlic, salt and pepper. Pour over vegetables and toss to coat.
2. Transfer to a greased 11x7-in. baking dish. Bake, covered, for 40 minutes. Uncover; sprinkle with chopped almonds. Bake until the vegetables are tender, 10-15 minutes longer.
¾ cup: 339 cal., 19g fat (7g sat. fat), 27mg chol., 290mg sod., 43g carb. (22g sugars, 7g fiber), 5g pro.

WINTER SQUASH WITH
MAPLE GLAZE

LATTICE CORN PIE

12-HOUR SALAD

❄ LATTICE CORN PIE

This unusual side dish is full of old-fashioned goodness, with tender diced potatoes and a fresh, sweet corn flavor. Once you've tasted this pie, you'll never want to serve corn another way!
—Kathy Spang, Manheim, PA

PREP: 25 min. • **BAKE:** 35 min.
MAKES: 8 servings

- 1 cup diced peeled potatoes
- ⅓ cup 2% milk
- 2 large eggs, room temperature
- 2 cups fresh or frozen corn, thawed
- 1 tsp. sugar
- ½ tsp. salt
- 2 sheets refrigerated pie crust

1. Preheat oven to 375°. Place potatoes in a small saucepan and cover with water. Bring to a boil. Reduce heat; cook, covered, until tender, 6-8 minutes. Drain and set aside.
2. In a blender, combine the milk, eggs, corn, sugar and salt; cover and process until blended.

3. Unroll 1 sheet crust into a 9-in. pie plate. Trim to ½ in. beyond rim of plate; flute edge. Spoon potatoes into crust; top with corn mixture (crust will be full). Roll out remaining crust; make a lattice top. Seal and flute edge.
4. Bake until crust is golden brown and filling is bubbly, 35-40 minutes.
1 piece: 308 cal., 16g fat (7g sat. fat), 57mg chol., 373mg sod., 37g carb. (5g sugars, 1g fiber), 5g pro.

┌─ **FREEZE OPTION** ─────
Place baked pie in the freezer, uncovered, until slightly firm (2-3 hours). Remove from freezer and tightly wrap in 2-3 layers of plastic wrap, covering all sides. Place in a large freezer bag and store in freezer. To use frozen pie, remove from freezer 30 minutes before baking. Place on a baking sheet and bake at 375° for 20 minutes or until filling is heated through, covering with foil if necessary.

🅟🅜 12-HOUR SALAD

This recipe was Mom's scrumptious scheme to get her kids to eat our vegetables. She never had any trouble when she served this colorful crunchy salad. Mom thought this salad was a real bonus for the cook since it must be made the night before.
—Dorothy Bowen, Thomasville, NC

PREP: 20 min. + chilling
MAKES: 12 servings

- 8 cups torn mixed salad greens
- 1½ cups chopped celery
- 2 medium green peppers, chopped
- 1 medium red onion, chopped
- 2½ cups frozen peas (about 10 oz.), thawed
- 1 cup mayonnaise
- 1 cup sour cream
- 3 Tbsp. sugar
- 1 cup shredded cheddar cheese
- ½ lb. bacon strips, cooked and crumbled

1. Place greens in a 3-qt. bowl or 13x9-in. dish. Layer with celery, peppers, onion and peas.
2. Mix mayonnaise, sour cream and sugar; spread over top. Sprinkle with cheese and bacon. Refrigerate, covered, 12 hours or overnight.
1 cup: 280 cal., 23g fat (7g sat. fat), 22mg chol., 347mg sod., 11g carb. (6g sugars, 3g fiber), 8g pro.

STEWED ZUCCHINI & TOMATOES

ITALIAN SPAGHETTI SALAD

This attractive, fresh-tasting salad can conveniently be prepared the night before. It makes enough for a crowd!
—Lucia Johnson, Massena, NY

PREP: 20 min. + chilling
MAKES: 16 servings

- 1 pkg. (16 oz.) thin spaghetti, halved
- 3 medium tomatoes, diced
- 3 small zucchini, diced
- 1 large cucumber, halved, seeded and diced
- 1 medium green pepper, diced
- 1 medium sweet red pepper, diced
- 1 bottle (8 oz.) Italian salad dressing
- 2 Tbsp. grated Parmesan cheese
- 1½ tsp. sesame seeds
- 1½ tsp. poppy seeds
- ½ tsp. paprika
- ¼ tsp. celery seed
- ⅛ tsp. garlic powder

1. Cook spaghetti according to package directions; drain and rinse in cold water. Place in a large bowl; add tomatoes, zucchini, cucumber and peppers.
2. Combine the remaining ingredients; pour over salad and toss to coat. Cover and refrigerate for at least 2 hours.
1 cup: 158 cal., 3g fat (1g sat. fat), 1mg chol., 168mg sod., 26g carb. (4g sugars, 2g fiber), 5g pro.
Diabetic exchanges: 1½ starch, 1 vegetable, ½ fat.

🍲 STEWED ZUCCHINI & TOMATOES

A fresh take on traditional vegetable sides, zucchini, tomatoes and green peppers star in this dish that you can prep in advance and cook while you do other things. Bubbly cheddar cheese adds a down-home feel.
—Barbara Smith, Salem, OR

PREP: 20 min. • **COOK:** 3½ hours
MAKES: 6 servings

- 3 medium zucchini, cut into ¼-in. slices
- 1 tsp. salt, divided
- ½ tsp. pepper, divided
- 1 medium onion, thinly sliced
- 1 medium green pepper, thinly sliced
- 3 medium tomatoes, sliced
- ⅔ cup condensed tomato soup, undiluted
- 1 tsp. dried basil
- 1 cup shredded cheddar cheese
  Minced fresh basil, optional

1. Place zucchini in a greased 3-qt. slow cooker. Sprinkle with ½ tsp. salt and ¼ tsp. pepper. Layer with onion, green pepper and tomatoes. In a small bowl, combine the soup, basil and remaining salt and pepper; spread over tomatoes.
2. Cover and cook on low for 3-4 hours or until vegetables are tender. Sprinkle with cheese. Cover and cook 30 minutes longer or until cheese is melted. If desired, top with fresh basil.
¾ cup: 126 cal., 6g fat (4g sat. fat), 20mg chol., 678mg sod., 14g carb. (8g sugars, 3g fiber), 7g pro.
Diabetic exchanges: 1 vegetable, 1 fat, ½ starch.

ITALIAN
SPAGHETTI SALAD

GREEN BEAN CASSEROLE

This green bean casserole has always been one of my favorite dishes—it's so easy to put together! You can make it before any guests arrive and keep it refrigerated until baking time.
—Anna Baker, Blaine, WA

PREP: 15 min. • **BAKE:** 30 min.
MAKES: 10 servings

- 2   cans (10¾ oz. each) condensed cream of mushroom soup, undiluted
- 1   cup whole milk
- 2   tsp. soy sauce
- ⅛   tsp. pepper
- 2   pkg. (16 oz. each) frozen green beans, cooked and drained
- 1   can (6 oz.) french-fried onions, divided

1. In a bowl, combine soup, milk, soy sauce and pepper. Gently stir in beans. Spoon half of the mixture into a 13x9-in. baking dish. Sprinkle with half of the onions. Spoon the remaining bean mixture over the top. Sprinkle with remaining onions.
2. Bake at 350° until heated through and the onions are brown and crispy, 30-35 minutes.

1 cup: 163 cal., 11g fat (3g sat. fat), 5mg chol., 485mg sod., 14g carb. (2g sugars, 1g fiber), 2g pro.

TEST KITCHEN TIP

For a little flavor twist, experiment with different types of cream soups—cream of mushroom with roasted garlic or cream of celery, for example.

GREEN BEAN CASSEROLE

DILL PICKLE POTATO SALAD

Dill pickles add some pizazz to this old-fashioned chilled potato salad. The creamy, well-dressed side dish makes a flavorful and attractive addition to a Fourth of July picnic or church supper.
—Nancy Holland, Morgan Hill, CA

PREP: 20 min. + chilling
BAKE: 20 min. + cooling
MAKES: 10 servings

- 3 lbs. potatoes (about 8 medium)
- 6 hard-boiled large eggs, chopped
- 3 celery ribs, chopped
- 6 green onions, chopped
- 2 medium dill pickles, finely chopped
- 1½ cups mayonnaise
- ¼ cup dill pickle juice
- 4½ tsp. prepared mustard
- 1 tsp. celery seed
- 1 tsp. salt
- ½ tsp. pepper
  Optional: Leaf lettuce and dill pickle slices

1. Place potatoes in a Dutch oven or large kettle and cover with water; bring to a boil. Reduce heat; cover and simmer until tender, 20-30 minutes. Drain and let cool.
2. Peel and cube potatoes; place in a large bowl. Add eggs, celery, onions and pickles.
3. In a small bowl, combine mayonnaise, pickle juice, mustard, celery seed, salt and pepper until blended. Pour over the potato mixture; mix well. Cover and refrigerate at least 4 hours. If desired, serve in a lettuce-lined bowl and top with pickle slices.
¾ cup: 415 cal., 30g fat (5g sat. fat), 139mg chol., 677mg sod., 30g carb. (2g sugars, 3g fiber), 7g pro.

PM CLASSIC MAKE-AHEAD MASHED POTATOES

This light holiday staple saves time on Christmas Day. No more frantically whipping the potatoes while hungry family and guests hang around the kitchen!
—Marty Rummel, Trout Lake, WA

PREP: 40 min. + chilling
BAKE: 55 min. • **MAKES:** 12 servings

- 5 lbs. potatoes, peeled and cut into wedges
- 1 pkg. (8 oz.) reduced-fat cream cheese, cubed
- 2 large egg whites, beaten
- 1 cup reduced-fat sour cream
- 2 tsp. onion powder
- 1 tsp. salt
- ½ tsp. pepper
- 1 Tbsp. butter, melted

1. Place potatoes in a Dutch oven; cover with water. Bring to a boil. Reduce heat; cover and cook until tender, 15-20 minutes. Drain.
2. In a large bowl, mash potatoes with cream cheese. Combine the egg whites, sour cream, onion powder, salt and pepper; stir into potatoes until blended. Transfer to a greased 3-qt. baking dish. Drizzle with butter. Cover and refrigerate overnight.
3. Remove from refrigerator 30 minutes before baking. Preheat oven to 350°. Bake, covered, 50 minutes. Uncover; bake 5-10 minutes longer or until a thermometer reads 160°.
¾ cup: 220 cal., 7g fat (4g sat. fat), 22mg chol., 316mg sod., 32g carb. (4g sugars, 3g fiber), 7g pro.
Diabetic exchanges: 2 starch, 1 fat.

DILL PICKLE POTATO SALAD

SAUCY BAKED BEANS

My family enjoys these beans with cornbread, but they also round out any cookout.
—*Phyllis Schmalz, Kansas City, KS*

PREP: 15 min. • **BAKE:** 1¼ hours
MAKES: 12 servings

- 2 cans (28 oz. each) pork and beans
- 1½ cups packed brown sugar
- ½ lb. sliced bacon, cooked and crumbled
- 1 cup finely chopped onion
- 1 cup cola
- 1 cup ketchup
- 2 Tbsp. ground mustard

Preheat oven to 325°. In a large bowl, mix all ingredients. Transfer to a greased 3-qt. baking dish. Bake, uncovered, 1¼-1½ hours or until bubbly.

¾ cup: 293 cal., 5g fat (1g sat. fat), 5mg chol., 793mg sod., 59g carb. (42g sugars, 7g fiber), 9g pro.

TO MAKE AHEAD
These baked beans will keep for 3-5 days in the refrigerator. Reheat in a saucepan over low heat until heated through.

HOMEMADE PIEROGI

❄ HOMEMADE PIEROGI

Pierogi are dumplings or tiny pies stuffed with a filling—often potatoes and cheese—and boiled, then cooked in butter. Our friends always ask us to bring them to potlucks.
—Diane Gawrys, Manchester, TN

PREP: 1 hour • **COOK:** 5 min./batch
MAKES: 6 dozen

- 5   cups all-purpose flour
- 1   tsp. salt
- 1   cup water
- 3   large eggs
- ½   cup butter, softened

FILLING
- 4   medium potatoes, peeled and cubed
- 2   medium onions, chopped
- 2   Tbsp. butter
- 5   oz. cream cheese, softened
- ½   tsp. salt
- ½   tsp. pepper

ADDITIONAL INGREDIENTS (FOR EACH SERVING)
- ¼   cup chopped onion
- 1   Tbsp. butter
     Minced fresh parsley

1. In a food processor, combine flour and salt; cover and pulse to blend. Add water, eggs and butter; cover and pulse until dough forms a ball, adding an additional 1 to 2 Tbsp. of water or flour if needed. Let rest, covered, 15 to 30 minutes.

2. Place potatoes in a large saucepan and cover with water. Bring to a boil over high heat. Reduce heat; cover and simmer until tender, 10-15 minutes. Meanwhile, in a large skillet over medium-high heat, saute onions in butter until tender.

3. Drain potatoes. Over very low heat, stir potatoes until steam has evaporated, 1-2 minutes. Press through a potato ricer or strainer into a large bowl. Stir in cream cheese, salt, pepper and onion mixture.

4. Divide dough into 4 parts. On a lightly floured surface, roll 1 portion of dough to ⅛-in. thickness; cut with a floured 3-in. biscuit cutter. Place 2 tsp. filling in center of each circle. Moisten edges with water; fold in half and press edges to seal. Repeat with remaining dough and filling.

5. Bring a Dutch oven of water to a boil over high heat; add pierogi in batches. Reduce heat to a gentle simmer; cook until pierogi float to the top and are tender, 1-2 minutes. Remove with a slotted spoon.

6. In a skillet, saute 4 pierogi and onion in butter until pierogi are lightly browned and heated through; sprinkle with parsley. Repeat with remaining pierogi.

4 pierogi: 373 cal., 22g fat (13g sat. fat), 86mg chol., 379mg sod., 38g carb. (3g sugars, 2g fiber), 6g pro.

FREEZE OPTION

Place cooled pierogi on waxed paper-lined 15x10x1-in. baking pans; freeze until firm. Transfer to an airtight freezer container; freeze for up to 3 months. To use, for each serving, in a large skillet, saute 4 pierogi and ¼ cup chopped onion in 1 Tbsp. butter until pierogi are lightly browned and heated through; sprinkle with minced fresh parsley.

ARROZ CON GANDULES
(RICE WITH PIGEON PEAS)

MAKE-AHEAD SOFRITO

Sofrito is a base used in many Puerto Rican recipes. Also try it on chilies, enchiladas and tacos. Separate and peel cloves of one head of garlic. Quarter 1 medium green pepper, 1 medium onion and 1 plum tomato. Place all in a food processor; add ½ cup fresh cilantro. Cover and process until finely chopped. Use immediately, refrigerate up to 1 week or freeze in small portions in resealable freezer bags for up to 1 month.

❄ ARROZ CON GANDULES (RICE WITH PIGEON PEAS)

Feed a crowd with this authentic Puerto Rican dish, which was handed down to me from my mom. It's a staple with the familiar at all our gatherings.
—Evelyn Robles, Oak Creek, WI

PREP: 15 min. • **COOK:** 30 min.
MAKES: 18 servings

- ½ cup SOFRITO (opposite page)
- 2 Tbsp. canola oil
- 4 cups uncooked long grain rice
- 1 envelope Goya sazon with coriander and annatto
- 7 cups water
- 1 can (15 oz.) pigeon peas, drained
- 2 cans (5 oz. each) Vienna sausage, drained and chopped
- ½ cup tomato sauce
- 1¼ tsp. salt
- 1 envelope Goya ham-flavored concentrate
- ½ tsp. chicken bouillon granules
- ¼ tsp. pepper

In a Dutch oven, cook sofrito in oil over medium-low heat, stirring occasionally, about 5 minutes. Add rice and sazon; cook and stir until rice is lightly toasted, 3-4 minutes. Add remaining ingredients. Bring to a boil. Reduce heat; simmer, covered, until tender, 15-20 minutes. Fluff with a fork.

┌─ **FREEZE OPTION** ─────
Chill in an even layer on greased baking sheets. Store in freezer-safe containers; freeze up to 2 months. To use, place in a microwave-safe bowl; cover with a damp paper towel. Cook in 2-minute intervals, stirring occasionally, until heated.

¾ cup: 220 cal., 5g fat (1g sat. fat), 14mg chol., 537mg sod., 38g carb. (1g sugars, 2g fiber), 6g pro.

FROZEN WALDORF SALAD

❄ FROZEN WALDORF SALAD

While I was growing up on a farm in Kansas, we always had lots of hungry men around during the harvest. We served this salad often since it was easy to increase and we could prepare it ahead of time.
—Mildred Hall, Topeka, KS

PREP: 25 min. + freezing
MAKES: 12 servings

- 1 can (20 oz.) crushed pineapple
- 1 cup sugar
- 2 large eggs, beaten
  Dash salt
- 1 cup chopped celery
- 2 medium red apples, chopped
- 1 cup chopped pecans
- 1 cup heavy whipping cream, whipped
  Lettuce leaves, optional

1. Drain pineapple, reserving juice. In a saucepan, combine pineapple juice with sugar, eggs and salt. Cook, stirring constantly, over medium-low heat until slightly thickened. Remove from heat; cool. Stir in pineapple, celery, apples and pecans. Fold in whipped cream.
2. Pour into a 9-in. square pan. Cover and freeze until firm. To serve, remove from the freezer and let stand at room temperature for 15 minutes before cutting. Serve on a bed of lettuce if desired.
1 piece: 257 cal., 15g fat (5g sat. fat), 63mg chol., 40mg sod., 30g carb. (26g sugars, 2g fiber), 3g pro.

THE BEST CHEESY SCALLOPED POTATOES

Here's my tried-and-true version of scalloped potatoes. I slice them extra thin and toss them in a rich, creamy cheese sauce. You can also finish these in the slow cooker instead of baking, so you can be done with your kitchen work early and the potatoes will be ready when you are.

—Aria Thornton, Milwaukee, WI

PREP: 40 min.
BAKE: 1¼ hours + standing
MAKES: 10 servings

- 4 Tbsp. butter
- ½ cup chopped onion
- 1 tsp. ground mustard
- 1 tsp. salt
- ½ tsp. coarsely ground pepper
- 2 garlic cloves, minced
- ¼ cup all-purpose flour
- 2 cups whole milk
- 3 blocks (4 oz. each) sharp cheddar cheese, shredded and divided
- 1 block (4 oz.) Monterey Jack cheese, shredded
- 3 lbs. russet potatoes, peeled and thinly sliced
- ¾ cup dry bread crumbs
  Minced chives, optional

1. Preheat oven to 350°. In a Dutch oven, melt butter over medium heat. Add the onion, mustard, salt and pepper; cook until onion is tender, 6-8 minutes. Add garlic; cook until fragrant. Whisk in flour; continue whisking 3-5 minutes.

2. Whisk in milk; bring to a boil. Reduce heat; simmer, uncovered, 8-10 minutes or until thickened slightly. Gradually stir in 2 cups shredded cheddar cheese; stir in Monterey Jack cheese. Add sliced potatoes and toss to coat. Simmer 10 minutes, stirring frequently.

3. Transfer potato mixture to a greased 13x9-in. baking dish. Top with remaining cheddar cheese. Bake, uncovered, for 1 hour. Top with bread crumbs; return to oven until potatoes are tender, 10-15 minutes. Let stand for 15 minutes before serving. If desired, sprinkle with chives.

¾ cup: 378 cal., 22g fat (13g sat. fat), 61mg chol., 646mg sod., 31g carb. (5g sugars, 2g fiber), 15g pro.

SLOW-COOKER OPTION

Simmer potatoes in cheese sauce on the stovetop for an additional 5-10 minutes, stirring frequently. Transfer to a greased 6-qt. slow cooker. Place 4 layers of paper towels under the lid; cover and cook on high 2 hours. Remove lid and paper towels; sprinkle potatoes with bread crumbs. Let stand for 15 minutes. If desired, sprinkle with chives.

THE BEST CHEESY SCALLOPED POTATOES

SLOW-COOKER
CITRUS CARROTS

SLOW-COOKER CITRUS CARROTS

These carrots are yummy and so simple. The recipe is from my mom, who tweaked it a bit to suit her tastes. You can make this tasty dish a day in advance and refrigerate it until needed. Then just reheat it before the party!
—Julie Puderbaugh, Berwick, PA

PREP: 10 min. • **COOK:** 4¼ hours
MAKES: 12 servings

- 12 **cups frozen sliced carrots (about 48 oz.), thawed**
- 1¾ **cups orange juice**
- ½ **cup sugar**
- 3 **Tbsp. butter, cubed**
- ½ **tsp. salt**
- 3 **Tbsp. cornstarch**
- ¼ **cup cold water**
  Minced fresh parsley, optional

1. In a 3- or 4-qt. slow cooker, combine the first 5 ingredients. Cook, covered, on low until carrots are tender, 4-5 hours.
2. In a small bowl, mix cornstarch and water until smooth; gradually stir into the slow cooker. Cook, covered, on high until the sauce is thickened, 15-30 minutes. If desired, garnish with minced fresh parsley.

¾ cup: 136 cal., 4g fat (2g sat. fat), 8mg chol., 208mg sod., 25g carb. (18g sugars, 5g fiber), 1g pro.

SAUSAGE-HERB
DRESSING

❄ FREEZER MASHED POTATOES

Can you freeze mashed potatoes? You bet you can! I always make these potatoes and give them to my kids when they go away to school. All they have to do is keep it in the freezer until it's mashed potato time!
—Jessie Fortune, Pocahontas, AR

PREP: 30 min. + freezing
BAKE: 30 min. • **MAKES:** 14 servings

- 5 lbs. potatoes (about 9 large), peeled and cut into chunks
- 2 Tbsp. butter, softened
- 1 cup sour cream
- 2 pkg. (3 oz. each) cream cheese, cubed
- ½ tsp. onion powder
- ½ tsp. salt
- ¼ tsp. pepper

1. Place potatoes in a large saucepan and cover with water. Bring to a boil. Reduce heat; cook, covered, until tender, 10-15 minutes. Drain.
2. In a large bowl, mash potatoes with butter. Beat in sour cream, cream cheese, onion powder, salt and pepper. Transfer to a greased 13x9-in. baking dish. Bake, uncovered, at 350° until heated through, 30-35 minutes. Or, transfer 1½ cup portions to greased 2-cup baking dishes. Cover and freeze up to 6 months.
3. To use frozen potatoes: Thaw in the refrigerator overnight. Bake at 350° until heated through, 30-35 minutes.
¾ cup: 195 cal., 6g fat (4g sat. fat), 19mg chol., 173mg sod., 31g carb. (4g sugars, 3g fiber), 6g pro.

🍲 SAUSAGE-HERB DRESSING

To make time for last-minute Thanksgiving essentials, I prep the sausage part of this recipe a day or two ahead of time, then finish the dressing in my slow cooker on the big day. It has passed the test two years running!
—Judy Batson, Tampa, FL

PREP: 20 min. • **COOK:** 2 hours
MAKES: 10 servings

- 1 lb. bulk sage pork sausage
- 1 medium sweet onion, chopped (about 2 cups)
- 2 celery ribs, chopped
- ¼ cup brewed coffee
- ½ tsp. poultry seasoning
- ½ tsp. dried oregano
- ½ tsp. rubbed sage
- ½ tsp. dried thyme
- ½ tsp. pepper
- 1½ cups chicken or turkey broth
- 1 pkg. (12 oz.) seasoned stuffing cubes (8 cups)
  Chopped fresh parsley

1. In a 6-qt. stockpot, cook and crumble sausage with onion and celery over medium heat 5-7 minutes or until meat is no longer pink; drain. Stir in coffee and seasonings; cook 3 minutes longer, stirring occasionally.
2. Add broth; bring to a boil. Remove from heat; stir in stuffing cubes. Transfer to a greased 4- or 5-qt. slow cooker.
3. Cook, covered, on low until heated through and the edges are lightly browned, 2-2½ hours, stirring once. Sprinkle with fresh parsley before serving.
¾ cup: 254 cal., 11g fat (3g sat. fat), 25mg chol., 919mg sod., 29g carb. (4g sugars, 2g fiber), 9g pro.

TEST KITCHEN TIP
Don't be tempted to add more broth. The dressing will moisten as it cooks. Stir once during cooking so the mixture heats evenly.

**FREEZER
MASHED POTATOES**

PM OVERNIGHT ROLLS

I've been making these light and tender rolls for 25 years. I once served them to a woman who had been in the restaurant business for half a century. She said they were the best rolls she'd ever tasted!

—Dorothy Yagodich, Charlerio, PA

PREP: 25 min. + chilling
BAKE: 15 min. • **MAKES:** 20 rolls

- 1 pkg. (¼ oz.) active dry yeast
- ½ cup plus ¾ tsp. sugar, divided
- 1⅓ cups plus 3 Tbsp. warm water (110° to 115°), divided
- ⅓ cup canola oil
- 1 large egg, room temperature
- 1 tsp. salt
- 4¾ to 5¼ cups all-purpose flour
  Melted butter, optional

1. In a bowl, dissolve yeast and ¾ tsp. sugar in 3 Tbsp. warm water. Add the remaining ½ cup sugar and 1⅓ cups warm water, the oil, egg, salt and 2 cups flour; mix well. Add enough remaining flour to form a soft dough.

2. Turn onto a floured surface; knead until smooth and elastic, 6-8 minutes. Place in a greased bowl, turning once to grease top. Cover and let rise in a warm place until doubled, about 1 hour.

3. Punch dough down. Shape into 20 balls. Roll each into an 8-in. rope; tie into a loose knot. Place on a greased baking sheet; cover and refrigerate overnight.

4. Allow rolls to sit at room temperature for 45 minutes before baking. Bake at 375° 12-15 minutes or until lightly browned. If desired, brush with melted butter. Remove to wire racks to cool.

1 roll: 165 cal., 4g fat (1g sat. fat), 11mg chol., 122mg sod., 28g carb. (6g sugars, 1g fiber), 4g pro.

FAVORITE MASHED SWEET POTATOES

My family begs me to make this recipe during the holidays. They like it because pumpkin pie spice enhances the flavor of the sweet potatoes. I like the fact that it can be made a day ahead and warmed before serving.

—Senja Merrill, Sandy, UT

TAKES: 25 min.
MAKES: 8 servings

- 3 lbs. sweet potatoes (about 6 medium), peeled and cubed
- 3 Tbsp. orange juice
- 2 Tbsp. brown sugar
- 2 Tbsp. maple syrup
- ¼ tsp. pumpkin pie spice

1. Place sweet potatoes in a 6-qt. stockpot; add water to cover. Bring to a boil. Reduce heat; cook, uncovered, until tender, 10-15 minutes. Drain; return to pan.

2. Mash the potatoes, gradually adding orange juice, brown sugar, syrup and pie spice to reach desired consistency.

⅔ cup: 117 cal., 0 fat (0 sat. fat), 0 chol., 10mg sod., 28g carb. (15g sugars, 3g fiber), 1g pro.

OVERNIGHT ROLLS

❄ Ⓟ APPLE, CHEDDAR & BACON BREAD PUDDING

I had this dish at a bridal brunch many years ago. It was so delicious that I created my own version, and this is the result. Now I make it all the time. Enjoy!
—Melissa Millwood, Lyman, SC

PREP: 30 min. + chilling
BAKE: 45 min. + standing
MAKES: 9 servings (1½ cups syrup)

- 3 Tbsp. butter
- 2 medium apples, peeled and chopped
- ¼ cup packed brown sugar
- 6 cups cubed day-old French bread
- 1 lb. bacon strips, cooked and crumbled
- 1½ cups shredded sharp cheddar cheese
- 5 large eggs
- 2¼ cups 2% milk
- ½ tsp. ground cinnamon
- ¼ tsp. salt

SYRUP
- 1 cup maple syrup
- ½ cup chopped walnuts

1. In a large skillet, heat butter over medium heat. Add apples; cook and stir until crisp-tender, 2-3 minutes. Reduce heat to medium-low; stir in brown sugar. Cook, uncovered, until apples are tender, 8-10 minutes, stirring occasionally. Cool completely.
2. In a greased 8-in. square baking dish, layer half of each of the following: bread, bacon, apples and cheese. Repeat layers. In a large bowl, whisk eggs, milk, cinnamon and salt; pour over top. Refrigerate, covered, several hours or overnight.
3. Preheat oven to 350°. Remove bread pudding from refrigerator; uncover and let stand while the oven heats. Bake until puffed and

APPLE, CHEDDAR & BACON BREAD PUDDING

golden, and a knife inserted in the center comes out clean, 45-55 minutes. Let stand 15 minutes before serving.
4. In a microwave-safe bowl, microwave syrup and walnuts until warmed, stirring once. Serve with bread pudding.
1 piece with 8 tsp. syrup: 505 cal., 26g fat (10g sat. fat), 155mg chol., 729mg sod., 50g carb. (35g sugars, 2g fiber), 19g pro.

⌐ FREEZE OPTION ─

After assembling, cover and freeze bread pudding. To use, partially thaw in refrigerator overnight. Remove from the refrigerator 30 minutes before baking. Preheat oven to 350°. Bake and serve bread pudding with syrup as directed.

CREAMED
PEARL ONIONS

🄿🄼 CREAMED PEARL ONIONS

At Christmas, this was one of many recipes I relied on that could be prepared a day in advance, which gave me more time to spend with guests. Everyone expected to see this vegetable dish on the table every year.
—Barbara Caserman, Lake Havasu City, AZ

PREP: 30 min. + chilling
BAKE: 25 min. • **MAKES:** 6 servings

- 4   cups pearl onions
- 3   Tbsp. butter
- 3   Tbsp. all-purpose flour
- ½   tsp. salt
  Dash pepper
- ¾   cup chicken broth
- ¾   cup half-and-half cream
- ¼   cup minced fresh parsley
- 3   Tbsp. grated Parmesan cheese
  Pimiento strips, optional

1. In a Dutch oven or large kettle, bring 8 cups water to a boil. Add pearl onions; boil until tender, 6-7 minutes. Drain and rinse in cold water; peel and set aside.
2. In a saucepan, melt butter. Stir in the flour, salt and pepper until smooth. Gradually stir in broth and cream. Bring to a boil; cook and stir until thickened, about 2 minutes or. Stir in the parsley, cheese and onions.
3. Pour into an ungreased 1½-qt. baking dish. Cover and refrigerate overnight. Remove from the refrigerator 30 minutes before baking. Cover and bake at 350° for 15 minutes; stir. Top with pimientos if desired. Uncover and bake until bubbly and heated through, about 10 minutes longer.
¾ cup: 151 cal., 10g fat (6g sat. fat), 33mg chol., 440mg sod., 12g carb. (5g sugars, 1g fiber), 3g pro.

PECAN RICE PILAF

❄ PECAN RICE PILAF

This is one of my standby side dishes, which can complement most meat and meatless entrees. It is special enough for company and quick enough for weeknights.
—Jacqueline Oglesby, Spruce Pine, NC

PREP: 15 min. • **COOK:** 20 min.
MAKES: 9 servings

- 1   cup chopped pecans
- 5   Tbsp. butter, divided
- 1   small onion, chopped
- 2   cups uncooked long grain rice
- 1   carton (32 oz.) chicken broth
- 3   Tbsp. minced fresh parsley, divided
- ½   tsp. salt
- ¼   tsp. dried thyme
- ⅛   tsp. pepper
- 1   cup shredded carrots

1. In a large saucepan, saute pecans in 2 Tbsp. butter until toasted; remove from the pan and set aside.
2. In the same pan, saute onion in remaining 3 Tbsp. butter until tender. Add rice; cook and stir until rice is lightly browned, 3-4 minutes. Stir in the broth, 2 Tbsp. parsley, salt, thyme and pepper. Bring to a boil. Reduce heat; cover and simmer for 10 minutes.
3. Add carrots; simmer until rice is tender, 3-5 minutes longer. Stir in toasted pecans and remaining 1 Tbsp. parsley. Fluff with a fork.
¾ cup: 313 cal., 16g fat (5g sat. fat), 19mg chol., 623mg sod., 37g carb. (2g sugars, 2g fiber), 5g pro.

┌─ **FREEZE OPTION** ─────────

Reserving pecans and 1 Tbsp. parsley, freeze cooled pilaf in a freezer container. To use, partially thaw in refrigerator overnight. Microwave, covered, on high in a microwave-safe dish, adding 2-3 Tbsp. water to moisten, until heated through. Serve with pecans and parsley.

MOM'S SWEET POTATO SALAD

My mother used to make this potato salad. We all liked it back then—and now my family likes it too!
—Willard Wilson, Woodsfield, OH

PREP: 10 min. + chilling
MAKES: 12 servings

- 3 lbs. sweet potatoes, cooked, peeled and cubed
- ½ cup chopped onion
- 1 cup chopped sweet red pepper
- 1¼ cups mayonnaise
- 1½ tsp. salt
- ½ tsp. pepper
- ¼ tsp. hot pepper sauce
  Sliced green onions, optional

In a large bowl, combine sweet potatoes, onion and red pepper. In a small bowl, combine next 4 ingredients; add to the potato mixture and toss to coat. Cover and refrigerate until serving. If desired, garnish with sliced green onions.

¾ cup: 292 cal., 19g fat (3g sat. fat), 8mg chol., 436mg sod., 29g carb. (7g sugars, 4g fiber), 2g pro.

TO MAKE AHEAD

You can make this salad up to 4 days in advance. If you do plan to keep it in the fridge for more than a few hours, mix in only half the dressing; add the other half right before serving and stir well. This ensures the salad is creamy and fresh.

MOM'S
SWEET POTATO
SALAD

BRIOCHE

PM BRIOCHE

These classic French rolls (pronounced BREE-osh) are rich in butter and eggs. The unique shape resembles a muffin.
—Wanda Kristoffersen, Owatonna, MN

PREP: 30 min. + rising
BAKE: 15 min. • **MAKES:** 1 dozen

- 3½ cups all-purpose flour
- ½ cup sugar
- 2 pkg. (¼ oz. each) active dry yeast
- 1 tsp. grated lemon zest
- ½ tsp. salt
- ⅔ cup butter, cubed
- ½ cup 2% milk
- 5 large eggs, room temperature

1. In a large bowl, combine 1½ cups flour, sugar, yeast, lemon zest and salt. In a small saucepan, heat butter and milk to 120°-130°. Add to the dry ingredients; beat until moistened. Add 4 eggs; beat on medium speed for 2 minutes. Add 1 cup flour. Beat until smooth. Stir in the remaining flour. Do not knead.

2. Spoon dough into a greased bowl, turning once to grease the top. Cover and let rise in a warm place until doubled, about 1 hour. Stir dough down. Cover and refrigerate overnight.

3. Preheat oven to 375°. Punch dough down. Turn onto a lightly floured surface. Cover; let rest for 15 minutes. Cut one-sixth from the dough; set aside. Shape remaining dough into 12 balls (about 2½ in.); place in well-greased muffin cups.

4. Divide the reserved dough into 12 small balls. Make an indentation in the top of each large ball; place a small ball in each indentation. Cover and let rise in a warm place until doubled, about 1 hour.

5. Beat remaining egg; brush over rolls. Bake until golden brown, 15-20 minutes. Remove from pan to wire racks to cool.

1 roll: 295 cal., 13g fat (7g sat. fat), 117mg chol., 234mg sod., 37g carb. (9g sugars, 1g fiber), 7g pro.

SOUR CREAM CUCUMBERS

It's been a tradition at our house to serve this dish with the other Hungarian specialties my mom learned to make from the women at church. It's especially good during the summer when the cucumbers are fresh-picked from the garden.
—Pamela Eaton, Monclova, OH

PREP: 15 min. + chilling
MAKES: 8 servings

- ½ cup sour cream
- 3 Tbsp. white vinegar
- 1 Tbsp. sugar
  Pepper to taste
- 4 medium cucumbers, peeled, if desired, and thinly sliced
- 1 small sweet onion, thinly sliced and separated into rings

In a large bowl, whisk sour cream, vinegar, sugar and pepper until blended. Add cucumbers and onion; toss to coat. Refrigerate, covered, at least 4 hours. Serve with a slotted spoon.
¾ cup: 62 cal., 3g fat (2g sat. fat), 10mg chol., 5mg sod., 7g carb. (5g sugars, 2g fiber), 2g pro. **Diabetic exchanges:** 1 vegetable, ½ fat.

TEST KITCHEN TIP
Peeling cucumbers for this salad is a personal preference. If you don't like the texture of the skin or aren't able to digest it easily, then peeling is the way to go. However, this recipe doesn't require it. Also, grocery-store cucumbers are often coated with a protective wax to prolong freshness; be sure to wash them if you're not peeling them.

CHEESE & HERB POTATO FANS

It's downright fun to make and serve these potatoes—and they taste incredible too. The herbs, butter and cheeses are just what a potato needs.
—Susan Curry, West Hills, CA

PREP: 20 min. • **BAKE:** 55 min.
MAKES: 8 servings

- 8 medium potatoes
- ½ cup butter, melted
- 2 tsp. salt
- ½ tsp. pepper
- ⅔ cup shredded cheddar cheese
- ⅓ cup shredded Parmesan cheese
- 2 Tbsp. each minced fresh chives, sage and thyme

1. Preheat oven to 425°. With a sharp knife, cut each potato crosswise into ⅛-in. slices, leaving slices attached at the bottom; fan potatoes slightly and place in a greased 13x9-in. baking dish. In a small bowl, mix butter, salt and pepper; drizzle over potatoes.
2. Bake, uncovered, until potatoes are tender, 50-55 minutes. In a small bowl, toss cheeses with herbs; sprinkle over potatoes. Bake until cheese is melted, about 5 minutes longer.
1 potato: 318 cal., 15g fat (10g sat. fat), 43mg chol., 797mg sod., 39g carb. (3g sugars, 4g fiber), 8g pro.

CHEESE & HERB POTATO FANS

❄ FAVORITE CHEESY POTATOES

My family loves these potatoes. I make a large batch in disposable pans and serve them at all our get-togethers. The holidays aren't the same without them. It's also a wonderful recipe for Christmas morning brunch.
—Brenda Smith, Curran, MI

PREP: 30 min. • **BAKE:** 45 min.
MAKES: 12 servings

- 3½ lbs. potatoes (about 7 medium), peeled and cut into ¾-in. cubes
- 1 can (10½ oz.) condensed cream of potato soup, undiluted
- 1 cup French onion dip
- ¾ cup 2% milk
- ⅔ cup sour cream
- 1 tsp. minced fresh parsley
- ¼ tsp. salt
- ¼ tsp. pepper
- 1 pkg. (16 oz.) Velveeta, cubed
  Additional minced fresh parsley

1. Preheat oven to 350°. Place potatoes in a Dutch oven; add water to cover. Bring to a boil. Reduce heat; cook, uncovered, until tender, 8-12 minutes. Drain. Cool slightly.
2. In a large bowl, mix soup, onion dip, milk, sour cream, parsley, salt and pepper; gently fold in potatoes and cheese. Transfer to a greased 13x9-in. baking dish.
3. Bake, covered, for 30 minutes. Uncover; bake until heated through and cheese is melted, 15-20 minutes longer. Just before serving, stir to combine; sprinkle with additional parsley. (Potatoes will thicken upon standing.)
½ cup: 294 cal., 16g fat (10g sat. fat), 42mg chol., 813mg sod., 26g carb. (6g sugars, 2g fiber), 10g pro.

FAVORITE
CHEESY POTATOES

FREEZE OPTION

Cover and freeze unbaked casserole. To use, partially thaw in refrigerator overnight. Remove from refrigerator 30 minutes before baking. Preheat oven to 350°. Cover casserole with foil; bake as directed until heated through and a thermometer inserted in center reads 165°, increasing covered time to 1¼-1½ hours. Uncover; bake until lightly browned, 15-20 minutes longer. Just before serving, stir to combine. If desired, sprinkle with additional parsley.

PAGE 136

PAGE 148

PAGE 134

Soups, Stews & Chilis

Few foods are as comforting as homemade soup, stew or chili—and few foods are easier to make ahead. Store a batch, freeze individual portions or slow-cook to suit your timeline—these recipes are just the thing!

PAGE 145

PAGE 125

TURKEY GINGER
NOODLE SOUP

🍲 ENGLISH PUB SPLIT PEA SOUP

*This family favorite is the same recipe
my grandmother used. Now with the
slow cooker, I can put it together, walk
away for 5 hours and come back when
soup's on. Finish it with more milk if
you like your soup a bit thinner.*
—Judy Batson, Tampa, FL

PREP: 15 min. • **COOK:** 5 hours
MAKES: 8 servings (2 qt.)

- 1 meaty ham bone
- 1⅓ cups dried green split peas, rinsed
- 2 celery ribs, chopped
- 1 large carrot, chopped
- 1 sweet onion, chopped
- 4 cups water
- 1 bottle (12 oz.) light beer
- 1 Tbsp. prepared English mustard
- ½ cup 2% milk
- ¼ cup minced fresh parsley
- ½ tsp. salt
- ¼ tsp. pepper
- ¼ tsp. ground nutmeg

1. Place ham bone in a 4-qt. slow cooker. Add peas, celery, carrot and onion. Combine the water, beer and mustard; pour over vegetables. Cook, covered, on high until split peas are tender, 5-6 hours.
2. Remove ham bone from soup. Cool slightly, trim away fat and remove meat from bone; discard fat and bone. Cut meat into bite-size pieces; return to slow cooker. Stir in the remaining ingredients. If desired, top with additional minced parsley.
1 cup: 141 cal., 1g fat (0 sat. fat), 1mg chol., 193mg sod., 25g carb. (6g sugars, 9g fiber), 9g pro.
Diabetic exchanges: 1½ starch, 1 lean meat.

🍲 TURKEY GINGER NOODLE SOUP

*I wanted something comforting yet
healthy, and ginger is my favorite spice,
so this recipe was a must-try for me.
It didn't disappoint!*
—Adina Monson, Nanaimo, BC

PREP: 20 min. • **COOK:** 4¼ hours
MAKES: 8 servings (3 qt.)

- 2 medium carrots, sliced
- 2 cans (8 oz. each) sliced water chestnuts, drained
- 3 to 4 Tbsp. minced fresh gingerroot
- 2 Tbsp. minced fresh parsley
- 2 tsp. chili powder
- 4 cups chicken stock
- 1 can (11.8 oz.) coconut water
- 3 Tbsp. lemon juice
- 2 lbs. boneless skinless turkey breast, cut into 1-in. cubes
- 2 tsp. pepper
- ½ tsp. salt
- 2 Tbsp. canola oil
- 1 cup frozen corn (about 5 oz.), thawed
- 1 cup frozen peas (about 4 oz.), thawed
- 8 oz. rice noodles or thin spaghetti

1. Place the first 8 ingredients in a 4- or 5-qt. slow cooker.
2. Toss turkey with pepper and salt. In a large skillet, heat oil over medium-high heat; brown the turkey in batches. Add to the slow cooker.
3. Cook, covered, on low until carrots are tender, 4-5 hours, Stir in corn and peas; heat through.
4. Cook noodles according to package directions; drain. Add to soup just before serving.
1½ cups: 351 cal., 6g fat (1g sat. fat), 65mg chol., 672mg sod., 41g carb. (5g sugars, 4g fiber), 33g pro.
Diabetic exchanges: 3 starch, 3 lean meat.

ENGLISH PUB
SPLIT PEA SOUP

❄ TURKEY CABBAGE STEW

Filled with ground turkey, cabbage, carrots and tomatoes, this stew delivers down-home comfort fast!
—Susan Lasken, Woodland Hills, CA

TAKES: 30 min.
MAKES: 6 servings

- 1 lb. lean ground turkey
- 1 medium onion, chopped
- 3 garlic cloves, minced
- 4 cups chopped cabbage
- 2 medium carrots, sliced
- 1 can (28 oz.) diced tomatoes, undrained
- ¾ cup water
- 1 Tbsp. brown sugar
- 1 Tbsp. white vinegar
- 1 tsp. salt
- 1 tsp. dried oregano
- ¼ tsp. dried thyme
- ¼ tsp. pepper

1. Cook the turkey, onion and garlic in a large saucepan over medium heat until the meat is no longer pink, 5-7 minutes, breaking up the turkey into crumbles; drain.
2. Add the remaining ingredients. Bring to a boil; cover and simmer until the vegetables are tender, 12-15 minutes.

1 cup: 180 cal., 6g fat (2g sat. fat), 52mg chol., 674mg sod., 16g carb. (10g sugars, 5g fiber), 17g pro.
Diabetic exchanges: 2 vegetable, 2 lean meat.

FREEZE OPTION

Freeze cooled stew in freezer containers. To use, partially thaw in refrigerator overnight. Heat through in a saucepan, stirring occasionally; add a little broth if necessary.

TURKEY
CABBAGE STEW

HEARTY HOMEMADE CHICKEN NOODLE SOUP

This satisfying soup with a hint of cayenne is brimming with vegetables, chicken and noodles. The recipe was my father-in-law's, but I made some adjustments to give it my own spin.
—*Norma Reynolds, Overland Park, KS*

PREP: 20 min. • **COOK:** 5½ hours
MAKES: 12 servings (3 qt.)

- 12 **fresh baby carrots,** cut into ½-in. pieces
- 4 **celery ribs,** cut into ½-in. pieces
- ¾ **cup finely chopped onion**
- 1 **Tbsp. minced fresh parsley**
- ½ **tsp. pepper**
- ¼ **tsp. cayenne pepper**
- 1½ **tsp. mustard seeds**
- 2 **garlic cloves, peeled and halved**
- 1¼ **lbs. boneless skinless chicken breast halves**
- 1¼ **lbs. boneless skinless chicken thighs**
- 4 **cans (14½ oz. each) chicken broth**
- 1 **pkg. (9 oz.) refrigerated linguine**
  Coarsely ground pepper, optional

1. In a 5-qt. slow cooker, combine the first 6 ingredients. Place the mustard seeds and garlic on a double thickness of cheesecloth; bring up corners of cloth and tie with kitchen string to form a bag. Place in slow cooker. Add chicken and broth. Cover and cook on low until meat is tender, 5-6 hours.

2. Discard the spice bag. Remove chicken; cool slightly. Stir linguine into soup; cover and cook on high until the linguine is tender, about 30 minutes.

3. Cut chicken into pieces and return to soup; heat through. If desired, sprinkle with coarsely ground pepper and additional minced fresh parsley.

1 cup: 199 cal., 6g fat (2g sat. fat), 73mg chol., 663mg sod., 14g carb. (2g sugars, 1g fiber), 22g pro.
Diabetic exchanges: 3 lean meat, 1 starch.

HEARTY HOMEMADE
CHICKEN NOODLE SOUP

SLOW-COOKED
BLACK BEAN SOUP

🍲 SLOW-COOKED BLACK BEAN SOUP

Life can get crazy with young children, but I never want to compromise when it comes to cooking. This recipe is healthy and so easy, thanks to the slow cooker!
—Angela Lemoine, Howell, NJ

PREP: 15 min. • **COOK:** 6 hours
MAKES: 8 servings

- 2 cans (15 oz. each) black beans, rinsed and drained
- 1 medium onion, finely chopped
- 1 medium sweet red pepper, finely chopped
- 4 garlic cloves, minced
- 2 tsp. ground cumin
- 2 cans (14½ oz. each) vegetable broth
- 1 tsp. olive oil
- 1 cup fresh or frozen corn
  Dash pepper
  Minced fresh cilantro

1. In a 3-qt. slow cooker, combine beans, onion, red pepper, garlic, cumin and broth. Cook, covered, on low until vegetables are softened, 6-8 hours.

2. Puree the soup using an immersion blender, or let cool slightly and puree in batches in a blender. Return to slow cooker and heat through.

3. In a small skillet, heat oil over medium heat. Add corn; cook and stir until golden brown, 4-6 minutes. Sprinkle soup with pepper. Garnish with corn and cilantro.

¾ cup: 117 cal., 1g fat (0 sat. fat), 0 chol., 616mg sod., 21g carb. (3g sugars, 5g fiber), 6g pro.
Diabetic exchanges: 1½ starch.

ANCIENT GRAIN BEEF STEW

ANCIENT GRAIN BEEF STEW

My version of beef stew is comfort food with a healthy twist. I use lentils and red quinoa rather than potatoes. If your leftover stew seems too thick, add more beef stock when reheating.
—Margaret Roscoe, Keystone Heights, FL

PREP: 25 min. • **COOK:** 6 hours
MAKES: 10 servings

2	Tbsp. olive oil
1	lb. beef stew meat, cut into 1-in. cubes
4	celery ribs with leaves, chopped
2	medium carrots, peeled and chopped
1	large onion, chopped
1½	cups dried lentils, rinsed
½	cup red quinoa, rinsed
5	large bay leaves
2	tsp. ground cumin
1½	tsp. salt
1	tsp. dried tarragon
½	tsp. pepper
2	cartons (32 oz. each) beef stock

1. Heat oil in a large skillet over medium heat. Add beef; brown on all sides. Transfer the meat and drippings to a 5- or 6-qt. slow cooker.
2. Stir in remaining ingredients. Cook, covered, on low until meat is tender, 6-8 hours. Discard the bay leaves.

1⅓ cups: 261 cal., 7g fat (2g sat. fat), 28mg chol., 797mg sod., 29g carb. (5g sugars, 5g fiber), 21g pro. **Diabetic exchanges:** 2 starch, 2 lean meat, ½ fat.

TEST KITCHEN TIP
Nutrient-dense quinoa has more protein than almost any other grain.

CREAM OF
BUTTERNUT SOUP

CREAM OF BUTTERNUT SOUP

Ginger, turmeric, cinnamon and sherry season this slightly sweet soup. The recipe was given to me by a friend from South Africa. It keeps in an airtight container in the fridge for three to four days, so it's a great make-ahead option!
—Shelly Snyder, Lafayette, CO

PREP: 35 min. • **COOK:** 30 min.
MAKES: 10 servings (2½ qt.)

- 1   cup chopped onion
- 2   celery ribs, chopped
- 2   Tbsp. butter
- 2   cans (14½ oz. each) reduced-sodium chicken broth
- 1   tsp. sugar
- 1   bay leaf
- ½   tsp. salt
- ½   tsp. ground ginger
- ½   tsp. ground turmeric
- ¼   tsp. ground cinnamon
- 1   butternut squash (2½ lbs.), peeled and cubed
- 3   medium potatoes, peeled and cubed
- 1½ cups 2% milk
- 2   Tbsp. sherry or additional reduced-sodium chicken broth
     Optional: Heavy whipping cream and fried sage

1. In a large saucepan coated with cooking spray, cook onion and celery in butter until tender, 3-5 minutes. Stir in the broth, sugar, bay leaf, salt, ginger, turmeric and cinnamon. Add squash and potatoes. Bring to a boil. Reduce heat; cover and simmer until vegetables are tender, 15-20 minutes.
2. Remove from the heat; cool slightly. Discard bay leaf. In a blender, puree vegetable mixture in batches. Return to the pan. Stir in milk and sherry; heat through

SLOW-COOKER MEATBALL STEW

(do not boil). If desired, serve with cream and sage.
1 cup: 145 cal., 3g fat (2g sat. fat), 8mg chol., 421mg sod., 27g carb. (7g sugars, 5g fiber), 5g pro.
Diabetic exchanges: 2 starch, ½ fat.

🍲 SLOW-COOKER MEATBALL STEW

This recipe was a lifesaver when I worked full time. Your young ones can help chop, peel, mix and pour. It doesn't matter if the veggies are different sizes—your kids will still devour this fun, tasty stew.
—Kallee Krong-McCreery, Escondido, CA

PREP: 20 min. • **COOK:** 6 hours
MAKES: 8 servings (2 qt.)

- 4   peeled medium potatoes, cut into ½-in. cubes
- 4   medium carrots, cut into ½-in. cubes
- 2   celery ribs, cut into ½-in. cubes
- 1   medium onion, diced
- ¼   cup frozen corn
- 1   pkg. (28 to 32 oz.) frozen fully cooked home-style meatballs
- 1½ cups ketchup
- 1½ cups water
- 1   Tbsp. white vinegar
- 1   tsp. dried basil
     Optional: Biscuits or dinner rolls

In a 5-qt. slow cooker, combine potatoes, carrots, celery, onion, corn and meatballs. In a bowl, mix ketchup, water, vinegar and basil; pour over the meatballs. Cook, covered, on low until the meatballs are cooked through, 6-8 hours. If desired, serve with biscuits or dinner rolls.
1 cup: 449 cal., 26g fat (12g sat. fat), 41mg chol., 1322mg sod., 40g carb. (17g sugars, 4g fiber), 16g pro.

❄ 🍲 Ⓟ KASHMIRI LAMB CURRY STEW

When I was growing up, I was taught that spicy foods are for lovers. So when I got married, this was the first meal I made for my husband. Every time we have a disagreement, I make this dish.
—Amber El, Pittsburgh, PA

PREP: 25 min. + marinating
COOK: 8 hours
MAKES: 11 servings (2¾ qt.)

- 1 cup plain yogurt
- 2 Tbsp. ghee or butter, melted
- ¼ cup lemon juice
- 4 tsp. curry powder
- 1 Tbsp. cumin seeds
- 1 tsp. each coriander seeds, ground ginger, ground cloves, ground cardamom, sugar and salt
- ½ tsp. each ground cinnamon and pepper
- 3 lbs. lamb stew meat, cut into 1-in. cubes
- 1 large onion, sliced
- 1 medium sweet potato, quartered
- 1 medium Yukon Gold potato, quartered
- 1 large tomato, chopped
- 1 cup frozen peas and carrots
- 3 garlic cloves, minced
- 2 dried hot chiles
- ½ cup chicken broth
- 1½ Tbsp. garam masala
  Optional: Hot cooked basmati rice, sliced green onion, mango chutney and raisins

1. In a large bowl, combine the yogurt, ghee and lemon juice; add curry powder, cumin seeds, coriander seeds, ginger, cloves, cardamom, sugar, salt, cinnamon and pepper. Add the cubed lamb, vegetables, garlic and chiles; turn to coat. Cover and refrigerate up to 24 hours.

2. Transfer lamb mixture and marinade to 6-qt. slow cooker; stir in broth and garam masala. Cook, covered, on low until meat is tender, 8-9 hours. If desired, serve with rice, green onion, mango chutney and raisins.

1 cup: 261 cal., 10g fat (4g sat. fat), 89mg chol., 384mg sod., 15g carb. (5g sugars, 3g fiber), 28g pro.
Diabetic exchanges: 4 lean meat, 1 starch.

FREEZE OPTION

Freeze cooled stew in freezer containers. To use, partially thaw in refrigerator overnight. Heat through in a saucepan, stirring occasionally; add broth if necessary.

KASHMIRI LAMB CURRY STEW

VEGETABLE LENTIL SOUP

❄ 🍲 VEGETABLE LENTIL SOUP

This healthy soup is ideal for vegetarians and those watching their weight. Butternut squash and lentils make it filling, while herbs and other veggies round out the flavor.
—Mark Morgan, Waterford, WI

PREP: 15 min. • **COOK:** 4½ hours
MAKES: 6 servings (2 qt.)

- 3 cups cubed peeled butternut squash
- 1 cup chopped carrots
- 1 cup chopped onion
- 1 cup dried lentils, rinsed
- 2 garlic cloves, minced
- 1 tsp. dried oregano
- 1 tsp. dried basil
- 4 cups vegetable broth
- 1 can (14½ oz.) Italian diced tomatoes, undrained
- 2 cups frozen cut green beans (about 8 oz.)

1. Place the first 8 ingredients in a 5-qt. slow cooker. Cook, covered, on low until lentils are tender, about 4 hours.
2. Stir in tomatoes and beans. Cook, covered, on high until soup is heated through, about 30 minutes.

1⅓ cups: 217 cal., 1g fat (0 sat. fat), 0 chol., 685mg sod., 45g carb. (11g sugars, 8g fiber), 11g pro.

┌─ **FREEZE OPTION** ─────────┐

You can store this soup in the refrigerator for several days. If you can't finish it that quickly, it's easy to freeze. Let the soup cool, then put it in an airtight container of your choice and freeze. Use within 6 months. To use, thaw soup overnight in the refrigerator, then heat in a saucepan.

└──────────────────────┘

CUBED BEEF & BARLEY SOUP

Here's a real stick-to-your-ribs soup. I've also used a chuck roast, rump roast or London broil that's been cut into bite-size pieces, with tremendous success.
—Jane Whittaker, Pensacola, FL

PREP: 20 min. • **COOK:** 8½ hours
MAKES: 8 servings (2 qt.)

1½ lbs. beef stew meat, cut into
   ½-in. cubes
1 Tbsp. canola oil
1 carton (32 oz.) beef broth
1 bottle (12 oz.) beer or
   nonalcoholic beer
1 small onion, chopped
½ cup medium pearl barley
3 garlic cloves, minced
1 tsp. dried oregano
1 tsp. dried parsley flakes
1 tsp. Worcestershire sauce
½ tsp. crushed red pepper
   flakes
½ tsp. pepper
¼ tsp. salt
1 bay leaf
2 cups frozen mixed
   vegetables, thawed

1. In a large skillet, brown cubed beef in oil; drain. Transfer to a 3-qt. slow cooker.
2. Add the broth, beer, onion, pearl barley, garlic, oregano, parsley, Worcestershire sauce, pepper flakes, pepper, salt and bay leaf. Cook, covered, on low for 8-10 hours.
3. Stir in vegetables; cover and cook until meat is tender and vegetables are heated through, about 30 minutes longer. Discard bay leaf.

1 cup: 233 cal., 8g fat (2g sat. fat), 53mg chol., 644mg sod., 18g carb. (3g sugars, 4g fiber), 20g pro.
Diabetic exchanges: 3 lean meat, 1 starch.

CUBED BEEF &
BARLEY SOUP

PORK & GREEN
CHILE STEW

❄️ 🍲 PORK & GREEN CHILE STEW

An easily adaptable stew, this delicious slow-cooked dish is ready in four hours if cooked on high.
—Paul Sedillo, Plainfield, IL

PREP: 40 min. • **COOK:** 7 hours
MAKES: 8 servings (2 qt.)

- 2 lbs. boneless pork shoulder butt roast, cut into ¾-in. cubes
- 1 large onion, cut into ½-in. pieces
- 2 Tbsp. canola oil
- 1 tsp. salt
- 1 tsp. coarsely ground pepper
- 4 large potatoes, peeled and cut into ¾-in. cubes
- 3 cups water
- 1 can (16 oz.) hominy, rinsed and drained
- 2 cans (4 oz. each) chopped green chiles
- 2 Tbsp. quick-cooking tapioca
- 2 garlic cloves, minced
- ½ tsp. dried oregano
- ½ tsp. ground cumin
- 1 cup minced fresh cilantro
  Sour cream, optional

1. In a large skillet, brown the cubed pork and onion in canola oil in batches. Sprinkle with salt and pepper. Transfer to a 5-qt. slow cooker.

2. Stir in the potatoes, water, hominy, chopped green chiles, quick-cooking tapioca, garlic, oregano and cumin. Cover and cook on low until meat is tender, 7-9 hours, stirring in cilantro during the last 30 minutes of cooking. If desired, serve stew with sour cream and additional minced fresh cilantro.

1 cup: 322 cal., 15g fat (4g sat. fat), 67mg chol., 723mg sod., 25g carb. (3g sugars, 3g fiber), 21g pro.
Diabetic exchanges: 3 medium-fat meat, 1½ starch, ½ fat.

FREEZE OPTION

Freeze cooled stew in freezer containers. To use, partially thaw in refrigerator overnight. Heat through in a saucepan, stirring occasionally; add a little broth if necessary.

BASIL TOMATO
SOUP WITH ORZO

POTATO & LEEK SOUP

Packed with veggies and bacon, with just a little tanginess from sour cream, this soup tastes just as good with sandwiches as with crackers.
—Melanie Wooden, Reno, NV

PREP: 20 min. • **COOK:** 8 hours
MAKES: 8 servings (2 qt.)

- 4 cups chicken broth
- 3 medium potatoes, peeled and cubed
- 1½ cups chopped cabbage
- 2 medium carrots, chopped
- 1 medium leek (white portion only), chopped
- 1 medium onion, chopped
- ¼ cup minced fresh parsley
- ½ tsp. salt
- ½ tsp. caraway seeds
- ½ tsp. pepper
- 1 bay leaf
- ½ cup sour cream
- 1 lb. bacon strips, cooked and crumbled

1. Combine first 11 ingredients in a 4- or 5-qt. slow cooker. Cover and cook on low until vegetables are tender, 8-10 hours.
2. Before serving, combine sour cream with 1 cup of the soup; return all to the slow cooker. Stir in bacon; discard bay leaf.
1 cup: 209 cal., 11g fat (4g sat. fat), 27mg chol., 1023mg sod., 18g carb. (4g sugars, 2g fiber), 10g pro.

WHY YOU'LL LOVE IT...

"This is delicious. Great texture and creaminess. I doubled the recipe but went light on the broth, around 6 cups. I'm saving [this recipe] to make again."
—AMYRICE, TASTEOFHOME.COM

BASIL TOMATO SOUP WITH ORZO

The soup is so scrumptious that it's worth the little time it takes to chop the onion, garlic and basil. It's even better the next day after the flavors have had a chance to blend, so it's great for advance planning!
—Tonia Billbe, Elmira, NY

PREP: 15 min. • **COOK:** 25 min.
MAKES: 16 servings (4 qt.)

- 1 large onion, chopped
- ¼ cup butter, cubed
- 2 garlic cloves, minced
- 3 cans (28 oz. each) crushed tomatoes
- 1 carton (32 oz.) chicken broth
- 1 cup loosely packed basil leaves, chopped
- 1 Tbsp. sugar
- ½ tsp. pepper
- 1¼ cups uncooked orzo pasta
- 1 cup heavy whipping cream
- ½ cup grated Romano cheese

1. In a Dutch oven, saute onion in butter for 3 minutes. Add garlic; cook until the onion is tender, 1-2 minutes longer. Stir in the tomatoes, broth, basil, sugar and pepper. Bring to a boil. Reduce heat; cover and simmer for 15 minutes.
2. Meanwhile, cook the orzo according to package directions; drain. Add orzo and cream to soup; heat through (do not boil). Sprinkle servings with cheese.
1 cup: 208 cal., 10g fat (6g sat. fat), 27mg chol., 607mg sod., 25g carb. (9g sugars, 3g fiber), 7g pro.

POTATO &
LEEK SOUP

🍲 SLOW-COOKED CORN CHOWDER

I combine the ingredients the night before and pop them in the refrigerator. The next morning, I start the slow cooker before leaving for work. When I come home, a hot tasty meal awaits!
—Mary Hogue, Rochester, PA

PREP: 10 min. • **COOK:** 6 hours
MAKES: 8 servings (2 qt.)

2½ cups 2% milk
1 can (14¾ oz.) cream-style corn
1 can (10¾ oz.) condensed cream of mushroom soup, undiluted
1¾ cups frozen corn
1 cup frozen shredded hash brown potatoes
1 cup cubed fully cooked ham
1 large onion, chopped
2 tsp. dried parsley flakes
2 Tbsp. butter
Salt and pepper to taste
Optional: Crumbled cooked bacon and minced parsley

In a 3-qt. slow cooker, combine all ingredients. Cover and cook on low for 6 hours. If desired, garnish with bacon and parsley.
1 cup: 196 cal., 8g fat (3g sat. fat), 26mg chol., 687mg sod., 26g carb. (7g sugars, 2g fiber), 9g pro.

TEST KITCHEN TIP
Store this corn chowder in an airtight container in the refrigerator for 3-4 days. Unfortunately, dairy-based soups and chowders such as this one do not freeze well.

SLOW-COOKED CORN CHOWDER

❄ THE BEST BEEF STEW

Our best beef stew recipe has tons of flavor, thanks to its blend of herbs and the addition of red wine and balsamic vinegar.
—James Schend, Pleasant Prairie, WI

PREP: 30 min. • **COOK:** 2 hours
MAKES: 6 servings (2¼ qt.)

- 1½ lbs. beef stew meat, cut into 1-in. cubes
- ½ tsp. salt, divided
- 6 Tbsp. all-purpose flour, divided
- ½ tsp. smoked paprika
- 1 Tbsp. canola oil
- 3 Tbsp. tomato paste
- 2 tsp. herbes de Provence
- 2 garlic cloves, minced
- 2 cups dry red wine
- 2 cups beef broth
- 1½ tsp. minced fresh rosemary, divided
- 2 bay leaves
- 3 cups cubed peeled potatoes
- 3 cups coarsely chopped onions (about 2 large)
- 2 cups sliced carrots
- 2 Tbsp. cold water
- 2 Tbsp. balsamic or red wine vinegar
- 1 cup fresh or frozen peas

1. In a small bowl, toss the beef and ¼ tsp. salt. In a large bowl, combine 4 Tbsp. flour and paprika. Add beef, a few pieces at a time, and toss to coat.
2. In a Dutch oven, brown beef in oil over medium heat. Stir in the tomato paste, herbes de Provence and garlic; cook until fragrant and color starts to darken slightly. Add wine; cook until mixture just comes to a boil. Simmer until reduced by half, about 5 minutes. Stir in broth, 1 tsp. rosemary and bay leaves. Bring to a boil. Reduce heat; cover and simmer until meat is almost tender, about 1½ hours.
3. Add the potatoes, onions and carrots. Cover; simmer until the meat and vegetables are tender, about 30 minutes longer.
4. Discard bay leaves. In a small bowl, combine remaining ½ tsp. rosemary, remaining ¼ tsp. salt and remaining 2 Tbsp. flour. Add cold water and vinegar; stir until smooth. Stir into stew. Bring to a boil; add peas. Cook, stirring, until thickened, about 2 minutes. If desired, top with additional fresh rosemary.
1½ cups: 366 cal., 11g fat (3g sat. fat), 71mg chol., 605mg sod., 40g carb. (9g sugars, 6g fiber), 28g pro.
Diabetic exchanges: 3 lean meat, 2½ starch, ½ fat.

THE BEST BEEF STEW

> **┌ FREEZE OPTION ─┐**
>
> Beef stew stores well in the refrigerator for up to 3 days, and you can freeze it for up to 3 months. Freeze in airtight containers; to use, partially thaw in the refrigerator overnight, then reheat in a saucepan over medium heat, adding a little water if necessary.

BUFFALO
CHICKEN CHILI

🍲 BUFFALO CHICKEN CHILI

This chili is rich in the best way. The cream cheese, blue cheese and tangy hot sauce join forces for a dinner recipe everyone will love.
—Peggy Woodward, Shullsburg, WI

PREP: 10 min. • **COOK:** 5½ hours
MAKES: 6 servings

- 1   can (15½ oz.) navy beans, rinsed and drained
- 1   can (14½ oz.) chicken broth
- 1   can (14½ oz.) fire-roasted diced tomatoes
- 1   can (8 oz.) tomato sauce
- ½   cup Buffalo wing sauce
- ½   tsp. onion powder
- ½   tsp. garlic powder
- 1   lb. boneless skinless chicken breast halves
- 1   pkg. (8 oz.) cream cheese, cubed and softened
     Optional: Crumbled blue cheese, chopped celery and chopped green onions

1. In a 4- or 5-qt. slow cooker, combine the first 7 ingredients. Add chicken. Cook, covered, on low until chicken is tender, 5-6 hours.
2. Remove chicken; shred with 2 forks. Return to slow cooker. Stir in cream cheese. Cover and cook on low until cheese is melted, about 30 minutes. Stir until blended. Serve with toppings as desired.
1¼ cups: 337 cal., 16g fat (8g sat. fat), 80mg chol., 1586mg sod., 25g carb. (5g sugars, 5g fiber), 25g pro.

SOUTHWESTERN
PORK & SQUASH SOUP

SOUTHWESTERN PORK & SQUASH SOUP

I adapted a pork and squash stew recipe by adding tomatoes and southwestern-style seasonings. My husband and sons loved it, and the leftovers were even better the next day!
—Molly Andersen, Portland, OR

PREP: 20 min. • **COOK:** 4 hours
MAKES: 6 servings (2¼ qt.)

FREEZE TOGETHER
+ Pork tenderloin (browned)
+ Onion
+ Butternut squash
+ Carrots
+ Seasonings

ADD WHEN COOKING
+ Chicken broth
+ Diced tomatoes

1   lb. pork tenderloin, cut into 1-in. cubes
1   medium onion, chopped
1   Tbsp. canola oil
3   cups reduced-sodium chicken broth
1   medium butternut squash, peeled and cubed
2   medium carrots, sliced
1   can (14½ oz.) diced tomatoes with mild green chiles, undrained
1   Tbsp. chili powder
1   tsp. ground cumin
1   tsp. dried oregano
½   tsp. pepper
¼   tsp. salt

In a large skillet, brown pork and onion in oil; drain. Transfer to a 4- or 5-qt. slow cooker. Stir in the remaining ingredients. Cover and cook on low for 4-5 hours or until meat is tender.

1½ cups: 220 cal., 5g fat (1g sat. fat), 42mg chol., 708mg sod., 26g carb. (10g sugars, 7g fiber), 19g pro. **Diabetic exchanges:** 4 vegetable, 2 lean meat, ½ fat.

WHY YOU'LL LOVE IT...

"This was super simple to make. I chopped the veggies the night before to make the morning a breeze putting this together ... Overall a great meal."
—RWIPPEL, TASTEOFHOME.COM

❄ CURRIED BEEF STEW

My mother, who was Japanese, made a dish very similar to this. After experimenting, I came up with a version that is close to hers. This recipe is special to me because it brings back memories of her.
—Gloria Gowins, Massillon, OH

PREP: 15 min. • **COOK:** 2 hours
MAKES: 4 servings

¾ lb. beef stew meat (1- to 1½-in. pieces)
¼ tsp. salt
⅛ tsp. pepper
2 Tbsp. all-purpose flour
1 Tbsp. canola oil
1 large onion, cut into ¾-in. pieces
2 Tbsp. curry powder
2 tsp. reduced-sodium soy sauce
2 bay leaves
3 cups beef stock
1½ lbs. potatoes (about 3 medium), cut into 1-in. cubes
2 large carrots, thinly sliced
1 Tbsp. white vinegar
Hot cooked rice, optional

1. Sprinkle beef with salt and pepper; toss with flour. In a Dutch oven, heat oil over medium heat; cook beef and onion until lightly browned, stirring occasionally. Stir in curry powder, soy sauce, bay leaves and stock; bring to a boil. Reduce heat; simmer, covered, 45 minutes.

2. Stir in potatoes and carrots; return to a boil. Reduce heat; simmer, covered, until meat and vegetables are tender, 1¼ hours, stirring occasionally. Remove bay leaves; stir in vinegar. If desired, serve with brown or white rice.

1½ cups: 362 cal., 10g fat (3g sat. fat), 53mg chol., 691mg sod., 44g carb. (7g sugars, 7g fiber), 24g pro. **Diabetic exchanges:** 3 starch, 3 lean meat, ½ fat.

FREEZE OPTION

Freeze cooled stew in freezer containers. To use, partially thaw in refrigerator overnight. Heat through in a saucepan, stirring occasionally; add water if necessary.

CURRIED BEEF STEW

🍲 ITALIAN SAUSAGE PIZZA SOUP

My mom's friend shared this recipe with her more than 50 years ago. I've tweaked it over the years, and it's still a family favorite. Warm garlic bread is heavenly on the side.

—Joan Hallford, North Richland Hills,

PREP: 15 min. • **COOK:** 6 hours
MAKES: 12 servings (3 qt.)

- 1 pkg. (1 lb.) Italian turkey sausage links
- 1 medium onion, chopped
- 1 medium green pepper, cut into strips
- 1 medium sweet red or yellow pepper, cut into strips
- 1 can (15 oz.) cannellini beans, rinsed and drained
- 1 can (14½ oz.) diced tomatoes, undrained
- 1 jar (14 oz.) pizza sauce
- 2 tsp. Italian seasoning
- 2 garlic cloves, minced
- 2 cans (14½ oz. each) beef broth
- 1 pkg. (5 oz.) Caesar salad croutons
   Shredded part-skim mozzarella cheese

1. Remove casings from sausage. In a large skillet over medium-high heat, cook and crumble sausage until no longer pink, 6-8 minutes. Add onion and peppers; cook until crisp-tender. Drain and transfer to a 6-qt. slow cooker.
2. Add the next 5 ingredients; pour in broth. Cook, covered, on low until vegetables are tender, 6-8 hours. Serve with croutons and mozzarella cheese.
1 cup: 158 cal., 5g fat (1g sat. fat), 15mg chol., 828mg sod., 19g carb. (4g sugars, 4g fiber), 9g pro.

BONNIE'S CHILI

❄️ 🍲 BONNIE'S CHILI

This chili is incredibly easy to make, and it tastes like it took all day to create! You can make this for people who like it hot or mild just by changing the salsa. To make it really spicy, add hot peppers and hot salsa.

—Bonnie Altig, North Pole, AK

PREP: 25 min. • **COOK:** 5 hours
MAKES: 8 servings (2½ qt.)

- 2 lbs. lean ground beef (90% lean)
- 2 cans (16 oz. each) kidney beans, rinsed and drained
- 2 cans (15 oz. each) tomato sauce
- 1½ cups salsa
- ½ cup water or reduced-sodium beef broth
- 4½ tsp. chili powder
- ½ tsp. garlic powder
- ½ tsp. pepper
- ¼ tsp. salt

Optional: Corn chips, sliced jalapeno peppers and shredded cheddar cheese

1. In a Dutch oven, cook the beef over medium heat until no longer pink, 8-10 minutes, breaking into crumbles; drain. Transfer to a 4- or 5-qt. slow cooker.
2. Stir in next 8 ingredients. Cook, covered, on low until heated through, 5-6 hours. If desired, serve with optional toppings.
1¼ cups: 323 cal., 10g fat (4g sat. fat), 71mg chol., 1027mg sod., 27g carb. (5g sugars, 8g fiber), 31g pro.

FREEZE OPTION

Freeze cooled chili in freezer containers. To use, partially thaw in refrigerator overnight. Heat through in a saucepan, stirring chili occasionally and adding a little water if necessary.

❄ 🍲 ITALIAN BEEF VEGETABLE SOUP

This hearty soup features a ton of fresh vegetables, perfect for using up all that summer produce. It's also fantastic during cooler weather. Serve this soup with breadsticks, rolls or flaky biscuits.
—Courtney Stultz, Weir, KS

PREP: 20 min. • **COOK:** 5 hours
MAKES: 6 servings

- ½ lb. lean ground beef (90% lean)
- ¼ cup chopped onion
- 2 cups chopped cabbage
- 2 medium carrots, chopped
- 1 cup fresh Brussels sprouts, quartered
- 1 cup chopped fresh kale
- 1 celery rib, chopped
- 1 Tbsp. minced fresh parsley
- ½ tsp. pepper
- ½ tsp. dried basil
- ¼ tsp. salt
- 3 cups beef stock
- 1 can (14½ oz.) Italian diced tomatoes, undrained

1. In a large skillet, cook beef with onion over medium-high heat until browned, 4-5 minutes, breaking the meat into crumbles. Transfer to a 3- or 4-qt. slow cooker. Stir in the remaining ingredients.
2. Cook, covered, on low until carrots are tender, 5-6 hours.
1 cup: 127 cal., 3g fat (1g sat. fat), 24mg chol., 617mg sod., 14g carb. (9g sugars, 3g fiber), 11g pro.
Diabetic exchanges: 1 starch, 1 lean meat.

> **FREEZE OPTION**
>
> Freeze cooled soup in freezer containers. To use, partially thaw in refrigerator overnight. Heat through in a saucepan, stirring occasionally.

🍲 CREAM OF POTATO & CHEDDAR SOUP

The Yukon Gold potatoes my daughter shares from her garden make this soup incredible. Add cheddar cheese and croutons, and it's just heavenly. Total comfort with the simplicity of good ingredients!
—Cindi Bauer, Marshfield, WI

PREP: 25 min. • **COOK:** 7½ hours
MAKES: 11 servings (2¾ qt.)

- 8 medium Yukon Gold potatoes, peeled and cubed
- 1 large red onion, chopped
- 1 celery rib, chopped
- 2 cans (14½ oz. each) reduced-sodium chicken broth
- 1 can (10¾ oz.) condensed cream of celery soup, undiluted
- 1 tsp. garlic powder
- ½ tsp. white pepper
- 1½ cups shredded sharp cheddar cheese
- 1 cup half-and-half cream
  Optional: Salad croutons, crumbled cooked bacon and chives

1. Combine potatoes, onion, celery, broth, condensed soup, garlic powder and white pepper in a 4- or 5-qt. slow cooker. Cover and cook on low until potatoes are tender, 7-9 hours.
2. Stir in the cheese and cream. Cover and cook until cheese is melted, about 30 minutes longer. If desired, garnish servings with croutons, bacon, chives and additional shredded cheese.
1 cup: 212 cal., 8g fat (5g sat. fat), 28mg chol., 475mg sod., 27g carb. (4g sugars, 3g fiber), 8g pro.
Diabetic exchanges: 2 starch, 1½ fat.

CREAM OF POTATO & CHEDDAR SOUP

COWBOY
STEW

❋ COWBOY STEW

I made up this dish back in the early 1970s when I was down to very little food in the house. A combination of barbecue sauce, hamburger, hot dogs and beans, this one-skillet meal is a hit with both children and adults.
—Val Rananawski, Millville, NJ

TAKES: 30 min.
MAKES: 11 servings

- 2 **lbs. ground beef**
- 4 **cans (16 oz. each) baked beans**
- 8 **hot dogs, sliced**
- ½ **cup barbecue sauce**
- ½ **cup grated Parmesan cheese**

In a Dutch oven, cook and crumble beef over medium heat until no longer pink; drain. Stir in remaining ingredients. Bring to a boil. Reduce heat; cover and simmer until flavors are blended, 4-6 minutes.
1 cup: 469 cal., 23g fat (9g sat. fat), 84mg chol., 1256mg sod., 39g carb. (5g sugars, 9g fiber), 28g pro.

TEST KITCHEN TIP

Store this stew in an airtight container in the refrigerator for up to 3 days. You can also freeze it in resealable freezer bags or containers for up to 3 months. To use, reheat the stew in a saucepan on the stovetop over low heat; add broth or water if necessary.

🍲 MEXI-STRONI SOUP

If you're a fan of classic minestrone but love bold Mexican flavors, this soup is for you! Spices, veggies and pasta make it a filling bowl of fun.
—Darlene Island, Lakewood, WA

PREP: 25 min. • **COOK:** 7½ hours
MAKES: 10 servings (3¾ qt.)

- 1½ lbs. beef stew meat (1-in. pieces)
- 1½ cups shredded carrots
- ½ cup chopped onion
- 1 jalapeno pepper, seeded and minced, optional
- 1 tsp. ground cumin
- 1 tsp. chili powder
- ¾ tsp. seasoned salt
- ½ tsp. Italian seasoning
- 2 cans (10 oz. each) diced tomatoes and green chiles, undrained
- 2 cups spicy hot V8 juice
- 1 carton (32 oz.) reduced-sodium beef broth
- 1 medium zucchini, halved and thinly sliced
- 2 cups finely shredded cabbage
- 2 celery ribs, thinly sliced
- 1 can (16 oz.) kidney beans, rinsed and drained
- 1 can (15 oz.) black beans, rinsed and drained
- 1 cup small pasta shells
- ¼ cup chopped fresh cilantro

1. Place first 11 ingredients in a 6- or 7-qt. slow cooker. Cook, covered, on low until meat is tender, 7-9 hours.
2. Stir in zucchini, cabbage, celery, beans and pasta. Cook, covered, on high until vegetables and pasta are tender, 30-45 minutes longer, stirring occasionally. Stir in cilantro.
1½ cups: 249 cal., 5g fat (2g sat. fat), 44mg chol., 816mg sod., 29g carb. (5g sugars, 6g fiber), 21g pro.

MEXI-STRONI SOUP

SAUSAGE & KALE LENTIL STEW

❄ SAUSAGE & KALE LENTIL STEW

I made a pot of this soup when visiting my sister and her family. Now I bring it along whenever I stop by. Sometimes I also pack up a few containers for my nephew, who appreciates a home-cooked meal while he's away at college.
—*Tiffany Ihle, Bronx, NY*

PREP: 20 min. • **COOK:** 45 min.
MAKES: 6 servings (2 qt.)

- 1   lb. bulk pork sausage
- 10 baby carrots, chopped (about ¾ cup)
- 1   small onion, finely chopped
- 4   garlic cloves, minced
- 4   plum tomatoes, halved
- ¾   cup roasted sweet red peppers
- 1   cup dried lentils, rinsed
- 2   cans (14½ oz. each) vegetable broth
- 1   bay leaf
- ½   tsp. ground cumin
- ¼   tsp. pepper
- 2   cups coarsely chopped fresh kale

1. In a Dutch oven, cook sausage, carrots and onion over medium-high heat until the sausage is no longer pink, breaking up sausage into crumbles, 8-10 minutes. Stir in garlic; cook 2 minutes longer. Drain.

2. Place tomatoes and red peppers in a food processor; process until finely chopped. Add to sausage mixture; stir in lentils, broth and seasonings. Bring to a boil. Reduce heat; simmer, covered, 20 minutes, stirring occasionally.

3. Stir in kale; cook until the lentils and the kale are tender, 10-15 minutes. Remove bay leaf.

1⅓ cups: 339 cal., 17g fat (5g sat. fat), 41mg chol., 1007mg sod., 29g carb. (5g sugars, 5g fiber), 17g pro.

┌─ **FREEZE OPTION** ─────────

Freeze cooled stew in freezer containers. To use, partially thaw in refrigerator overnight. Heat through in a saucepan, stirring occasionally.

SQUASH & LENTIL LAMB STEW

🍲 SQUASH & LENTIL LAMB STEW

My family lived in New Zealand many years ago. Every Sunday my mother made a lamb stew—it was Dad's favorite! I changed the recipe to suit my family's more modern palates, but it seems just as exotic and delicious.
—Nancy Heishman, Las Vegas, NV

PREP: 30 min. • **COOK:** 6 hours
MAKES: 8 servings (2½ qt.)

- 1 can (13.66 oz.) coconut milk
- ½ cup creamy peanut butter
- 2 Tbsp. red curry paste
- 1 Tbsp. hoisin sauce
- 1 tsp. salt
- ½ tsp. pepper
- 1 can (14½ oz.) chicken broth
- 3 tsp. olive oil, divided
- 1 lb. lamb or beef stew meat (1½-in. pieces)
- 2 small onions, chopped
- 1 Tbsp. minced fresh gingerroot
- 3 garlic cloves, minced
- 1 cup dried brown lentils, rinsed
- 4 cups cubed peeled butternut squash (about 1 lb.)
- 2 cups chopped fresh spinach
- ¼ cup minced fresh cilantro
- ¼ cup lime juice

1. In a 5- or 6-qt. slow cooker, whisk together the first 7 ingredients. In a large skillet, heat 2 tsp. oil over medium heat; brown lamb in batches. Add to the slow cooker.
2. In same skillet, saute onions in remaining 1 tsp. oil over medium heat until tender, 4-5 minutes. Add ginger and garlic; cook and stir 1 minute. Add to slow cooker. Stir in lentils and squash.
3. Cook, covered, on low until the meat and lentils are tender, 6-8 hours. Stir in spinach until wilted. Stir in minced cilantro and lime juice.
1¼ cups: 411 cal., 21g fat (11g sat. fat), 38mg chol., 777mg sod., 34g carb. (7g sugars, 6g fiber), 23g pro.

🍲 SPICY MEATLESS CHILI

Before I retired, this recipe was a mainstay in our house. I could prepare the ingredients the night before, and then on the way out the door in the morning I would throw everything in the slow cooker. When I got home, I just had to make the toppings and supper was done!
—Jane Whittaker, Pensacola, FL

PREP: 25 min. • **COOK:** 8 hours
MAKES: 5 servings

- 2 cans (14½ oz. each) Mexican diced tomatoes, undrained
- 1 can (15 oz.) black beans, rinsed and drained
- 2 cups frozen corn, thawed
- 1 cup salsa
- 1 medium zucchini, cut into ½-in. pieces
- 1 medium green pepper, coarsely chopped
- 1 small onion, coarsely chopped
- 1 celery rib, chopped
- 3 Tbsp. chili powder
- 1 tsp. dried oregano
- 2 garlic cloves, minced
- ¾ tsp. salt
- ¾ tsp. pepper
- ½ tsp. ground cumin
- ¼ tsp. cayenne pepper
  Optional: Sour cream, shredded cheddar cheese and sliced jalapeno pepper

In a 4-qt. slow cooker, combine the first 15 ingredients. Cover and cook on low until vegetables are tender, 8-10 hours. If desired, top with sour cream, cheddar cheese and jalapeno pepper.
1½ cups: 224 cal., 2g fat (0 sat. fat), 0 chol., 1290mg sod., 48g carb. (15g sugars, 11g fiber), 9g pro.

SPICY
MEATLESS CHILI

🍲 MEXICAN-INSPIRED CHICKEN SOUP

This zesty soup is loaded with chicken, corn and black beans in a mildly spicy red broth. As a busy mom of three young children, I'm always looking for dinner recipes that can be prepared in the morning. The kids love the taco taste of this easy soup.
—Marlene Kane, Lainesburg, MI

PREP: 10 min. • **COOK:** 3 hours
MAKES: 6 servings (2¼ cups)

- 1½ lbs. boneless skinless chicken breasts, cubed
- 2 tsp. canola oil
- ½ cup water
- 1 envelope reduced-sodium taco seasoning
- 1 can (32 oz.) V8 juice
- 1 jar (16 oz.) salsa
- 1 can (15 oz.) black beans, rinsed and drained
- 1 pkg. (10 oz.) frozen corn, thawed
  Optional: Shredded cheddar cheese, sour cream and chopped fresh cilantro

1. In a large nonstick skillet, saute chicken in oil until no longer pink. Add water and taco seasoning; simmer, uncovered, until chicken is well coated.
2. Transfer to a 5-qt. slow cooker. Stir in the V8 juice, salsa, beans and corn. Cover and cook on low until heated through, 3-4 hours. If desired, serve with toppings.
1½ cups: 304 cal., 5g fat (1g sat. fat), 63mg chol., 1199mg sod., 35g carb. (11g sugars, 5g fiber), 29g pro.

MEXICAN-INSPIRED CHICKEN SOUP

❄ SPECIAL OCCASION BEEF BOURGUIGNON

I've found many rich and satisfying variations on classic beef bourguignon, including an intriguing peasant version that used beef cheeks for the meat and a rustic table wine. To make this stew gluten-free, use white rice flour instead of all-purpose flour.
—Leo Cotnoir, Johnson City, NY

PREP: 50 min. • **BAKE:** 2 hours
MAKES: 8 servings

- 4 bacon strips, chopped
- 1 beef sirloin tip roast (2 lbs.), cut into 1½-in. cubes and patted dry
- ¼ cup all-purpose flour
- ½ tsp. salt
- ½ tsp. pepper
- 1 Tbsp. canola oil
- 2 medium onions, chopped
- 2 medium carrots, coarsely chopped
- ½ lb. medium fresh mushrooms, quartered
- 4 garlic cloves, minced
- 1 Tbsp. tomato paste
- 2 cups dry red wine
- 1 cup beef stock
- 2 bay leaves
- ½ tsp. dried thyme
- 8 oz. uncooked egg noodles
  Minced fresh parsley

1. Preheat oven to 325°. In a Dutch oven, cook bacon over medium-low heat until crisp, stirring occasionally. Remove with a slotted spoon, reserving drippings; drain on paper towels.
2. In batches, brown beef in bacon drippings over medium-high heat. Remove beef from pot; toss with flour, salt and pepper.
3. In the same pot, heat 1 Tbsp. oil over medium heat; saute onions, carrots and mushrooms until the onions are tender, 4-5 minutes. Add garlic and tomato paste; cook and stir for 1 minute. Add wine and stock, stirring to loosen any browned bits from pan. Add bay leaves, thyme, bacon and beef; bring to a boil.
4. Transfer to oven; bake, covered, until meat is tender, 2-2¼ hours. Remove the bay leaves.
5. To serve, cook noodles according to package directions; drain. Serve stew with noodles; sprinkle with parsley.

⅔ cup stew with ⅔ cup noodles: 422 cal., 14g fat (4g sat. fat), 105mg chol., 357mg sod., 31g carb. (4g sugars, 2g fiber), 31g pro. **Diabetic exchanges:** 4 lean meat, 2 fat, 1½ starch, 1 vegetable.

SPECIAL OCCASION
BEEF BOURGUIGNON

FREEZE OPTION

Freeze cooled stew in freezer containers. To use, partially thaw in refrigerator overnight. Heat through in a saucepan, stirring occasionally; add a little stock or broth if necessary.

RICH SEAFOOD
CHOWDER

RICH SEAFOOD CHOWDER

This delectable soup is even better the next day. It also works well with scallops or a flaky whitefish. Swap half-and-half or heavy cream for all or part of the milk to make it even richer.
—Anita Culver, Royersford, PA

PREP: 30 min. • **COOK:** 25 min.
MAKES: 8 servings (2 qt.)

- 2 Tbsp. butter
- 1 small onion, chopped
- 1 celery rib, chopped
- 1 medium carrot, shredded
- 2 Tbsp. all-purpose flour
- ½ cup 2% milk
- 3 cups seafood stock
- 1 medium potato, peeled and diced
- 1 Tbsp. Worcestershire sauce
- 1 tsp. salt
- ½ tsp. pepper
- 1 lb. uncooked shrimp (41-50 per lb.), peeled and deveined
- 2 cans (6½ oz. each) chopped clams, drained
- 2 cans (6 oz. each) lump crabmeat, drained
- 1 pkg. (8 oz.) cream cheese, cubed
  Minced fresh parsley

1. In a Dutch oven, heat butter over medium-high heat. Add the onion, celery and carrot; cook and stir until crisp-tender, 2-3 minutes. Stir in flour until blended; gradually add the milk. Bring to a boil; cook and stir until thickened, about 2 minutes.
2. Add the stock, diced potato, Worcestershire sauce, salt and pepper; return to a boil. Reduce heat; cover and simmer until potato is tender, 10-15 minutes.
3. Add the shrimp, clams, crab and cream cheese; cook and stir until shrimp turn pink and cheese is melted, 4-5 minutes. Garnish with parsley.

1 cup: 272 cal., 15g fat (8g sat. fat), 164mg chol., 1076mg sod., 11g carb. (3g sugars, 1g fiber), 24g pro.

SOUTHWEST CHICKEN CHILI

🍲 SOUTHWEST CHICKEN CHILI

Chicken thighs are a nice change of pace in this easy chili. I also add a smoked ham hock and fresh cilantro to add flavor and keep the dish interesting.
—Phyllis Beatty, Chandler, AZ

PREP: 15 min. • **COOK:** 6 hours
MAKES: 5 servings

- 1½ lbs. boneless skinless chicken thighs, cut into 1-in. cubes
- 1 Tbsp. olive oil
- 1 smoked ham hock
- 1 can (15½ oz.) great northern beans, rinsed and drained
- 1 can (14½ oz.) chicken broth
- 1 can (4 oz.) chopped green chiles
- ¼ cup chopped onion
- 2 Tbsp. minced fresh cilantro
- 1 tsp. garlic powder
- 1 tsp. ground cumin
- ½ tsp. dried oregano
- ⅛ to ¼ tsp. crushed red pepper flakes
  Optional: Sour cream and sliced jalapeno

1. In a large skillet, brown chicken in oil over medium-high heat. Transfer to a 3-qt. slow cooker. Add the ham hock, beans, broth, chiles, onion, cilantro and the seasonings. Cover chili and cook on low until the ham is tender, 6 to 8 hours.
2. Remove ham bone. When cool enough to handle, remove meat from bone; discard the bone. Cut meat into bite-sized pieces and return to slow cooker. If desired, serve chili with sour cream and sliced jalapeno.
1 cup: 343 cal., 16g fat (4g sat. fat), 104mg chol., 735mg sod., 16g carb. (1g sugars, 5g fiber), 33g pro.

BACON
CHEESEBURGER SOUP

🍲 BACON CHEESEBURGER SOUP

This creamy recipe brings two of my absolute favorite foods together in one! The tomato, fresh lettuce and crisp bacon make this soup taste as if it's burger time.
—Geoff Bales, Hemet, CA

PREP: 20 min. • **COOK:** 4 hours
MAKES: 6 servings

- 1½ lbs. lean ground beef (90% lean)
- 1 large onion, chopped
- ⅓ cup all-purpose flour
- ½ tsp. pepper
- 2½ cups chicken broth
- 1 can (12 oz.) evaporated milk
- 1½ cups shredded cheddar cheese
- 8 slices American cheese, chopped
- 1½ cups shredded lettuce
- 2 medium tomatoes, chopped
- 6 bacon strips, cooked and crumbled

1. In a large skillet, cook beef with onion over medium-high heat until meat is no longer pink, 6-8 minutes, breaking beef into crumbles; drain. Stir in flour and pepper; transfer the mixture to a 5-qt. slow cooker.
2. Stir in broth and milk. Cook, covered, on low until flavors are blended, 4-5 hours. Stir in the cheeses until melted. Top individual servings with lettuce, tomatoes and bacon.
1 cup: 557 cal., 32g fat (17g sat. fat), 135mg chol., 1160mg sod., 18g carb. (10g sugars, 1g fiber), 42g pro.

SLOW-COOKER CASSOULET WITH CRUMB TOPPING

🍲 SLOW-COOKER CASSOULET WITH CRUMB TOPPING

Classically inspired, this dish is loaded with chicken thighs, pork and smoked sausage. Tomatoes, beans and wine round out the hearty French stew, and bread crumbs thicken it slightly.
—Marie Rizzio, Interlochen, MI

PREP: 20 min. • **COOK:** 7 hours
MAKES: 8 servings (2½ qt.)

- 1 cup soft bread crumbs
- 2 lbs. boneless skinless chicken thighs
- 1 lb. boneless pork shoulder, trimmed and cut into 1-in. pieces
- 8 oz. kielbasa, halved lengthwise and cut into ½-in. thick slices
- 2 cans (15 oz. each) cannellini beans, rinsed and drained
- 1 can (14½ oz.) petite diced tomatoes, drained
- 1 cup chopped onion
- 1 cup chicken broth
- ¾ cup white wine
- 1 Tbsp. tomato paste
- ½ tsp. salt
- ½ tsp. pepper
- 2 garlic cloves, crushed
- 2 fresh thyme sprigs
- 1 bay leaf
  Minced fresh parsley, optional

1. Preheat oven to 350°. Place bread crumbs in a 15x10x1-in. baking pan. Bake, uncovered, stirring occasionally, until lightly browned, 8-12 minutes. Set aside.
2. Combine remaining ingredients in a 5- or 6-qt. slow cooker. Cook, covered, on low until the meat is tender, about 7 hours.
3. Remove and discard thyme sprigs and bay leaf. Stir in ¾ cup bread crumbs. Top individual servings with remaining bread crumbs. If desired, sprinkle with minced parsley.
1¼ cups: 482 cal., 22g fat (7g sat. fat), 129mg chol., 802mg sod., 24g carb. (4g sugars, 6g fiber), 40g pro.

THE BEST EVER CHILI

After my honeymoon in New Mexico, inspired by the fresh and fragrant chile peppers at the Santa Fe farmers market, I introduced my chili-loving family to this spicy, meaty version with a touch of masa harina. While this chili is fantastic right out of the pot, it tastes even better the next day. To make ahead, make a double batch and freeze leftovers in individual portions— they'll keep for at least six months.
—Sarah Farmer, Waukesha, WI

PREP: 20 min. + standing
COOK: 1 hour 20 min.
MAKES: 8 servings (3½ qt.)

- 3 dried ancho or guajillo chiles
- 1 to 2 cups boiling water
- 2 Tbsp. tomato paste
- 3 garlic cloves
- ¼ cup chili powder
- 1½ tsp. smoked paprika
- 2 tsp. ground cumin
- 1 lb. ground beef
- 1½ tsp. Montreal steak seasoning
- 2 lbs. beef tri-tip roast, cut into ½-in. cubes
- 2 tsp. salt, divided
- 2 tsp. coarsely ground pepper, divided
- 2 Tbsp. canola oil, divided
- 1 large onion, chopped (about 2 cups)
- 1 poblano pepper, seeded and chopped
- 1 tsp. dried oregano
- 1½ tsp. crushed red pepper flakes
- 3 cups beef stock
- 1 bottle (12 oz.) beer
- 2 cans (14½ oz. each) fire-roasted diced tomatoes, undrained
- 1 can (16 oz.) kidney beans, drained
- 3 Tbsp. masa harina
Optional: American cheese slices, sour cream, shredded cheddar cheese, diced red onion, sliced jalapenos, cilantro and corn chips

1. Combine chiles and enough boiling water to cover; let stand until softened, about 15 minutes. Drain, reserving ⅓ cup of the soaking liquid. Discard stems and seeds. Process the chiles, tomato paste, garlic and reserved soaking liquid until smooth.
2. In a small skillet, toast chili powder, paprika and cumin over medium heat 3-4 minutes or until aromatic; remove and set aside.
3. In a Dutch oven, cook and stir ground beef and steak seasoning over medium-high heat until beef is no longer pink, about 5 minutes; remove and drain.
4. Sprinkle steak cubes with 1 tsp. each of salt and pepper. In same Dutch oven, brown beef cubes in batches in 1 Tbsp. oil over medium-high heat; remove and set aside.
5. Saute onion and poblano in remaining 1 Tbsp. oil until tender, about 5 minutes. Stir in toasted spices, oregano and pepper flakes. Add the cooked meats, stock, beer, tomatoes, beans, remaining salt and pepper and chile paste mixture. Cook over medium heat 20 minutes; reduce heat to low. Stir in masa harina; simmer 30-45 minutes longer. Serve with desired toppings.
1¾ cups: 473 cal., 20g fat (6g sat. fat), 103mg chol., 1554mg sod., 29g carb. (8g sugars, 7g fiber), 41g pro.

THE BEST EVER CHILI

SPICED SPLIT PEA SOUP

🍲 SPICED SPLIT PEA SOUP

A hint of curry adds the perfect amount of kick to this family-pleasing soup. Just assemble the ingredients in the slow cooker and go about your day while it simmers.
—Sue Mohre, Mt. Gilead, OH

PREP: 25 min. • **COOK:** 8 hours
MAKES: 10 servings (2½ qt.)

- 1 cup dried green split peas
- 2 medium potatoes, chopped
- 2 medium carrots, halved and thinly sliced
- 1 medium onion, chopped
- 1 celery rib, thinly sliced
- 3 garlic cloves, minced
- 3 bay leaves
- 4 tsp. curry powder
- 1 tsp. ground cumin
- ½ tsp. coarsely ground pepper
- ½ tsp. ground coriander
- 1 carton (32 oz.) reduced-sodium chicken broth
- 1 can (28 oz.) diced tomatoes, undrained

1. In a 4-qt. slow cooker, combine the first 12 ingredients. Cook, covered, on low until the split peas are tender, 8-10 hours.
2. Stir in tomatoes; heat through. Discard bay leaves.

1 cup: 139 cal., 0 fat (0 sat. fat), 0 chol., 347mg sod., 27g carb. (7g sugars, 8g fiber), 8g pro.
Diabetic exchanges: 1 starch, 1 lean meat, 1 vegetable.

WHY YOU'LL LOVE IT...

"[This soup] was delicious on its own, but I imagine a little plain yogurt would be delicious stirred in. I served this with homemade naan brushed with garlic butter for sopping, and it was divine."
—CARLYFACE, TASTEOFHOME.COM

PAGE 181

PAGE 161

PAGE 172

Make-Ahead Main Courses

Your time may be limited, but that doesn't mean your meal options must be! It'll look as if you worked magic when these tantalizing and satisfying home-cooked entrees land on the dinner table.

PAGE 173

PAGE 182

CHOCOLATE
MOLASSES
PORK ROAST

🥘 CHOCOLATE MOLASSES PORK ROAST

This new twist on pork roast has a rich molasses flavor with a tantalizing hint of chocolate. It's easy to make, yet elegant enough for entertaining. Serve this roast with mashed potatoes on the side so as not to waste a drop of the delicious gravy.
—Avionne Huppert, Adams, NY

PREP: 20 min. • **COOK:** 6 hours
MAKES: 10 servings

- ½ cup packed brown sugar
- ½ cup maple syrup
- ¼ cup beef broth
- ¼ cup Worcestershire sauce
- ¼ cup ketchup
- ¼ cup molasses
- 2 Tbsp. baking cocoa
- 2 tsp. garlic powder
- 2 tsp. onion powder
- ¾ tsp. salt
- ½ tsp. ground ginger
- ½ tsp. ground mustard
- 1 boneless pork loin roast (4 to 5 lbs.)
- 3 Tbsp. cornstarch
- 3 Tbsp. water

1. In a small bowl, mix the first 12 ingredients. Cut roast in half; place in a 5- or 6-qt. slow cooker. Pour sauce over top. Cover and cook on low until meat is tender, 6-8 hours.
2. Remove pork to a serving platter; keep warm. Skim fat from cooking juices. Transfer juices to a small saucepan; bring to a boil. In a small bowl, mix the cornstarch and water until smooth; gradually stir into pan. Return to a boil; cook and stir for 2 minutes or until thickened. Serve with pork.
5 oz. cooked pork with ⅓ cup sauce: 355 cal., 9g fat (3g sat. fat), 90mg chol., 403mg sod., 33g carb. (27g sugars, 0 fiber), 35g pro.

FLAKY CHICKEN WELLINGTON

❄ FLAKY CHICKEN WELLINGTON

This cozy chicken Wellington takes a classic recipe and makes it super easy! I like to cook the chicken a day or so ahead of time to make it even simpler to throw together on busy nights.
—Kerry Dingwall, Wilmington, NC

PREP: 30 min. • **BAKE:** 15 min.
MAKES: 2 pastries (3 servings each)

- 2 cups cubed cooked chicken
- 1 pkg. (10 oz.) frozen chopped spinach, thawed and squeezed dry
- 3 hard-boiled large eggs, chopped
- ½ cup finely chopped dill pickles
- ⅓ cup finely chopped celery
- 2 tubes (8 oz. each) refrigerated crescent rolls
- 2 tsp. prepared mustard, divided
- 1 cup sour cream
- 2 Tbsp. dill pickle juice

1. Preheat oven to 350°. Combine first 5 ingredients. Unroll 1 tube of crescent dough into 1 long rectangle; press perforations to seal.
2. Spread half the mustard over dough; top with half the chicken mixture to within ¼ in. of edges. Roll up jelly-roll style, starting with a long side; pinch seam to seal. Place seam side down on a parchment-lined baking sheet. Cut slits in the top. Repeat with the remaining crescent dough, mustard and chicken mixture.
3. Bake until golden brown, 15-20 minutes. Meanwhile, combine sour cream and pickle juice; serve with pastries.
⅓ pastry with about 3 Tbsp. sauce: 495 cal., 28g fat (6g sat. fat), 144mg chol., 830mg sod., 37g carb. (10g sugars, 2g fiber), 25g pro.

┌─ **FREEZE OPTION** ─────
Cover and freeze unbaked pastries on a parchment-lined baking sheet until firm. Transfer to a freezer container; return to freezer. To use, bake pastries on a parchment-lined baking sheet in a preheated 350° oven until golden brown, 30-35 minutes. Prepare sauce as directed.
└────────────────

❄ HOMEMADE SLOPPY JOES

I simmer a big batch of this hot, tangy sandwich filling and freeze the extras. Then I just thaw and reheat it when I need a quick dinner.
—Sandra Castillo, Janesville, WI

PREP: 10 min. • **COOK:** 30 min.
MAKES: 12 servings

- 2 lbs. ground beef
- 2 medium onions, chopped
- 2 to 3 garlic cloves, minced
- 2 cups ketchup
- 1 cup barbecue sauce
- ¼ cup packed brown sugar
- ¼ cup cider vinegar
- 2 Tbsp. prepared mustard
- 1 tsp. Italian seasoning
- 1 tsp. onion powder
- ½ tsp. pepper
- 12 hamburger buns, split

1. In a large skillet, cook beef, onions and garlic over medium heat until meat is no longer pink, 6-8 minutes, breaking meat into crumbles; drain.
2. Stir in ketchup, barbecue sauce, brown sugar, vinegar, mustard and seasonings. Bring to a boil. Reduce heat; simmer, uncovered, for 20 minutes. Serve on buns.

1 sandwich: 368 cal., 11g fat (4g sat. fat), 47mg chol., 1029mg sod., 49g carb. (27g sugars, 1g fiber), 18g pro.

┌─ **FREEZE OPTION** ─────────

Freeze cooled meat mixture in freezer containers. To use, partially thaw in refrigerator overnight. Heat through in a saucepan, stirring occasionally; add water if necessary.
└──────────────────────────

HOMEMADE SLOPPY JOES

❄ ALL-AMERICAN TURKEY POTPIE

Ever since my sister-in-law shared this recipe with me, I haven't made any other kind of potpie. The crust is very easy to work with.
—Laureen Naylor, Factoryville, PA

PREP: 30 min. + chilling
BAKE: 45 min. • **MAKES:** 6 servings

- 2½ cups all-purpose flour
- ½ tsp. salt
- ½ cup finely shredded aged sharp cheddar cheese
- 14 Tbsp. cold butter
- 10 to 12 Tbsp. ice water

FILLING
- 1 cup cubed potatoes
- ½ cup thinly sliced carrots
- ⅓ cup chopped celery
- ¼ cup chopped onion
- 1 Tbsp. butter
- 1 garlic clove, minced
- 1 cup chicken broth
- 2 Tbsp. all-purpose flour
- ½ cup 2% milk
- 1½ cups shredded cooked turkey
- ½ cup frozen peas, thawed
- ½ cup frozen corn, thawed
- ½ tsp. salt
- ¼ tsp. dried tarragon
- ¼ tsp. pepper
  Egg wash, optional

1. In a food processor, combine flour and salt; cover and pulse to blend. Add cheese; pulse until fine crumbs form. Add butter; pulse until coarse crumbs form. While processing, gradually add 10 Tbsp. water; if needed, add remaining water, 1 Tbsp. at a time, until dough forms a ball.

2. Divide dough in half with 1 ball slightly larger than the other. Wrap both halves; refrigerate for 30 minutes.

3. Preheat oven to 400°. For filling, in a large saucepan or Dutch oven, saute potatoes, carrots, celery and onion in butter for 5 minutes. Add the garlic; cook 1 minute longer. Stir in broth; cover and cook until vegetables are tender, 10-15 minutes.

4. Combine flour and milk until smooth; gradually add to the vegetable mixture. Bring to a simmer; cook and stir until thickened, 3-5 minutes. Add the next 6 ingredients; cook until heated through, about 5 minutes longer.

5. Roll out the larger pastry ball to fit a 9-in. pie plate; transfer to pie plate. Trim crust even with edge. Pour hot turkey filling into crust. Roll out remaining pastry to fit top of pie; place over filling. Trim, seal and flute edges. Cut slits in top or make decorative cutouts in top crust. If desired, brush with egg wash.

6. Bake for 10 minutes; reduce oven temperature to 375°. Bake until the crust is golden brown, 35-45 minutes longer, covering edges of crust with foil if needed during the last few minutes to keep from overbrowning.

1 piece: 609 cal., 35g fat (21g sat. fat), 123mg chol., 898mg sod., 54g carb. (3g sugars, 3g fiber), 21g pro.

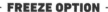

⌐ FREEZE OPTION

Cover and freeze unbaked pie. To use, remove from freezer 30 minutes before baking (do not thaw). Preheat oven to 425°. Place pie on baking sheet; cover edges loosely with foil. Bake 30 minutes. Reduce oven setting to 350°; bake 70-80 minutes longer or until crust is golden brown and a thermometer inserted in center reads 165°.

ALL-AMERICAN TURKEY POTPIE

SLOW-COOKER SHORT RIBS

🍲 SLOW-COOKER SHORT RIBS

These are an easy alternative to traditionally braised short ribs—you don't need to pay any attention to them once you get them started.
—*Rebekah Beyer, Sabetha, KS*

PREP: 30 min. • **COOK:** 6¼ hours
MAKES: 6 servings

- 3 lbs. bone-in beef short ribs
- ½ tsp. salt
- ½ tsp. pepper
- 1 Tbsp. canola oil
- 4 medium carrots, cut into 1-in. pieces
- 1 cup beef broth
- 4 fresh thyme sprigs
- 1 bay leaf
- 2 large onions, cut into ½-in. wedges
- 6 garlic cloves, minced
- 1 Tbsp. tomato paste
- 2 cups dry red wine or beef broth
- 4 tsp. cornstarch
- 3 Tbsp. cold water
  Salt and pepper to taste

1. Sprinkle ribs with salt and pepper. In a skillet, heat oil over medium heat. In batches, brown ribs on all sides; transfer to 4- or 5-qt. slow cooker. Add carrots, broth, thyme and bay leaf.
2. Add onions to the same skillet; cook and stir over medium heat 8-9 minutes or until tender. Add the garlic and tomato paste; cook and stir 1 minute longer. Stir in wine. Bring to a boil; cook 8-10 minutes or until liquid is reduced by half. Add to slow cooker. Cook, covered, on low until meat is tender, 6-8 hours.
3. Remove ribs and vegetables; keep warm. Transfer cooking juices to a small saucepan; skim off fat. Discard thyme and bay leaf. Bring juices to a boil. In a small bowl, mix cornstarch and water until smooth; stir into cooking juices. Return to a boil; cook and stir 1-2 minutes or until thickened. If desired, sprinkle with additional salt and pepper. Serve with ribs and vegetables.
1 serving: 250 cal., 13g fat (5g sat. fat), 55mg chol., 412mg sod., 12g carb. (4g sugars, 2g fiber), 20g pro.

MEXICAN MEAT LOAF

✳ MEXICAN MEAT LOAF

Being a working mother with a small budget and little time, I often rely on ground beef. When our son was getting bored with meat loaf, I made this taco-seasoned version. Everyone loves it with sour cream and extra salsa.
—Alice McCauley, Beaumont, TX

PREP: 10 min.
BAKE: 65 min. + standing
MAKES: 8 servings

> 4 **cups cooked shredded hash brown potatoes**
> ¼ **cup salsa**
> 1 **large egg, lightly beaten**
> 2 **Tbsp. vegetable soup mix**
> 2 **Tbsp. taco seasoning**
> 2 **cups shredded cheddar cheese, divided**
> 2 **lbs. ground beef**
> **Optional: Additional salsa, sour cream**

1. Preheat oven to 350°. Combine hash browns, salsa, egg, soup mix, taco seasoning and 1 cup cheese. Crumble beef over the mixture and mix well. Shape into a 12-in. loaf. Place in a 13x9-in. baking dish.
2. Bake, uncovered, for 1 hour or until a thermometer reads 160°. Sprinkle with remaining cheese; bake until the cheese is melted, 5 minutes longer. Let stand for 10 minutes before slicing. If desired, serve with additional salsa and sour cream.
1 piece: 376 cal., 23g fat (11g sat. fat), 121mg chol., 699mg sod., 12g carb. (1g sugars, 1g fiber), 28g pro.

FREEZE & STORE

Cover and freeze unbaked meat loaf in an airtight container. Cover and freeze remaining 1 cup cheese. To use, thaw in the refrigerator overnight. Bake, uncovered, at 350° until a thermometer reads 160°, about 1 hour. Sprinkle with remaining cheese; bake until cheese is melted, about 5 minutes longer. Let stand 10 minutes before slicing. If desired, serve with additional ingredients.

❉ HAM & COLLARDS QUICHE

I love quiche and wanted to make something that incorporates my southern roots. With eggs, cheese, ham and nutritious collard greens in a flaky crust, it's a complete meal.
—Billie Williams-Henderson, Bowie, MD

PREP: 20 min.
BAKE: 35 min. + standing
MAKES: 6 servings

- 1 sheet refrigerated pie crust
- 2 Tbsp. olive oil
- 1 cup frozen chopped collard greens, thawed and drained
- 1 small onion, chopped
- 1 garlic clove, minced
- ¼ tsp. salt
- ¼ tsp. pepper
- 2 cups shredded Colby-Monterey Jack cheese
- ¾ cup cubed fully cooked ham
- 6 large eggs
- 1 cup 2% milk

1. Preheat oven to 375°. Unroll crust into a 9-in. pie plate; flute edge. Chill while preparing filling.
2. In a large skillet, heat oil over medium-high heat. Add collard greens and onion; cook and stir until onion is tender, 5-7 minutes. Add garlic; cook 1 minute longer. Stir in the salt and pepper. Cool slightly; stir in cheese and ham. Spoon into crust.
3. In a large bowl, whisk eggs and milk until blended. Pour over top.
4. Bake on lower oven rack until a knife inserted in center comes out clean, 35-40 minutes. Cover edge loosely with foil during the last 15 minutes if needed to prevent overbrowning. Remove foil. Let quiche stand for 10 minutes before cutting.
1 piece: 457 cal., 31g fat (15g sat. fat), 240mg chol., 766mg sod., 23g carb. (4g sugars, 1g fiber), 21g pro

HAM & COLLARDS QUICHE

FREEZE OPTION

Cover and freeze unbaked quiche. To use, remove from freezer 30 minutes before baking (do not thaw). Preheat oven to 375°. Place quiche on a baking sheet. Bake as directed, increasing time to 50-60 minutes.

CUTS-LIKE-BUTTER
BBQ BRISKET

❄ CUTS-LIKE-BUTTER BBQ BRISKET

With just a few ingredients and steps, this recipe is nearly impossible to mess up. The thin, fall-apart-tender slices are delicious on their own but also make everything from tacos to Frito pies taste better.
—Darla Andrews, Boerne, TX

PREP: 15 min. • **BAKE:** 6 hours 5 min. **MAKES:** 20 servings

- 1 whole fresh beef brisket (about 10 lbs.), deckle fat removed
- 1 bottle (21.5 oz.) Asian honey barbecue sauce and marinade
- 1 cup packed brown sugar
- 2 Tbsp. garlic powder
- 2 Tbsp. ground cumin
- 1 Tbsp. salt
- 1 Tbsp. chili powder
- 1 Tbsp. pepper

1. Preheat oven to 300°. Place brisket, fat side up, in a large roasting pan. Pour marinade over brisket. Bake, covered, 4 hours. Combine remaining ingredients; sprinkle over the brisket. Bake, covered, until tender, 2-4 hours longer (a thermometer inserted in the brisket should read about 200°).
2. Preheat broiler; uncover the brisket. Broil 3-4 in. from heat until fat is bubbly and slightly charred, 4-5 minutes. Cut beef diagonally across the grain into thin slices. If desired, skim fat from cooking juices and serve juices with brisket.
6 oz. cooked beef: 345 cal., 10g fat (4g sat. fat), 97mg chol., 523mg sod., 14g carb. (12g sugars, 0 fiber), 47g pro.

> ### FREEZE OPTION
> Freeze the cooled meat mixture and juices in freezer containers. To use, partially thaw in refrigerator overnight. Heat through in a saucepan, stirring occasionally.

🍲 SLOW-COOKED COFFEE BEEF ROAST

Coffee is the key to a flavorful beef roast that simmers in the slow cooker until it's fall-apart tender. Try it once, and I'm sure you'll cook it again.
—Charles Trahan, San Dimas, CA

PREP: 15 min. • **COOK:** 8 hours
MAKES: 6 servings

- 1 beef sirloin tip roast (2½ lbs.), cut in half
- 2 tsp. canola oil
- 1½ cups sliced fresh mushrooms
- ⅓ cup sliced green onions
- 2 garlic cloves, minced
- 1½ cups brewed coffee
- 1 tsp. liquid smoke, optional
- ½ tsp. salt
- ½ tsp. chili powder
- ¼ tsp. pepper
- ¼ cup cornstarch
- ⅓ cup cold water

1. In a large nonstick skillet, brown roast on all sides in oil over medium-high heat. Place in a 5-qt. slow cooker. In the same skillet, saute mushrooms, onions and garlic until tender; stir in the coffee, liquid smoke if desired, salt, chili powder and pepper. Pour over roast.
2. Cover and cook on low until the meat is tender, 8-10 hours. Remove roast and keep warm. Pour cooking juices into a 2-cup measuring cup; skim fat.
3. In a small saucepan, combine the cornstarch and water until smooth. Gradually stir in 2 cups cooking juices. Bring to a boil; cook and stir until thickened, about 2 minutes. Serve with beef.
5 oz. cooked beef: 281 cal., 10g fat (3g sat. fat), 120mg chol., 261mg sod., 6g carb. (1g sugars, 0 fiber), 39g pro. **Diabetic exchanges:** 5 lean meat, ½ starch.

🍲 PULLED PORK TATERS

This recipe is as hearty as it gets—part barbecued pork, part potatoes, but completely delicious. My family can't get enough of this comforting, warm-you-up baked potato dish.
—Shannon Harris, Tyler, TX

PREP: 15 min. • **COOK:** 6 hours
MAKES: 6 servings

- 1 **boneless pork loin roast (2 to 3 lbs.)**
- 1 **medium onion, chopped**
- 1 **cup ketchup**
- 1 **cup root beer**
- ¼ **cup cider vinegar**
- 2 **Tbsp. Worcestershire sauce**
- 1 **Tbsp. Louisiana-style hot sauce**
- 2 **tsp. salt**
- 2 **tsp. pepper**
- 1 **tsp. ground mustard**
- 6 **large russet potatoes**
- 1 **Tbsp. cornstarch**
- 1 **Tbsp. cold water**
- 6 **Tbsp. butter**
- 6 **Tbsp. sour cream**
- 1½ **cups shredded cheddar cheese**
  Thinly sliced green onions, optional

1. Place roast in a 5-qt. slow cooker. Top with onion. Combine the ketchup, root beer, vinegar, Worcestershire, hot sauce, salt, pepper and mustard; pour over top. Cook, covered, on low until meat is tender, 6-8 hours.

2. Meanwhile, scrub and pierce potatoes. Bake at 400° until tender, 50-55 minutes.

3. Remove pork; shred meat with 2 forks and set aside. Skim fat from cooking juices; transfer to a large saucepan. Bring liquid to a boil. Combine cornstarch and water until smooth; gradually stir into the pan. Return to a boil; cook and stir until thickened, 2 minutes. Add shredded meat; heat through.

4. With a sharp knife, cut an "X" in a long side of each potato; fluff with a fork. Top each with butter, pork mixture and sour cream. Sprinkle with cheese and, if desired, green onions.

1 filled potato: 795 cal., 29g fat (18g sat. fat), 145mg chol., 1677mg sod., 89g carb. (24g sugars, 7g fiber), 44g pro.

TEST KITCHEN TIP

As cheese ages, its flavor becomes more pronounced, or sharper. Using aged cheese in your recipes adds complexity and rich flavor.

PULLED PORK TATERS

LOUISIANA RED BEANS & RICE

❄ 🍲 LOUISIANA RED BEANS & RICE

Smoked sausage and red pepper flakes add zip to this slow-cooked version of the New Orleans classic. For extra heat, add red pepper sauce.
—Julia Bushree, Menifee, CA

PREP: 20 min. • **COOK:** 3 hours
MAKES: 8 servings

- 4 cans (16 oz. each) kidney beans, rinsed and drained
- 1 can (14½ oz.) diced tomatoes, undrained
- 1 pkg. (14 oz.) smoked turkey sausage, sliced
- 3 celery ribs, chopped
- 1 large onion, chopped
- 1 cup chicken broth
- 1 medium green pepper, chopped
- 1 small sweet red pepper, chopped
- 6 garlic cloves, minced
- 1 bay leaf
- ½ tsp. crushed red pepper flakes
- 2 green onions, chopped
  Hot cooked rice

1. In a 4- or 5-qt. slow cooker, combine the first 11 ingredients. Cook, covered, on low until the vegetables are tender, 3-4 hours.
2. Remove bay leaf; stir. Serve with green onions and rice.
1 cup: 291 cal., 3g fat (1g sat. fat), 32mg chol., 1070mg sod., 44g carb. (8g sugars, 13g fiber), 24g pro.

┌─ **FREEZE OPTION** ─────────

Remove bay leaf; freeze cooled bean mixture in freezer containers. To use, partially thaw in refrigerator overnight. Heat in a saucepan, stirring occasionally; add a little broth or water if necessary.

FREEZE & STORE
Cover and freeze unbaked lasagna. To use, partially thaw in refrigerator overnight. Remove from refrigerator 30 minutes before baking. Preheat oven to 350°. Bake lasagna as directed until heated through and a thermometer inserted in center reads 165°, increasing cooking time to 1-1½ hours.

PERFECT FOUR-CHEESE LASAGNA

❄ PERFECT FOUR-CHEESE LASAGNA

Lasagna is one of my favorite meals, and this is the recipe I've made since I was a teenager. It's a tantalizing combo of pasta, meat sauce, cheese and more cheese that really lives up to its name!
—Lauren Delaney-Wallace, Glen Carbon, IL

PREP: 25 min.
BAKE: 50 min. + standing
MAKES: 12 servings

- 1 lb. ground beef
- 1 medium onion, chopped
- 2 garlic cloves, minced
- 1 tsp. dried oregano
- 1 tsp. dried basil
- 2 cans (15 oz. each) tomato sauce
- 2 large eggs, lightly beaten
- 2 cups 4% cottage cheese
- ⅔ cup grated Parmesan cheese
- ¼ cup shredded cheddar cheese
- 1½ cups shredded part-skim mozzarella cheese, divided
- 12 no-cook lasagna noodles (about 7 oz.)
- 1 tsp. Italian seasoning

1. Preheat oven to 350°. In a large skillet, cook and crumble beef with onion and garlic over medium-high heat until meat is browned, 5-7 minutes; drain. Stir in herbs and tomato sauce. In a bowl, mix eggs, cottage cheese, Parmesan cheese, cheddar cheese and ½ cup mozzarella cheese.
2. Spread 1 cup meat sauce into a greased 13x9-in. baking dish; layer with 4 noodles, cottage cheese mixture, an additional 4 noodles and half the remaining meat sauce. Repeat last 2 layers. Sprinkle with Italian seasoning and the remaining mozzarella.
3. Cover with greased foil; bake until the cheese is melted, 50-55 minutes. Let stand 10 minutes before serving.
1 piece: 279 cal., 13g fat (6g sat. fat), 72mg chol., 662mg sod., 22g carb. (4g sugars, 2g fiber), 20g pro.

HONEY CHIPOTLE RIBS

Nothing is better than a barbecue sauce with the perfect slather consistency. Here's one that'll ensure a lip-smacking feast. Go ahead and make the sauce up to a week ahead for an easier grilling experience.
—Caitlin Hawes, Westwood, MA

PREP: 10 min. • **GRILL:** 1½ hours
MAKES: 12 servings

- 6 lbs. pork baby back ribs
BARBECUE SAUCE
- 3 cups ketchup
- 2 bottles (11.2 oz. each) Guinness beer
- 2 cups barbecue sauce
- ⅔ cup honey
- 1 small onion, chopped
- ¼ cup Worcestershire sauce
- 2 Tbsp. chopped chipotle peppers in adobo sauce
- 4 tsp. ground chipotle pepper
- 2 Tbsp. Dijon mustard
- 1 tsp. salt
- 1 tsp. garlic powder
- ½ tsp. pepper

1. Wrap ribs in large pieces of heavy-duty foil; seal edges of foil. Grill, covered, over indirect medium heat for 1-1½ hours or until tender.
2. In a large saucepan, combine all the sauce ingredients; bring to a boil. Reduce heat; simmer, uncovered, for about 45 minutes or until thickened, stirring occasionally.
3. Carefully remove ribs from foil. Place over direct heat; baste with some of the sauce. Grill, covered, over medium heat until browned, about 30 minutes, turning once and basting occasionally with additional sauce. Serve with the remaining sauce.
1 serving: 515 cal., 21g fat (8g sat. fat), 81mg chol., 1674mg sod., 54g carb. (49g sugars, 1g fiber), 23g pro.

HONEY CHIPOTLE RIBS

FORGOTTEN JAMBALAYA

❄ 🍲 FORGOTTEN JAMBALAYA

During chilly times of the year, I fix this jambalaya at least once a month. It's so easy—just chop the vegetables, dump everything in the slow cooker and forget it! Even my sons, who are picky about spicy things, like this dish.
—Cindi Coss, Coppell, TX

PREP: 35 min. • **COOK:** 4¼ hours
MAKES: 11 servings

- 1 **can (14½ oz.) diced tomatoes, undrained**
- 1 **can (14½ oz.) beef or chicken broth**
- 1 **can (6 oz.) tomato paste**
- 3 **celery ribs, chopped**
- 2 **medium green peppers, chopped**
- 1 **medium onion, chopped**
- 5 **garlic cloves, minced**
- 3 **tsp. dried parsley flakes**
- 2 **tsp. dried basil**
- 1½ **tsp. dried oregano**
- 1¼ **tsp. salt**
- ½ **tsp. cayenne pepper**
- ½ **tsp. hot pepper sauce**
- 1 **lb. boneless skinless chicken breasts, cut into 1-in. cubes**
- 1 **lb. smoked sausage, halved and cut into ¼-in. slices**
- ½ **lb. uncooked shrimp (31-40 per pound), peeled and deveined**
  Hot cooked rice

1. In a 5-qt. slow cooker, combine the tomatoes, broth and tomato paste. Stir in next 10 ingredients. Stir in chicken and sausage.
2. Cook, covered, until the chicken is no longer pink, 4-6 hours. Stir in shrimp. Cook, covered, until shrimp turn pink, 15-30 minutes longer. Serve with rice.
1 cup: 230 cal., 13g fat (5g sat. fat), 75mg chol., 1016mg sod., 9g carb. (5g sugars, 2g fiber), 20g pro.

┌─ **FREEZE OPTION** ─────
Place individual portions of cooled stew in freezer containers and freeze. To use, partially thaw in refrigerator overnight. Heat through in a saucepan, stirring occasionally; add a little water if necessary.

🍲 PENNSYLVANIA POT ROAST

This heartwarming one-dish meal is adapted from a Pennsylvania Dutch recipe. I start the roast before I leave for church, add the vegetables when I get home, then just relax until it's done.
—Donna Wilkinson, Monrovia, MD

PREP: 10 min. • **COOK:** 5 hours
MAKES: 6 servings

- 1 **boneless pork shoulder butt roast (2½ to 3 lbs.), halved**
- 1½ **cups beef broth**
- ½ **cup sliced green onions**
- 1 **tsp. dried basil**
- 1 **tsp. dried marjoram**
- ½ **tsp. salt**
- ½ **tsp. pepper**
- 1 **bay leaf**
- 6 **medium red potatoes, cut into 2-in. chunks**
- 4 **medium carrots, cut into 2-in. chunks**
- ½ **lb. medium fresh mushrooms, quartered**
- ¼ **cup all-purpose flour**
- ½ **cup cold water**
  Browning sauce, optional

1. Place roast in a 5-qt. slow cooker; add broth, onions and seasonings. Cook, covered, on high for 4 hours. Add potatoes, carrots and mushrooms. Cook, covered, on high until vegetables are tender, about 1 hour longer. Remove meat and vegetables; keep warm. Discard bay leaf.
2. In a saucepan, combine flour and cold water until smooth; stir in 1½ cups cooking juices. Bring to a boil. Cook and stir until thickened, 2 minutes. If desired, add browning sauce. Serve with roast and vegetables.
1 serving: 331 cal., 12g fat (4g sat. fat), 78mg chol., 490mg sod., 28g carb. (5g sugars, 4g fiber), 26g pro.

**PENNSYLVANIA
POT ROAST**

SPECIAL SLOW-COOKED BEEF

This hearty entree is easy to prepare for Sunday dinner. While the beef cooks, the chef has lots of time to attend to the other details. With mashed potatoes on the side, it's comfort food for the cool months.
—Juli George, Grandville, MI

PREP: 35 min. • **COOK:** 6 hours
MAKES: 8 servings

- 1 boneless beef chuck roast (3 lbs.), cubed
- 1 Tbsp. canola oil
- 1 Tbsp. Italian seasoning
- 1 tsp. salt
- 1 garlic clove, minced
- ½ cup sliced ripe olives, drained
- ⅓ cup oil-packed sun-dried tomatoes, drained and chopped
- 1 cup beef broth
- ½ cup fresh pearl onions, peeled
- 1 Tbsp. cornstarch
- 2 Tbsp. cold water

1. In a large skillet, brown meat in oil in batches; drain. Transfer to a 5-qt. slow cooker. Sprinkle with the Italian seasoning, salt and garlic; top with olives and tomatoes. Add broth and onions. Cook, covered, on low until the meat is tender, 6-8 hours.

2. With a slotted spoon, remove the beef and onions to a serving platter; keep warm. Pour cooking juices into a small saucepan; skim fat.

3. Combine cornstarch and water until smooth; gradually stir into cooking juices. Bring to a boil; cook and stir until thickened, about 2 minutes. Spoon over beef mixture.

1 serving: 332 cal., 20g fat (7g sat. fat), 111mg chol., 551mg sod., 3g carb. (0 sugars, 1g fiber), 34g pro.

SPECIAL SLOW-COOKED BEEF

❄ SHEPHERD'S PIE TWICE-BAKED POTATOES

This recipe captures the best of two classics—baked potatoes and shepherd's pie. Serve it with a green salad, and satisfaction's guaranteed.
—Cyndy Gerken, Naples, FL

PREP: 1¾ hours • **BAKE:** 25 min.
MAKES: 6 servings

- 6 large russet potatoes
- 2 Tbsp. olive oil
- 1 lb. ground beef
- 1 medium onion, chopped
- 1 medium green pepper, chopped
- 1 medium sweet red pepper, chopped
- 4 garlic cloves, minced
- 1 pkg. (16 oz.) frozen mixed vegetables
- 3 Tbsp. Worcestershire sauce
- 1 Tbsp. tomato paste
- 1 Tbsp. steak seasoning
- ¼ tsp. salt
- ⅛ tsp. pepper
  Dash cayenne pepper
- 2 tsp. paprika, divided
- ½ cup butter, cubed
- ¾ cup heavy whipping cream
- ¼ cup sour cream
- 1 cup shredded Monterey Jack cheese
- 1 cup shredded cheddar cheese
- ¼ cup shredded Parmesan cheese
- 2 Tbsp. minced chives

TOPPINGS
- ½ cup shredded cheddar cheese
- 1 Tbsp. minced chives
- 1 tsp. paprika

1. Scrub and pierce potatoes; rub with oil. Bake at 375° until tender, about 1 hour.

2. In a large skillet, cook and crumble beef with onion, peppers and garlic over medium heat until the beef is no longer pink; drain. Add mixed vegetables, Worcestershire sauce, tomato paste, steak seasoning, salt, pepper, cayenne and 1 tsp. paprika. Cook and stir until vegetables are tender.

3. When the potatoes are cool enough to handle, cut a thin slice off the top of each; discard tops. Scoop out the pulp, leaving thin shells.

4. In a large bowl, mash pulp with butter. Add whipping cream, sour cream, cheeses and chives. Mash until combined.

5. Spoon 1 cup meat mixture into each potato shell; top with ½ cup potato mixture. Sprinkle with the remaining 1 tsp. paprika.

6. Place on a baking sheet. Bake at 375° for 20 minutes. Sprinkle with cheese; bake until melted, about 5 minutes longer. Sprinkle with chives and paprika.

1 stuffed potato: 986 cal., 56g fat (32g sat. fat), 183mg chol., 1066mg sod., 86g carb. (12g sugars, 11g fiber), 37g pro.

> ┌ **FREEZE OPTION** ─────────
>
> Before the second bake, wrap stuffed potatoes and freeze in a freezer container. To use, partially thaw in refrigerator overnight. Follow directions for the second bake, adding additional time until heated through.

SHEPHERD'S PIE TWICE-BAKED POTATOES

❄ 🍲 GARDEN CHICKEN CACCIATORE

Treat company to this perfect Italian meal. You'll have time to visit with your guests while it simmers, and it often earns rave reviews. I like to serve it with couscous, green beans and a dry red wine. Chop the onions, peppers and garlic ahead of time to make this dish even more convenient.
—*Martha Schirmacher,*
Sterling Heights, MI

PREP: 15 min. • **COOK:** 8½ hours
MAKES: 12 servings

12 boneless skinless
    chicken thighs (about 3 lbs.)
2   medium green peppers,
    chopped
1   can (14½ oz.) diced tomatoes
    with basil, oregano and
    garlic, undrained
1   can (6 oz.) tomato paste
1   medium onion, chopped
½   cup reduced-sodium
    chicken broth
¼   cup dry red wine or
    additional reduced-sodium
    chicken broth
3   garlic cloves, minced
¾   tsp. salt
⅛   tsp. pepper
2   Tbsp. cornstarch
2   Tbsp. cold water
    Minced fresh parsley,
    optional

1. Place chicken in a 4- or 5-qt. slow cooker. In a medium bowl, combine green peppers, tomatoes, tomato paste, onion, broth, wine, garlic, salt and pepper; pour over the chicken. Cook, covered, on low 8-10 hours or until chicken is tender.

2. In a small bowl, mix cornstarch and water until smooth; gradually stir into the slow cooker. Cook, covered, on high 30 minutes or until sauce is thickened. If desired, sprinkle with parsley before serving.

3 oz. cooked chicken with about ½ cup sauce: 207 cal., 9g fat (2g sat. fat), 76mg chol., 410mg sod., 8g carb. (4g sugars, 1g fiber), 23g pro. **Diabetic exchanges:** 3 lean meat, 1 vegetable, ½ fat.

FREEZE TOGETHER
+ Chicken thighs
+ Green peppers
+ Onion
+ Garlic

ADD WHEN COOKING
+ Tomatoes
+ Tomato paste
+ Broth
+ Wine
+ Salt & pepper
+ Cornstarch & water

GARDEN CHICKEN
CACCIATORE

 **BAJA PORK TACOS**

This delicious recipe is my copycat version of the most excellent Mexican food we ever had. The original recipe used beef, but this pork version comes mighty close to the same taste.
—Ariella Winn, Mesquite, TX

PREP: 10 min. • **COOK:** 8 hours
MAKES: 12 servings

- 1 **boneless pork sirloin roast (3 lbs.)**
- 5 **cans (4 oz. each) chopped green chiles**
- 2 **Tbsp. reduced-sodium taco seasoning**
- 3 **tsp. ground cumin**
- 24 **corn tortillas (6 in.), warmed**
- 3 **cups shredded lettuce**
- 1½ **cups shredded part-skim mozzarella cheese**

1. Cut the roast in half; place in a 3- or 4-qt. slow cooker. Mix chiles, taco seasoning and cumin; spoon over pork. Cook, covered, on low until the meat is tender, 8-10 hours.
2. Remove pork; cool slightly. Skim fat from cooking juices. Shred meat with 2 forks. Return to slow cooker; heat through.
3. Serve in tortillas with lettuce and cheese.
2 tacos: 320 cal., 11g fat (4g sat. fat), 77mg chol., 434mg sod., 26g carb. (1g sugars, 4g fiber), 30g pro. **Diabetic exchanges:** 3 medium-fat meat, 2 starch.

FREEZE OPTION

Place cooled pork mixture in freezer containers; freeze up to 3 months. To use, partially thaw in refrigerator overnight. Heat through in a covered saucepan, stirring occasionally; add a little broth if necessary.

TILAPIA FLORENTINE
FOIL PACKETS

TILAPIA FLORENTINE FOIL PACKETS

I just love fish and serving healthy food to my family. It's ultraconvenient to prep these packets ahead and have them ready for grilling!
—Shanna Belz, Prineville, OR

PREP: 30 min. • **GRILL:** 15 min.
MAKES: 4 servings

- 12 cups fresh baby spinach
- 1 Tbsp. butter
- 1 Tbsp. extra virgin olive oil, divided
- 4 tilapia fillets (6 oz. each)
- ½ tsp. salt
- ¼ tsp. pepper
- ½ large sweet or red onion, thinly sliced
- 2 Tbsp. fresh lemon juice
- 2 garlic cloves, minced
   Lemon wedges, optional

1. Prepare grill for medium-high heat or preheat oven to 475°. In a large skillet, cook spinach in butter and 1 tsp. oil over medium-high heat until wilted, 8-10 minutes.
2. Divide spinach among four 18x12-in. pieces of heavy-duty nonstick foil, placing food on dull side of foil. Place tilapia on top of spinach; sprinkle with salt and pepper. Top with onion, lemon juice, garlic and remaining 2 tsp. olive oil. Fold foil around mixture, sealing tightly.
3. Place packets on grill or on a baking pan in oven. Cook until fish just begins to flake easily with a fork, 12-15 minutes. Open packets carefully to allow steam to escape. Serve with lemon wedges if desired.
1 packet: 233 cal., 8g fat (3g sat. fat), 90mg chol., 453mg sod., 8g carb. (3g sugars, 2g fiber), 35g pro.
Diabetic exchanges: 5 lean meat, 1 vegetable, 1 fat.

MEXICAN CHICKEN ALFREDO

❄ MEXICAN CHICKEN ALFREDO

One family member likes Italian; another likes Mexican. They'll never have to argue when this rich and creamy sensation is on the menu!
—Tia Woodley, Stockbridge, GA

PREP: 25 min. • **BAKE:** 30 min.
MAKES: 2 casseroles
(4 servings each)

- 1 pkg. (16 oz.) gemelli or spiral pasta
- 2 lbs. boneless skinless chicken breasts, cubed
- 1 medium onion, chopped
- ¼ tsp. salt
- ¼ tsp. pepper
- 1 Tbsp. canola oil
- 2 jars (15 oz. each) Alfredo sauce
- 1 cup grated Parmesan cheese
- 1 cup medium salsa
- ¼ cup 2% milk
- 2 tsp. taco seasoning

1. Preheat oven to 350°. Cook pasta according to package directions.
2. Meanwhile, in a large skillet over medium heat, cook chicken, onion, salt and pepper in oil until chicken is no longer pink. Stir in Alfredo sauce; bring to a boil. Stir in cheese, salsa, milk and taco seasoning.
3. Drain the pasta; toss with the chicken mixture. Divide between 2 greased 8-in. square baking dishes. Bake, covered, until bubbly, 30-35 minutes.
1½ cups: 559 cal., 20g fat (11g sat. fat), 102mg chol., 899mg sod., 55g carb. (4g sugars, 3g fiber), 40g pro.

┌─ **FREEZE OPTION** ───────

Cover and freeze unbaked casserole up to 3 months. To use, thaw in refrigerator overnight. Remove from refrigerator 30 minutes before baking. Preheat oven to 350°. Bake casserole, covered, until bubbly, 50-60 minutes.

❄ 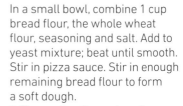 PIZZA STROMBOLI

When I owned a bakery, this was one of our customers' favorites. Once they smelled the aroma and sampled these tempting spiral slices, they just couldn't resist taking some home.
—John Morcom, Oxford, MI

PREP: 25 min. + rising
BAKE: 25 min.
MAKES: 1 loaf (12 pieces)

- 1 pkg. (¼ oz.) active dry yeast
- ¾ cup warm water (110° to 115°)
- 4½ tsp. honey
- 1 Tbsp. nonfat dry milk powder
- 2 cups bread flour
- ½ cup whole wheat flour
- 2 tsp. Italian seasoning
- 1 tsp. salt
- 4½ tsp. pizza sauce
- ¾ cup chopped pepperoni
- ½ cup shredded cheddar cheese, divided
- ¼ cup shredded Parmesan cheese
- ¼ cup shredded part-skim mozzarella cheese, divided
- 2 Tbsp. finely chopped onion
- 1 Tbsp. each chopped ripe olives, chopped pimiento-stuffed olives and chopped canned mushrooms

1. In a large bowl, dissolve yeast in warm water. Stir in honey and milk powder until well blended.

In a small bowl, combine 1 cup bread flour, the whole wheat flour, seasoning and salt. Add to yeast mixture; beat until smooth. Stir in pizza sauce. Stir in enough remaining bread flour to form a soft dough.

2. Turn onto a floured surface; knead until smooth and elastic, 6-8 minutes. Place in a greased bowl, turning once to grease top. Cover; let rise in a warm place until doubled, about 1 hour.

3. Punch dough down. Turn onto a lightly floured surface; roll into a 14x12-in. rectangle. Sprinkle with pepperoni, ¼ cup cheddar cheese, Parmesan cheese, 2 Tbsp. mozzarella cheese, onion, olives and mushrooms to within ½ in. of edges.

4. Roll up jelly-roll style, starting with a long side; pinch seam to seal and tuck ends under. Place seam side down on a greased baking sheet. Cover and let rise for 45 minutes.

5. Sprinkle with remaining cheddar and mozzarella cheeses. Bake at 350° until golden brown, 25-30 minutes. Remove from pan to a wire rack to cool slightly. Serve warm. Refrigerate leftovers.

1 piece: 192 cal., 7g fat (3g sat. fat), 15mg chol., 478mg sod., 24g carb. (3g sugars, 1g fiber), 8g pro.

TO MAKE AHEAD
Tightly wrap assembled stromboli, then place it in the refrigerator and bake it the next day. For best results, bring it to room temperature before baking. Store baked stromboli in the refrigerator up to 4 days, or in an airtight container in the freezer for up to 3 months.

PIZZA STROMBOLI

BAKED CHICKEN CHIMICHANGAS

❄ BAKED CHICKEN CHIMICHANGAS

I developed this recipe through trial and error— these are much healthier than deep-fried chimichangas.
—*Rickey Madden, Clinton, SC*

PREP: 20 min. • **BAKE:** 20 min.
MAKES: 6 servings

- 1½ cups cubed cooked chicken breast
- 1½ cups picante sauce, divided
- ½ cup shredded reduced-fat cheddar cheese
- ⅔ cup chopped green onions, divided
- 1 tsp. ground cumin
- 1 tsp. dried oregano
- 6 flour tortillas (8 in.), warmed
- 1 Tbsp. butter, melted
  Sour cream, optional

1. Preheat oven to 375°. Combine chicken, ¾ cup picante sauce, cheese, ¼ cup onions, cumin and oregano. Spoon ½ cup mixture down the center of each tortilla. Fold sides and ends over filling and roll up. Place seam side down in a 15x10x1-in. baking pan coated with cooking spray. Brush with butter.
2. Bake, uncovered, until heated through, 20-25 minutes. Broil until browned, about 1 minute. Top with remaining picante sauce and onions. If desired, serve with sour cream.

1 serving: 269 cal., 8g fat (3g sat. fat), 39mg chol., 613mg sod., 31g carb. (3g sugars, 1g fiber), 17g pro.

┌ FREEZE OPTION ─────

Cool baked chimichangas; wrap and freeze for up to 3 months. Place on a baking sheet coated with cooking spray. Bake at 400° until heated through, 10-15 minutes.

PM MARINATED BEEF TENDERLOIN

My three grown children and my grandkids enjoy this tempting tenderloin. Leftovers make wonderful sandwiches with fresh bread and Dijon mustard. I sometimes substitute a marinated eye of round roast and it turns out fine.
—Connie Scheffer, Salina, KS

PREP: 10 min. + marinating
BAKE: 55 min. + standing
MAKES: 8 servings

- 1 cup soy sauce
- ¾ cup beef broth
- ½ cup olive oil
- 2 Tbsp. red wine vinegar
- 4 to 5 garlic cloves, minced
- 1 tsp. coarsely ground pepper
- 1 tsp. dried thyme
- ½ tsp. salt
- ½ tsp. hot pepper sauce
- 1 bay leaf
- 1 beef tenderloin roast (3½ to 4 lbs.)

1. In a bowl, combine the first 9 ingredients; mix well. Cover and refrigerate 1 cup for basting. Pour the remaining marinade into a shallow dish; add bay leaf and tenderloin. Turn to coat; cover and refrigerate overnight.
2. Drain the beef, discarding marinade and bay leaf. Place tenderloin on a rack in a shallow roasting pan. Bake, uncovered, at 425° for 55-60 minutes or until meat reaches desired doneness (for medium-rare, a thermometer should read 135°; medium, 140°; medium-well, 145°), basting often with reserved marinade. Let roast stand 15 minutes before slicing.
4 oz. cooked beef: 610 cal., 40g fat (12g sat. fat), 169mg chol., 2191mg sod., 1g carb. (0 sugars, 0 fiber), 58g pro.

FREEZE & STORE
Assemble lasagna as directed, reserving final addition of 1 cup cheese. Cover and freeze lasagna and remaining cheese separately. To use, preheat oven to 375°. Bake frozen lasagna, covered, for 50 minutes. Sprinkle with the 1 cup shredded mozzarella cheese. Bake, uncovered, until a thermometer inserted in center reads 165°, 50-55 minutes longer. If desired, sprinkle with additional cheese. Let stand 10 minutes before serving.

ZUCCHINI
LASAGNA

❄ ZUCCHINI LASAGNA

I plant zucchini every year, and we always seem to have more than we can use! This is a particularly delicious way to use an abundant crop.
—Charlotte McDaniel, Williamsville, IL

PREP: 20 min.
BAKE: 40 min. + standing
MAKES: 6 servings

- 1 lb. lean ground beef (90% lean)
- ¼ cup chopped onion
- ½ tsp. dried oregano
- ½ tsp. dried basil
- ¼ tsp. salt
- ¼ tsp. pepper
- 1 can (15 oz.) tomato sauce
- 1 large egg, lightly beaten
- 1 cup 2% cottage cheese
- 4 medium zucchini (about 1¾ lbs.)
- 3 Tbsp. all-purpose flour
- 1 cup shredded part-skim mozzarella cheese
  Additional shredded mozzarella cheese, optional

1. Preheat oven to 375°. In large skillet, cook and crumble beef with onion over medium-high heat until meat is no longer pink, 5-7 minutes. Stir in seasonings and tomato sauce. Bring to a boil; simmer, uncovered, 5 minutes. In a bowl, mix the egg and the cottage cheese.
2. Trim the ends of zucchini; cut lengthwise into ¼-in.-thick slices. Toss zucchini with flour. Layer half the slices in a greased 13x9-in. baking dish. Top with cottage cheese mixture and half the meat sauce. Add remaining zucchini slices; sprinkle with any remaining flour. Spread with remaining meat sauce; sprinkle with 1 cup mozzarella cheese.
3. Bake, uncovered, until heated through, about 40 minutes. If desired, sprinkle with additional cheese. Let stand 10 minutes before serving.

1 serving: 273 cal., 13g fat (5g sat. fat), 92mg chol., 725mg sod., 14g carb. (6g sugars, 3g fiber), 27g pro.
Diabetic exchanges: 3 lean meat, 1 starch, 1 fat.

TEST KITCHEN TIP

There are several ways to keep your zucchini lasagna from being watery.

- Keep your zucchini slices thin—no more than ¼ in. thick. (A mandoline is a perfect tool for this.)
- Sprinkle the zucchini slices with salt and let them sit for 15 minutes. Salt brings water to the surface; blot it away with a paper towel.
- Precook the zucchini slices. Grill, broil or boil them for 5-7 minutes. Let them cool and blot them dry before assembling the lasagna.
- Let the lasagna sit for 10-15 minutes before cutting to let the moisture reabsorb evenly throughout the dish.

LIGHT-BUT-HEARTY
TUNA CASSEROLE

❄ LIGHT-BUT-HEARTY TUNA CASSEROLE

My boyfriend grew up loving his mother's tuna casserole and says he can't tell this one is light! We have it at least once a month.
—Heidi Carofano, Brooklyn, NY

PREP: 20 min. • **BAKE:** 25 min.
MAKES: 4 servings

- 3 cups uncooked yolk-free noodles
- 1 can (10¾ oz.) reduced-fat reduced-sodium condensed cream of mushroom soup, undiluted
- ½ cup fat-free milk
- 2 Tbsp. reduced-fat mayonnaise
- ½ tsp. ground mustard
- 1 jar (6 oz.) sliced mushrooms, drained
- 1 can (5 oz.) albacore white tuna in water
- ¼ cup chopped roasted sweet red pepper

TOPPING
- ¼ cup dry bread crumbs
- 1 Tbsp. butter, melted
- ½ tsp. paprika
- ¼ tsp. Italian seasoning
- ¼ tsp. pepper

1. Preheat oven to 400°. Cook noodles according to package directions.
2. In a large bowl, combine soup, milk, mayonnaise and mustard. Stir in the mushrooms, tuna and red pepper. Drain noodles; add to soup mixture and stir until blended. Transfer to a greased 8-in. square baking dish.
3. Combine topping ingredients; sprinkle over casserole. Bake until bubbly, 25-30 minutes.
1½ cups: 322 cal., 9g fat (3g sat. fat), 32mg chol., 843mg sod., 39g carb. (7g sugars, 4g fiber), 18g pro.

FREEZE OPTION

For perfectly portioned meals, place cooled casserole in freezer-safe containers. Freeze for up to 1 month. Microwaving is the easiest way to reheat it, or warm it slowly over low heat in a saucepan with a little water.

🍲 SLOW-COOKER SWISS STEAK SUPPER

Here's a satisfying dinner that's loaded with veggies. To save a step, I like to season the steak with peppered seasoned salt instead of using both seasoned salt and pepper.
—Kathleen Romaniuk, Chomedey, QC

PREP: 20 min. • **COOK:** 5 hours
MAKES: 6 servings

- 1½ lbs. beef top round steak
- ½ tsp. seasoned salt
- ¼ tsp. coarsely ground pepper
- 1 Tbsp. canola oil
- 3 medium potatoes
- 1½ cups fresh baby carrots
- 1 medium onion, sliced
- 1 can (14½ oz.) Italian diced tomatoes
- 1 jar (12 oz.) home-style beef gravy
- 1 Tbsp. minced fresh parsley

1. Cut steak into 6 serving-size pieces; flatten to ¼-in. thickness. Rub with seasoned salt and pepper. In a large skillet, brown beef in oil on both sides; drain.
2. Cut each potato into 8 wedges. In a 5-qt. slow cooker, layer the potatoes, carrots, beef and onion. Combine tomatoes and gravy; pour over top.
3. Cook, covered, on low until meat and vegetables are tender, 5-6 hours. Sprinkle with parsley.
1 serving: 402 cal., 6g fat (2g sat. fat), 67mg chol., 822mg sod., 53g carb. (10g sugars, 5g fiber), 33g pro.

CHICKEN BACON RANCH CASSEROLE

This casserole is a dinner that both of my wonderful (but picky!) children will eat. I can easily make it ahead and then bake it right before serving. Sometimes I add 2 cups of cooked veggies, such as peas or chopped broccoli, for a complete meal.
—Rebekah Schultz, Mantua, NJ

PREP: 30 min. • **COOK:** 15 min.
MAKES: 10 cups

- 1 pkg. (16 oz.) uncooked spiral pasta
- 1½ cups 2% milk
- ½ cup ranch salad dressing
- 1 envelope ranch salad dressing mix
- 1 pkg. (8 oz.) cream cheese, cubed
- 2 cups cubed cooked chicken
- 8 bacon strips, cooked and crumbled
- 2 cups shredded Colby cheese, divided
  Sliced green onions, optional

1. Preheat oven to 400°. Cook pasta according to package directions. Drain and transfer to a large bowl.
2. In the same pan, combine milk, ranch salad dressing and salad dressing mix until smooth. Stir in cream cheese. Cook and stir over medium heat until cream cheese is melted; pour over pasta. Stir in chicken, bacon and 1 cup shredded cheese. Transfer to a greased 13x9-in. baking dish. Top with remaining 1 cup cheese.
3. Bake, uncovered, until heated through and cheese is melted, 15-20 minutes. If desired, sprinkle with green onions.
1 cup: 495 cal., 26g fat (12g sat. fat), 80mg chol., 710mg sod., 40g carb. (4g sugars, 1g fiber), 24g pro.

CHICKEN BACON RANCH
CASSEROLE

 BEEF OSSO BUCCO

Our osso bucco recipe boasts a thick, savory sauce complemented by the addition of gremolata, a chopped herb condiment made of lemon zest, garlic and parsley.

—Taste of Home *Test Kitchen*

PREP: 30 min. • **COOK:** 7 hours
MAKES: 6 servings

- ½ cup all-purpose flour
- ¾ tsp. salt, divided
- ½ tsp. pepper
- 6 beef shanks (14 oz. each)
- 2 Tbsp. butter
- 1 Tbsp. olive oil
- ½ cup white wine or beef broth
- 1 can (14½ oz.) diced tomatoes, undrained
- 1½ cups beef broth
- 2 medium carrots, chopped
- 1 medium onion, chopped
- 1 celery rib, sliced
- 1 Tbsp. dried thyme
- 1 Tbsp. dried oregano
- 2 bay leaves
- 3 Tbsp. cornstarch
- ¼ cup cold water

GREMOLATA
- ⅓ cup minced fresh parsley
- 1 Tbsp. grated lemon zest
- 1 Tbsp. grated orange zest
- 2 garlic cloves, minced
  Polenta, optional

1. In a large resealable container, combine the flour, ½ tsp. salt and the pepper. Add beef, a few pieces at a time, and shake to coat.

2. In a large skillet, brown beef in butter and oil. Transfer meat and drippings to a 6-qt. slow cooker. Add wine to skillet, stirring to loosen browned bits from pan; pour over meat. Add tomatoes, broth, carrots, onion, celery, thyme, oregano, bay leaves and remaining ¼ tsp. salt.

3. Cook, covered, on low until the meat is tender, 7-9 hours.

4. Discard bay leaves. Skim fat from cooking juices; transfer juices to a large saucepan. Bring to a boil. Combine cornstarch and water until smooth; gradually stir into pan. Bring to a boil; cook and stir until thickened, 2 minutes.

5. In a small bowl, combine the 4 gremolata ingredients. Serve beef with gremolata and sauce. If desired, serve over polenta.

1 shank with 1 cup sauce and 4 tsp. gremolata: 398 cal., 15g fat (6g sat. fat), 112mg chol., 640mg sod., 17g carb. (5g sugars, 4g fiber), 47g pro.

TEST KITCHEN TIP

Pair this with French bread, or serve it over polenta, mashed potatoes or pasta. This dish reheats well, so you can easily make it ahead.

BEEF OSSO
BUCCO

MINI
PORK
PIES

❋ MINI PORK PIES

As a child, I discovered my love of pork pies. I used to help my father deliver oil on Saturdays, and we would stop at a local place to have these for lunch.
—*Renee Murby, Johnston, RI*

PREP: 1 hour • **BAKE:** 15 min.
MAKES: 10 servings

- 1 Tbsp. cornstarch
- 1¼ cups reduced-sodium chicken broth
- 2 lbs. ground pork
- 3 garlic cloves, minced
- 1½ tsp. salt
- ½ tsp. pepper
- ⅛ to ¼ tsp. ground cloves
- ⅛ to ¼ tsp. ground nutmeg
- ⅛ tsp. cayenne pepper
- 4 sheets refrigerated pie crust
- 1 large egg
- 2 tsp. 2% milk

1. Preheat oven to 425°. In a small saucepan, mix cornstarch and broth until blended; bring to a boil, stirring constantly. Cook and stir until thickened, 1-2 minutes. Remove from heat.
2. In a skillet, cook pork, garlic and seasonings over medium heat until pork is no longer pink, 6-8 minutes, breaking the pork into crumbles. Drain. Add the broth mixture; cook, stirring until thickened, 1-2 minutes. Cool slightly.
3. Unroll each pie crust. Roll each into a 12-in. circle. Using floured round cookie cutters, cut twenty 4-in. circles and twenty 2¾-in. circles, rerolling scraps as needed. Place large circles in ungreased muffin cups, pressing crusts on bottoms and up sides.
4. Fill each with 3 Tbsp. pork mixture. Place small circles over filling; press edges with a fork to seal. Whisk egg and milk; brush over tops. Cuts slits in crust.
5. Bake pies until golden brown, 15-20 minutes. Carefully remove pies to wire racks. Serve warm.
2 pies: 561 cal., 35g fat (14g sat. fat), 94mg chol., 776mg sod., 40g carb. (3g sugars, 0 fiber), 21g pro.

FREEZE OPTION

Freeze cooled pies in freezer containers. To use, partially thaw in refrigerator overnight. Reheat on ungreased baking sheets in a preheated 350° oven for 14-17 minutes or until heated through.

STEAK STROGANOFF

STEAK STROGANOFF

This slow-cooker recipe makes a traditional dinner completely fuss free. Serve it over noodles for a home-style meal that your whole family is sure to request time and again.
—Lisa VanEgmond, Annapolis, IL

PREP: 25 min. • **COOK:** 7 hours
MAKES: 12 servings

- 3 to 4 lbs. beef top sirloin steak, cubed
- 2 cans (14½ oz. each) chicken broth
- 1 lb. sliced fresh mushrooms
- 1 can (12 oz.) regular cola
- ½ cup chopped onion
- 1 envelope onion soup mix
- 1 to 2 tsp. garlic powder
- 2 tsp. dried parsley flakes
- ½ tsp. pepper
- 2 envelopes country gravy mix
- 2 cups sour cream
  Hot cooked noodles
  Minced fresh parsley, optional

1. In a 5-qt. slow cooker, combine first 9 ingredients. Cook, covered, on low until the beef is tender, 7-8 hours.
2. With a slotted spoon, remove the beef and mushrooms. Place gravy mix in a large saucepan; gradually whisk in cooking liquid. Bring to a boil; cook and stir until thickened, about 2 minutes.
3. Remove from heat; stir in sour cream. Add beef and mushrooms to the gravy. Serve with noodles. If desired, sprinkle with parsley.
1 cup: 345 cal., 20g fat (11g sat. fat), 65mg chol., 840mg sod., 11g carb. (7g sugars, 1g fiber), 29g pro.

RAVIOLI
LASAGNA

RAVIOLI LASAGNA

When you taste this casserole, you'll think it came from a complicated, from-scratch recipe. Really, though, it starts with frozen ravioli and has only a few other ingredients. You can assemble this earlier in the day and put it in the oven when you're ready.
—Patricia Smith, Asheboro, NC

PREP: 25 min. • **BAKE:** 40 min.
MAKES: 8 servings

- 1 lb. ground beef
- 1 jar (28 oz.) spaghetti sauce
- 1 pkg. (25 oz.) frozen sausage or cheese ravioli
- 1½ cups shredded part-skim mozzarella cheese
  Minced fresh basil, optional

1. Cook and crumble beef over medium heat until no longer pink, 5-7 minutes; drain. In a greased 2½-qt. baking dish, layer a third of the spaghetti sauce, half the ravioli and beef, and ½ cup cheese; repeat layers. Top with remaining sauce and cheese.
2. Bake, covered, at 400° until heated through, 40-45 minutes. If desired, top with basil to serve.
1 cup: 438 cal., 18g fat (7g sat. fat), 77mg chol., 1178mg sod., 42g carb. (7g sugars, 5g fiber), 26g pro.
SPINACH RAVIOLI LASAGNA: Replace the beef with 3 cups fresh baby spinach (do not cook); use meatless spaghetti sauce. Assemble and bake as directed.
ULTIMATE CHEESE RAVIOLI: Replace the beef with 2 cups small-curd 4% cottage cheese; use cheese ravioli. Increase mozzarella to 4 cups. Assemble and bake as directed, layering 2 cups mozzarella each time. Sprinkle ¼ cup grated Parmesan cheese over the top. Bake as directed, uncovering during the last 10 minutes.

BACON SWISS QUICHE

❄ BACON SWISS QUICHE

With a quiche like this, you don't need lots of side dishes. It's got everything— eggs, bacon, cheese and a touch of apple juice for a salty-sweet fix.
—Colleen Belbey, Warwick, RI

PREP: 15 min.
BAKE: 40 min. + standing
MAKES: 6 servings

- 1 sheet refrigerated pie crust
- ¼ cup sliced green onions
- 1 Tbsp. butter
- 6 large eggs
- 1½ cups heavy whipping cream
- ¼ cup unsweetened apple juice
- 1 lb. sliced bacon, cooked and crumbled
- ⅛ tsp. salt
- ⅛ tsp. pepper
- 2 cups shredded Swiss cheese

1. Line a 9-in. pie plate with crust; trim and flute edges. Set aside. In a small skillet, saute green onions in butter until tender.
2. In a large bowl, whisk eggs, cream and juice. Stir in bacon, salt, pepper and green onions. Pour into crust; sprinkle with shredded cheese.
3. Bake at 350° until a knife inserted in the center comes out clean, 40-45 minutes. Let stand 10 minutes before cutting.
1 piece: 739 cal., 60g fat (31g sat. fat), 359mg chol., 781mg sod., 22g carb. (4g sugars, 0 fiber), 27g pro.

FREEZE OPTION

Let quiche cool. Securely wrap individual portions in parchment and then in foil; freeze. To use, partially thaw in the refrigerator overnight. Remove from refrigerator 30 minutes before baking. Preheat oven to 350°. Unwrap the quiche; reheat in oven until heated through and a thermometer inserted in center reads 165°.

❋ FAVORITE BAKED SPAGHETTI

This is a fancied-up version of my grandchildren's favorite baked spaghetti. It feels like such a special dinner, and it's so cozy for winter.
—Louise Miller, Westminster, MD

PREP: 25 min.
BAKE: 1 hour + standing
MAKES: 10 servings

- 1 pkg. (16 oz.) spaghetti
- 1 lb. ground beef
- 1 medium onion, chopped
- 1 jar (24 oz.) pasta sauce
- ½ tsp. seasoned salt
- 2 large eggs
- ⅓ cup grated Parmesan cheese
- 5 Tbsp. butter, melted
- 2 cups 4% cottage cheese
- 4 cups shredded part-skim mozzarella cheese
  Chopped fresh basil, optional

1. Preheat oven to 350°. Cook spaghetti according to the package directions for al dente. Meanwhile, in a large skillet, cook beef and onion over medium heat until beef is no longer pink and onion is tender, 6-8 minutes, breaking beef into crumbles; drain. Stir in pasta sauce and seasoned salt; set aside.

2. In a large bowl, whisk the eggs, Parmesan cheese and butter. Drain spaghetti; add to egg mixture and toss to coat.

3. Place half the spaghetti mixture in a greased 13x9-in. or 3-qt. baking dish. Top with half the cottage cheese, meat sauce and mozzarella cheese. Repeat layers. Place baking dish on a rimmed baking sheet.

4. Bake, covered, 40 minutes. Uncover; bake until heated through, 20-25 minutes longer. Let stand 15 minutes before serving. If desired, sprinkle with basil.

1¼ cups: 526 cal., 24g fat (13g sat. fat), 127mg chol., 881mg sod., 45g carb. (9g sugars, 3g fiber), 31g pro.

BAKED SPAGHETTI PUTTANESCA: Add 1 Tbsp. minced garlic while cooking ground beef mixture. After draining, stir in 3 Tbsp. rinsed and drained capers, 1 cup coarsely chopped black olives, 3 finely chopped anchovy fillets and ¾ tsp. red pepper flakes. Proceed as directed, topping with additional olives and capers before serving.

FAVORITE BAKED SPAGHETTI

TO MAKE AHEAD

Cover the assembled, unbaked casserole, and keep it either in the refrigerator for up to 2 days or in the freezer for up to 3 months. To use, let it thaw in the refrigerator, then proceed with baking as directed. You can also bake this directly from frozen, but be sure to add additional time.

BLACK BEAN
ENCHILADAS

❄ BLACK BEAN ENCHILADAS

Picante sauce gives lots of zip to the tasty filling in these meatless enchiladas. Each generous serving is packed with fresh-tasting ingredients—and fiber too.
—Wendy Stenman, Germantown, WI

TAKES: 30 min.
MAKES: 6 servings

- 1 large onion, chopped
- 1 medium green pepper, chopped
- 2 Tbsp. chicken or vegetable broth
- 2 cans (15 oz. each) black beans, rinsed and drained, divided
- 1½ cups picante sauce, divided
- 12 flour tortillas (6 in.)
- 2 medium tomatoes, chopped
- ½ cup shredded cheddar cheese
- ½ cup shredded part-skim mozzarella cheese
- 3 cups shredded lettuce
  Sour cream

1. Preheat oven to 350°. In a nonstick skillet, cook and stir onion and green pepper in broth until tender, 2-3 minutes. Mash 1 can black beans. Add to skillet with ¾ cup of picante sauce and remaining beans; heat through.
2. Spoon ¼ cup mixture down the center of each tortilla. Roll up and place, seam side down, in a 13x9-in. baking dish coated with cooking spray. Combine tomatoes and remaining picante sauce; spoon over enchiladas.

3. Bake, covered, 15 minutes. Uncover; sprinkle with cheeses. Bake 5 minutes longer. Serve with lettuce and sour cream.
2 enchiladas: 442 cal., 12g fat (5g sat. fat), 15mg chol., 1261mg sod., 63g carb. (7g sugars, 10g fiber), 17g pro.

FREEZE OPTION

Assemble enchiladas up to the point of baking. Wrap tightly with foil, and freeze for up to 3 months. (Do not sprinkle with cheese until ready to bake.) To use, let them thaw in the refrigerator overnight; then add cheese and bake as directed.

CHICKEN SOFT TACOS

My family loves these tacos. The chicken cooks in the slow cooker, so it's convenient to throw together before I leave for work. Then we just roll it up in tortillas with the remaining ingredients and dinner's ready in minutes.
—Cheryl Newendorp, Pella, IA

PREP: 30 min. • **COOK:** 5 hours
MAKES: 5 servings

- 1   broiler/fryer chicken (3½ lbs.), cut up and skin removed
- 1   can (8 oz.) tomato sauce
- 1   can (4 oz.) chopped green chiles
- ⅓   cup chopped onion
- 2   Tbsp. chili powder
- 2   Tbsp. Worcestershire sauce
- ¼   tsp. garlic powder
- 10 flour tortillas (8 in.), warmed
- 1¼ cups shredded cheddar cheese
- 1¼ cups salsa
- 1¼ cups shredded lettuce
- 1   large tomato, chopped
      Sour cream, optional

1. Place chicken in a 4-qt. slow cooker. In a small bowl, combine tomato sauce, chiles, onion, chili powder, Worcestershire sauce and garlic powder; pour over chicken. Cook, covered, on low until chicken is tender and juices run clear, 5-6 hours.

2. Remove chicken. Shred meat with 2 forks and return to the slow cooker; heat through.

3. Spoon ½ cup chicken mixture down the center of each tortilla. Top with cheese, salsa, lettuce, tomato and, if desired, sour cream; roll up.

2 tacos: 749 cal., 29g fat (13g sat. fat), 157mg chol., 1454mg sod., 64g carb. (6g sugars, 5g fiber), 52g pro.

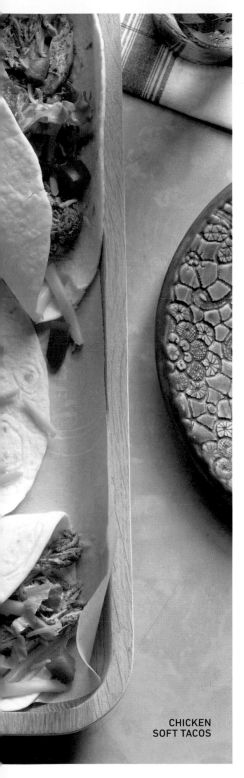

**CHICKEN
SOFT TACOS**

❄ 🍲 ALL-DAY RED BEANS & RICE

My family loves New Orleans-style cooking, so I make this dish often. I appreciate how simple it is, and the smoky ham flavor is scrumptious.
—Celinda Dahlgren, Napa, CA

PREP: 20 min. + soaking
COOK: 8½ hours
MAKES: 6 servings

- 1 cup dried red beans
- 2 smoked ham hocks
- 1 medium onion, chopped
- 1½ tsp. minced garlic
- 1 tsp. ground cumin
- 3 cups water
- 1 medium tomato, chopped
- 1 medium green pepper, chopped
- 1 tsp. salt
- 4 cups hot cooked rice

1. Sort beans and rinse in cold water. Place beans in a 3-qt. slow cooker. Add 4 cups water; cover and let stand overnight.
2. Drain and rinse the beans, discarding liquid. Return beans to slow cooker; add the ham hocks, onion, garlic, cumin and 3 cups water. Cook, covered, on low until beans are tender, 8-10 hours.
3. Remove ham hocks; cool slightly. Remove meat from bones. Finely chop meat and return to slow cooker; discard bones. Stir in tomato, pepper and salt; cook, covered, on high until pepper is tender, 30 minutes. Serve with rice.

⅔ cup bean mixture with ⅔ cup rice: 297 cal., 7g fat (3g sat. fat), 33mg chol., 441mg sod., 50g carb. (3g sugars, 12g fiber), 17g pro

┌─ **FREEZE OPTION** ───────

Freeze cooled bean mixture in freezer containers. To use, partially thaw in refrigerator overnight. Microwave, covered, on high in a microwave-safe dish until heated through, stirring occasionally; add a little water if necessary.

PAGE 206

PAGE 209

PAGE 190

Delicious Desserts

You can't talk about comfort food without including dessert! Whether you need a last-minute delight to pass at a potluck or a sweet ending to a weeknight dinner, these make-ahead treats will help you beat the clock!

PAGE 191

PAGE 192

CLASSIC CREME BRULEE

*My favorite dessert is creme brulee,
so I quickly learned to successfully
make this recipe myself. Recently,
I attended a party where guests had
the opportunity to caramelize their
own portions using a small torch.
What a clever idea!*
—Joylyn Trickel, Helendale, CA

PREP: 30 min.
BAKE: 25 min. + cooling
MAKES: 8 servings

- 4 **cups heavy whipping cream**
- 9 **large egg yolks**
- ¾ **cup sugar**
- 1 **tsp. vanilla extract**
  Brown sugar

1. In a large saucepan, combine
the cream, egg yolks and sugar.
Cook and stir over medium heat
until mixture reaches 160° or is
thick enough to coat the back of
a metal spoon. Stir in vanilla.
2. Transfer mixture to eight 6-oz.
ramekins or custard cups. Place
the cups in a baking pan; add
1 in. of boiling water to the pan.
Bake, uncovered, at 325° for
25-30 minutes or until centers
are just set (mixture will jiggle).
Remove ramekins from the
water bath; cool for 10 minutes.
Cover and refrigerate custard for
at least 4 hours.
3. One hour before serving,
place the custards on a baking
sheet. Sprinkle each with 1-2 tsp.
brown sugar. Broil 8 in. from the
heat until sugar is caramelized,
4-7 minutes. Refrigerate
any leftovers.
1 serving: 551 cal., 50g fat (29g sat.
fat), 402mg chol., 53mg sod., 22g
carb. (22g sugars, 0 fiber), 6g pro.

**CLASSIC
CREME BRULEE**

PM DIRTY BANANA TRIFLE

The addition of Kahlua takes the classic banana pudding trifle up a notch. Feel free to adjust the amount of coffee liqueur to suit your taste.
—Laurie Handlin, Ocean View, DE

PREP: 40 min. + chilling
MAKES: 24 servings

- 2 pkg. (8 oz. each) cream cheese, softened, divided
- 2 cans (14 oz. each) sweetened condensed milk, divided
- 1½ cups Kahlua (coffee liqueur), chilled
- 2½ cups cold 2% milk, divided
- 2 pkg. (3.9 oz. each) instant chocolate pudding mix
- 3 cartons (8 oz. each) frozen whipped topping, thawed, divided
- 9 whole chocolate graham crackers, coarsely crushed
- 2 pkg. (3.4 oz. each) instant banana cream pudding mix
- 1½ cups coarsely crushed vanilla wafers (about 45 wafers)
- 5 medium bananas, sliced
  Additional wafers, crushed chocolate graham crackers and sliced bananas

1. In a large bowl, beat 1 package of cream cheese and 1 can of condensed milk until blended. Beat in Kahlua, ½ cup milk and chocolate pudding mixes until thickened, about 2 minutes. Fold in 1 carton whipped topping, then the chocolate graham crackers.

2. In another large bowl, beat remaining cream cheese and condensed milk until blended. Beat in the remaining 2 cups milk and the banana pudding mixes until thickened, about 2 minutes. Fold in 1 carton whipped topping, vanilla wafers and bananas.

3. Spread chocolate pudding mixture in the bottom of a 6- or 7-qt. trifle bowl or glass bowl. Layer with 1½ cups whipped topping and banana pudding mixture; top with remaining 1½ cups whipped topping. Cover trifle and refrigerate overnight.

4. Garnish trifle with additional wafers, crushed chocolate graham crackers and sliced bananas before serving.

1 cup: 381 cal., 16g fat (11g sat. fat), 33mg chol., 326mg sod., 46g carb. (33g sugars, 1g fiber), 5g pro.

DIRTY
BANANA TRIFLE

WHY YOU'LL LOVE IT...

"Loved the addition of Kahlua! It gives a nice new spin on the usual banana pudding (which is great already!). Be sure to allow enough time for it to chill overnight, so that the vanilla wafers achieve the correct temperature. I also sprinkled some chopped pecans over the top for additional texture and flavor. It was an excellent dessert!"
—LVARNER, TASTEOFHOME.COM

ROOT BEER COOKIES

When it's too difficult to take along root beer floats on a picnic, take these cookies instead! I've found the flavor is even better the next day. The hard part is convincing my family to wait that long before sampling them.
—Violette Bawden, West Valley City, UT

PREP: 20 min.
BAKE: 10 min./batch + cooling
MAKES: 6 dozen

- 1 cup butter, softened
- 2 cups packed brown sugar
- 2 large eggs, room temperature
- 1 cup buttermilk
- ¾ tsp. root beer concentrate or extract
- 4 cups all-purpose flour
- 1 tsp. baking soda
- 1 tsp. salt
- 1½ cups chopped pecans

FROSTING
- 3½ cups confectioners' sugar
- ¾ cup butter, softened
- 3 Tbsp. water
- 1¼ tsp. root beer concentrate or extract

1. In a large bowl, cream butter and brown sugar. Add eggs, 1 at a time, beating well after each addition. Beat in buttermilk and root beer concentrate. Combine the flour, baking soda and salt; gradually add to creamed mixture. Stir in pecans.
2. Drop by tablespoonfuls 3 in. apart onto ungreased baking sheets. Bake at 375° until lightly browned, 10-12 minutes. Remove to wire racks to cool. In a small bowl, combine the frosting ingredients; beat until smooth. Frost cooled cookies.

1 cookie: 130 cal., 6g fat (3g sat. fat), 17mg chol., 96mg sod., 18g carb. (12g sugars, 0 fiber), 1g pro.

ⓅⓂ NEW YORK CHEESECAKE WITH SHORTBREAD CRUST

This traditional New York Cheesecake takes some time but is well worth the effort. Made with a shortbread crust and topped with a triple berry sauce, it is guaranteed to melt in your mouth.
—Karen Nielson, St. George, UT

PREP: 50 min.
BAKE: 1¼ hours + chilling
MAKES: 16 servings

- 1 cup all-purpose flour
- ¼ cup sugar
- 1 tsp. grated lemon zest
- ½ cup cold butter, cubed
- 2 large egg yolks, room temperature
- 1 tsp. vanilla extract

FILLING
- 5 pkg. (8 oz. each) cream cheese, softened
- 1¾ cups sugar
- ½ cup heavy whipping cream
- 3 Tbsp. all-purpose flour
- 2 tsp. vanilla extract
- 2 tsp. lemon juice
- 1½ tsp. grated lemon zest
- 5 large eggs, room temperature, lightly beaten
- 2 large egg yolks, room temperature

TRIPLE BERRY SAUCE
- 1¼ cups sugar
- ¼ cup cornstarch
- 2 cups cranberry juice
- 1 tsp. lemon juice
- 2 cups fresh or frozen unsweetened raspberries, divided
- 1 Tbsp. butter
- 1 cup fresh or frozen blueberries
- 1 cup fresh or frozen blackberries or boysenberries

1. Preheat oven to 325°. Place a greased 9-in. springform pan on a double thickness of heavy-duty foil (about 18 in. square). Wrap foil securely around pan. Place on a baking sheet.
2. In a small bowl, mix flour, sugar and lemon zest; cut in butter until crumbly. Add egg yolks and vanilla, tossing with a fork until mixture pulls together.
3. Press mixture onto bottom and 1½ in. up side of prepared pan. Bake until lightly browned, 12-16 minutes. Let cool on a wire rack.
4. Beat cream cheese and sugar until smooth. Beat in cream, flour, vanilla, lemon juice and zest. Add eggs and egg yolks; beat on low speed just until blended. Pour into crust. Place springform pan in a larger baking pan; add 1 in. of hot water to larger pan.
5. Bake until center is just set and top appears dull, 1¼ to 1½ hours. Remove springform pan from water bath. Cool cheesecake on a wire rack 10 minutes. Loosen side from pan with a knife; remove foil. Cool 1 hour longer. Refrigerate overnight, covering when completely cooled. Remove rim of pan.
6. In a small saucepan, combine sugar and cornstarch. Gradually add the cranberry and lemon juices. Stir in 1 cup raspberries. Bring to a boil; cook and stir until thickened, about 2 minutes. Remove from the heat; stir in the butter.
7. Strain sauce; discard seeds. Cool to room temperature. Stir in the blueberries, blackberries and remaining 1 cup raspberries. Serve with cheesecake.

1 piece: 494 cal., 36g fat (21g sat. fat), 200mg chol., 295mg sod., 37g carb. (28g sugars, 0 fiber), 8g pro.

NEW YORK CHEESECAKE
WITH SHORTBREAD CRUST

LEMON ANGEL CAKE BARS

LEMON ANGEL
CAKE BARS

A neighbor gave me this dessert recipe years ago, and it's been in my baking rotation ever since. It can be made in advance and serves a large group.
—*Marina Castle-Kelley,*
Canyon Country, CA

PREP: 15 min.
BAKE: 20 min. + chilling
MAKES: 4 dozen

- 1 **pkg. (16 oz.) angel food cake mix**
- 1 **can (15¾ oz.) lemon pie filling**
- 1 **cup unsweetened finely shredded coconut**

FROSTING
- 1 **pkg. (8 oz.) cream cheese, softened**
- ½ **cup butter, softened**
- 1 **tsp. vanilla extract**
- 2½ **cups confectioners' sugar**
- 3 **tsp. grated lemon zest**

1. Preheat oven to 350°. In a large bowl, mix cake mix, pie filling and coconut until blended; spread the batter into a greased 15x10x1-in. baking pan.
2. Bake until toothpick inserted in the center comes out clean, 20-25 minutes. Cool completely in pan on a wire rack.
3. Meanwhile, in a large bowl, beat cream cheese, butter and vanilla until smooth. Gradually beat in confectioners' sugar. Spread over cooled bars; sprinkle with lemon zest. Refrigerate for at least 4 hours. Cut into bars or triangles.
1 bar: 116 cal., 5g fat (3g sat. fat), 10mg chol., 135mg sod., 18g carb. (12g sugars, 0 fiber), 1g pro.

**FROZEN BANANA
SPLIT PIE**

*This dessert is the perfect finale to a
yummy meal of burgers and fries. The
pie is so tall and pretty, and the flavors
are just like the classic frozen banana
split. Make it ahead to save time.*
—Joy Collins, Birmingham, AL

PREP: 25 min. + freezing
MAKES: 8 servings

- 3 Tbsp. chocolate hard-shell
  ice cream topping
- 1 graham cracker crust (9 in.)
- 2 medium bananas, sliced
- ½ tsp. lemon juice
- ½ cup pineapple ice cream
  topping
- 1 qt. strawberry ice cream,
  softened
- 2 cups whipped topping
- ½ cup chopped walnuts, toasted
  Chocolate syrup
- 8 maraschino cherries
  with stems

1. Pour chocolate topping into
crust; freeze for 5 minutes or
until chocolate is firm.
2. Meanwhile, place bananas
in a small bowl; toss with lemon
juice. Arrange bananas over
chocolate topping. Layer with
pineapple topping, ice cream,
whipped topping and walnuts.
3. Cover and freeze until firm.
Remove pie from the freezer
15 minutes before cutting.
Garnish with chocolate syrup
and cherries.
1 piece: 459 cal., 22g fat (9g sat.
fat), 19mg chol., 174mg sod.,
64g carb. (26g sugars, 2g fiber),
5g pro.

**FROZEN BANANA
SPLIT PIE**

**SLOW-COOKER
PEACH CRUMBLE**

🍲 SLOW-COOKER PEACH CRUMBLE

I look forward to going on our beach vacation every year, but I don't always relish the time I spend cooking for everybody. This slow-cooker dessert gives me more time to lie in the sun and enjoy the waves. A scoop of melty ice cream on top is a must.
—Colleen Delawder, Herndon, VA

PREP: 20 min. • **COOK:** 3 hours
MAKES: 8 servings

- 1 Tbsp. butter, softened
- 6 large ripe peaches, peeled and sliced (about 6 cups)
- 2 Tbsp. light brown sugar
- 1 Tbsp. lemon juice
- 1 Tbsp. vanilla extract
- 2 Tbsp. coconut rum, optional

TOPPING
- 1 cup all-purpose flour
- ¾ cup packed light brown sugar
- 1½ tsp. baking powder
- 1 tsp. ground cinnamon
- ½ tsp. baking soda
- ⅛ tsp. salt
- 1 cup old-fashioned oats
- 6 Tbsp. cold butter, cubed
  Whipped cream, optional

1. Grease a 6-qt. oval slow cooker with 1 Tbsp. softened butter. Toss peaches with brown sugar, lemon juice, vanilla and, if desired, rum; spread evenly in slow cooker.
2. Whisk together first 6 topping ingredients; stir in oats. Cut in butter until crumbly; sprinkle over peaches. Cook, covered, on low until peaches are tender, 3-4 hours. If desired, serve with whipped cream.
¾ cup: 339 cal., 11g fat (7g sat. fat), 27mg chol., 293mg sod., 57g carb. (36g sugars, 4g fiber), 4g pro.

BANANA CREAM PIE

BANANA CREAM PIE

Made from our farm-fresh dairy products, this pie was a sensational creamy treat any time Mom served it. Her recipe is a real treasure, and I've never found one that tastes better!
—Bernice Morris, Marshfield, MO

PREP: 35 min. + chilling
COOK: 10 min. + cooling
MAKES: 8 servings

- 1 sheet refrigerated pie pastry
- ¾ cup sugar
- ⅓ cup all-purpose flour
- ¼ tsp. salt
- 2 cups whole milk
- 3 large egg yolks, room temperature, lightly beaten
- 2 Tbsp. butter
- 1 tsp. vanilla extract
- 3 firm medium bananas
  Optional: Whipped cream and additional sliced bananas

1. Unroll pie pastry into a 9-in. pie plate. Trim pastry to ½ in. beyond the rim of the pie plate; flute edge. Refrigerate for 30 minutes. Preheat oven to 425°.

2. Line the crust with a double thickness of foil. Fill with pie weights, dried beans or uncooked rice. Bake on a lower oven rack until the edge is golden brown, 20-25 minutes. Remove foil and pie weights; bake until the bottom is golden brown, 3-6 minutes longer. Cool on a wire rack.
3. Meanwhile, in a saucepan, combine sugar, flour and salt; stir in milk and mix well. Cook over medium-high heat until mixture is thickened and bubbly. Cook and stir 2 minutes longer. Remove from heat. Stir a small amount into the egg yolks; return all to saucepan. Bring to a gentle boil. Cook and stir 2 minutes; remove from the heat. Add butter and vanilla; cool slightly.
4. Slice bananas into crust; pour filling over the top. Cool on wire rack for 1 hour. Store pie in the refrigerator. If desired, garnish the pie with whipped cream and additional sliced bananas.
1 piece: 338 cal., 14g fat (7g sat. fat), 101mg chol., 236mg sod., 49g carb. (30g sugars, 1g fiber), 5g pro.

PM DOUBLE CHOCOLATE ALMOND CHEESECAKE

A friend gave me the recipe for this cheesecake. It's easy to make, but a challenge to wait a day to devour it!
—Darlene Brenden, Salem, OR

PREP: 25 min. + chilling
BAKE: 50 min. + chilling
MAKES: 16 servings

CRUST
- 1 pkg. (9 oz.) chocolate wafer cookies, crushed (about 2 cups)
- ¼ cup sugar
- ¼ tsp. ground cinnamon
- ¼ cup butter, melted

FILLING
- 2 pkg. (8 oz. each) cream cheese, softened
- 1 cup sugar
- 1 cup sour cream
- 8 oz. semisweet chocolate, melted and cooled
- ½ tsp. almond extract
- 2 large eggs, room temperature, lightly beaten

TOPPING
- 1 cup sour cream
- ¼ tsp. baking cocoa
- 2 Tbsp. sugar
- ½ tsp. almond extract
  Sliced almonds, toasted, optional

1. Preheat oven to 350°. Combine crust ingredients; reserve 2 Tbsp. for garnish. Press remaining crumbs evenly onto the bottom and 2 in. up the side of a 9-in. springform pan. Chill.
2. For filling, in a large bowl, beat cream cheese and sugar until smooth. Beat in the sour cream, chocolate and extract. Add eggs; beat on low speed just until combined. Pour into crust.
3. Place pan on a baking sheet. Bake for 40 minutes (the filling will not be set). Remove from the oven and let stand for 5 minutes.
4. Meanwhile, combine topping ingredients. Gently spread over filling. Sprinkle with reserved crumbs. Bake 10 minutes longer.
5. Cool on a wire rack for 10 minutes. Carefully run a knife around edge of pan to loosen; cool 1 hour longer. Refrigerate overnight. Garnish with sliced, toasted almonds if desired.
1 piece: 315 cal., 19g fat (11g sat. fat), 78mg chol., 215mg sod., 31g carb. (19g sugars, 1g fiber), 4g pro.

TEST KITCHEN TIP
When adding the eggs into the cheesecake batter, mix until just combined—no longer. The more you beat the eggs, the more air you whip into the batter. Extra air in the batter can cause your cake to crack, so avoid it wherever possible..

DOUBLE CHOCOLATE ALMOND CHEESECAKE

ANGEL FOOD
CAKE ROLL

❄ ANGEL FOOD CAKE ROLL

There's always room for dessert—especially when it's this eye-catching frozen fare. We like strawberry yogurt in the filling, but other flavors work well, too. The make-ahead treat is often requested at parties and potlucks.
—Joan Colbert, Sigourney, IA

PREP: 30 min. + freeezing
BAKE: 15 min. + cooling
MAKES: 12 servings

- 1 pkg. (16 oz.) angel food cake mix
  Confectioners' sugar
- 1 cup (8 oz.) strawberry yogurt
- 1 pkg. (3.4 oz.) instant vanilla pudding mix
- 3 drops red food coloring, optional
- 2 cups whipped topping

1. Preheat oven to 350°. Line an ungreased 15x10x1-in. pan with parchment.
2. Prepare cake batter according to package directions. Transfer to prepared pan. Bake until the top springs back when lightly touched, 15-20 minutes. Cool for 5 minutes. Invert onto a tea towel dusted with confectioners' sugar. Gently peel off paper. Roll up the cake in the towel jelly-roll style, starting with a short side. Cool completely on a wire rack.
3. Whisk together yogurt, pudding mix and, if desired, food coloring. Fold in whipped topping.
4. Unroll cake; spread yogurt mixture over cake to within ½ in. of edges. Roll up again, without towel. Cover tightly and freeze. Remove from freezer 30 minutes before slicing.
1 piece: 243 cal., 3g fat (3g sat. fat), 1mg chol., 427mg sod., 50g carb. (37g sugars, 0 fiber), 4g pro.

EASY OATMEAL
CREAM PIES

LEMONY LIMONCELLO TIRAMISU

Here's a great citrus twist on a classic Italian dessert. It's always a favorite at holiday meals and family gatherings!
—Deena Resnick, Oregon City, OR

PREP: 25 min. + chilling
MAKES: 12 servings

- 2 cartons (8 oz. each) mascarpone cheese
- 6 large egg yolks
- ¾ cup sugar
- ⅔ cup 2% milk
- 1¼ cups heavy whipping cream
- ½ tsp. vanilla extract
- ¼ cup lemon juice
- ½ cup limoncello
- 1 pkg. (7 oz.) crisp ladyfinger cookies
- 1 jar (10 oz.) lemon curd
  Candied lemon slices, optional

1. Stir mascarpone; let stand at room temperature 30 minutes.
2. Whisk egg yolks, sugar and milk in the top of a double boiler until thickened (ribbon stage) and a thermometer reads 160°. Remove from the heat; cool completely. Whisk in mascarpone cheese until almost smooth.
3. Whip heavy cream and vanilla until soft peaks form.
4. In a shallow bowl, combine the lemon juice and limoncello. Briefly dip 24 ladyfingers into lemon mixture and place in the bottom of an 11x7-in. baking dish. Top with half the mascarpone mixture, half the lemon curd and half the whipped cream. Repeat layers. Refrigerate, covered, for 6 hours or overnight. To serve, garnish with candied lemon slices as desired.
1 piece: 509 cal., 31g fat (17g sat. fat), 204mg chol., 80mg sod., 47g carb. (40g sugars, 0 fiber), 7g pro.

❄ EASY OATMEAL CREAM PIES

If you're craving those nostalgic store-bought oatmeal sandwich cookies, you'll love these simple morsels. Treats are always more delicious from your own kitchen!
—Crystal Schlueter, Northglenn, CO

PREP: 20 min. + chilling
BAKE: 10 min./batch + cooling
MAKES: 1½ dozen

- ¾ cup butter, softened
- 2 large eggs, room temperature
- 1 pkg. spice cake mix (regular size)
- 1 cup quick-cooking oats
- 1 can (16 oz.) vanilla frosting

1. Beat butter and eggs until blended. Beat in cake mix and oats. Refrigerate, covered, until firm enough to roll, 2 hours (dough will remain fairly soft).

2. Preheat oven to 350°. On a well-floured surface, roll half of the dough to ¼-in. thickness. Cut with a floured 2½-in. round cookie cutter. Place 1 in. apart on parchment-lined baking sheets. Bake until set, 8-10 minutes. Remove from pans to wire racks to cool completely. Repeat with remaining dough.
3. Spread frosting on bottoms of half of the cookies; cover with remaining cookies.
1 sandwich cookie: 296 cal., 13g fat (8g sat. fat), 41mg chol., 316mg sod., 42g carb. (26g sugars, 0 fiber), 3g pro.

┌─ **FREEZE OPTION** ─

Freeze assembled sandwich cookies in freezer containers, separating layers with waxed paper. To use, thaw the cookies before serving.

LEMONY LIMONCELLO TIRAMISU

❋ RUSTIC HONEY CAKE

When my boys were young, they couldn't have milk but could have yogurt. I included this cake in their diet with confidence. It also isn't overly sweet, which is a nice change of pace.
—Linda Leuer, Hamel, MN

PREP: 15 min.
BAKE: 30 min. + cooling
MAKES: 12 servings

- ½ cup butter, softened
- 1 cup honey
- 2 large eggs, room temperature
- ½ cup plain yogurt
- 1 tsp. vanilla extract
- 2 cups all-purpose flour
- 2 tsp. baking powder
- ½ tsp. salt
    Assorted fresh fruit and additional honey
    Chopped pistachios, optional

1. Preheat oven to 350°. Grease a 9-in. cast-iron skillet.
2. In a large bowl, beat butter and honey until blended. Add eggs, 1 at a time, beating well after each addition. Beat in yogurt and vanilla. In another bowl, whisk flour, baking powder and salt; add to butter mixture. Transfer batter to prepared skillet.
3. Bake until a toothpick inserted in the center comes out clean, 30-35 minutes. Cool completely in pan on a wire rack. Serve with fruit, additional honey and, if desired, chopped pistachios.
1 piece: 248 cal., 9g fat (5g sat. fat), 53mg chol., 257mg sod., 40g carb. (24g sugars, 1g fiber), 4g pro.

┌─ **FREEZE OPTION** ─────────
  Securely wrap cooled cake in foil; freeze. To use, thaw at room temperature and top as directed.
└──────────────────────────

RUSTIC
HONEY CAKE

PEANUT-CASHEW
MARSHMALLOW PIE

PEANUT-CASHEW MARSHMALLOW PIE

This pie appeals to kids and adults! The chocolate crust and caramel topping make it all the more special. I like the nice contrast of the creamy marshmallow filling with the crunchy peanuts. An added bonus is that the pie can be made ahead of time.
—Lisa Varner, El Paso, TX

PREP: 20 min. + chilling
COOK: 5 min. • **MAKES:** 8 servings

- 4 cups miniature marshmallows
- 1 cup 2% milk
- 1 Tbsp. butter
- 2 tsp. vanilla extract
- 1 cup cold heavy whipping cream
- ½ cup lightly salted dry-roasted peanuts, coarsely chopped
- ½ cup salted cashews, coarsely chopped
- 1 chocolate crumb crust (9 in.)
- ¼ cup hot caramel ice cream topping
- 2 Tbsp. chocolate syrup, optional

1. In a large saucepan, combine marshmallows and milk over medium heat, stirring often, until marshmallows are melted and mixture is smooth. Remove from heat. Transfer mixture to a bowl; stir in butter and vanilla. Place bowl in a pan of ice water. Gently stir until mixture is cool and starts to thicken, about 5 minutes.

2. In a large bowl, whip heavy cream at high speed until soft peaks form. Gently fold whipped cream into marshmallow mixture. In a small bowl, mix together peanuts and cashews; reserve ¼ cup for topping. Fold remaining nut mixture into the marshmallow mixture. Spoon the marshmallow mixture into prepared crumb crust. Sprinkle reserved ¼ cup nuts over top. Refrigerate, covered, for at least 6 hours or overnight. Drizzle with caramel topping and, if desired, chocolate syrup before serving.

1 piece: 441 cal., 26g fat (11g sat. fat), 40mg chol., 259mg sod., 47g carb. (30g sugars, 2g fiber), 7g pro.

ⓅⓂ SPICED RUM FRUITCAKE

Not only can this fruitcake be made weeks ahead, it tastes better that way! You can substitute Brazil nuts, pecans and hazelnuts for the walnuts—or use a combination of your favorites.
—*Jason Boor, Manchester, NY*

PREP: 25 min.
BAKE: 1¼ hours + cooling
MAKES: 1 loaf (16 pieces)

- ¾ cup all-purpose flour
- ½ tsp. baking powder
- ¼ tsp. salt
- 2 cups chopped walnuts
- 1 pkg. (8 oz.) pitted dates, chopped
- 1 cup maraschino cherries, halved
- ½ cup dried mangoes, chopped
- 3 large eggs, room temperature
- ¾ cup packed brown sugar
- 1 cup spiced rum, divided

1. Preheat oven to 300°. Line a 9x5-in. loaf pan with parchment, letting ends extend up sides of pan; grease parchment.
2. In a large bowl, mix the flour, baking powder and salt. Add the walnuts, dates, cherries and mangoes; toss to coat. In a small bowl, whisk the eggs, brown sugar and ½ cup rum until blended; stir into fruit mixture. Transfer to prepared pan.
3. Bake until a toothpick inserted in the center comes out clean, 1¼ to 1½ hours. Cool in pan on a wire rack 20 minutes. Slowly pour remaining rum over cake. Cool completely. Wrap tightly and store in a cool, dry place overnight. Cut fruitcake with a serrated knife.
1 piece: 256 cal., 11g fat (1g sat. fat), 35mg chol., 96mg sod., 35g carb. (25g sugars, 3g fiber), 4g pro.

SPICED RUM FRUITCAKE

CONTEST-WINNING EGGNOG CAKE

This gorgeous cake is full of eggnog flavor. It makes a showstopping dessert for the holidays.
—Debra Frappolli, Wayne, NJ

PREP: 30 min. + cooling
BAKE: 25 min. + cooling
MAKES: 16 servings

- ½ cup butter, softened
- 1¼ cups sugar
- 3 large eggs, room temperature
- ½ tsp. vanilla extract
- ½ tsp. rum extract
- 2 cups all-purpose flour
- 2 tsp. baking powder
- 1 tsp. salt
- 1 cup eggnog

FROSTING
- ¼ cup all-purpose flour
- ¼ tsp. salt
- 1½ cups eggnog
- 1 cup butter, softened
- 1½ cups confectioners' sugar
- 1½ tsp. vanilla extract
  Pearlized nonpareils, optional

CONTEST-WINNING EGGNOG CAKE

1. Preheat oven to 350°. In a large bowl, cream butter and sugar until light and fluffy, 5-7 minutes. Add eggs, 1 at a time, beating well after each addition. Add the extracts. Combine flour, baking powder and salt; gradually add to creamed mixture alternately with eggnog, beating well after each addition. Pour into 2 greased 9-in. round baking pans.
2. Bake until a toothpick inserted in the center comes out clean, 25-30 minutes. Cool in pans for 10 minutes before removing to wire racks to cool completely.
3. For the frosting, in a small saucepan, combine the flour and salt. Gradually stir in eggnog until smooth. Bring mixture to a boil over medium heat whisking constantly; cook and stir until thickened, about 2 minutes. Cool to room temperature.
4. In a large bowl, cream butter and confectioners' sugar until light and fluffy, 5-7 minutes. Gradually beat in eggnog mixture and vanilla until smooth. Spread between layers and over top and side of cake. If desired, pipe additional frosting for decoration and top with nonpareils. Store in the refrigerator.
1 piece: 372 cal., 20g fat (12g sat. fat), 104mg chol., 417mg sod., 44g carb. (30g sugars, 0 fiber), 5g pro.

TO MAKE AHEAD

The frosted cake can be stored in the refrigerator for up to 5 days. You can make the layers about a month ahead of time, then individually wrap them and freeze. To use, thaw for an hour at room temperature before frosting. The frosting should be made fresh.

SOUTHERN BANANA PUDDING

This old southern recipe features a comforting custard layered with sliced bananas and vanilla wafers and topped with meringue. It's great in summer, but I serve it all year long.

—Jan Campbell, Hattiesburg, MS

PREP: 30 min.
BAKE: 15 min. + chilling
MAKES: 8 servings

- ¾ cup sugar
- ⅓ cup all-purpose flour
- 2 cups 2% milk
- 2 large egg yolks, lightly beaten
- 1 Tbsp. butter
- 1 tsp. vanilla extract
- 36 vanilla wafers
- 3 medium ripe bananas, cut into ¼-in. slices

MERINGUE

- 2 large egg whites, room temperature
- 1 tsp. vanilla extract
- ⅛ tsp. cream of tartar
- 3 Tbsp. sugar

1. Preheat oven to 350°. In a large saucepan, combine sugar and flour. Stir in milk until smooth. Cook and stir over medium-high heat until thickened and bubbly. Reduce the heat; cook and stir 2 minutes longer.

2. Remove from the heat. Stir a small amount of hot milk mixture into the egg yolks; return all to pan, stirring constantly. Bring to a gentle boil; cook and stir for 2 minutes longer. Remove from the heat; gently stir in the butter and vanilla.

3. In an ungreased 8-in. square baking dish, layer a third of the vanilla wafers, bananas and filling. Repeat layers twice.

4. For meringue, beat egg whites, vanilla and cream of tartar on medium speed until soft peaks form. Gradually beat in sugar, 1 Tbsp. at a time, on high until stiff peaks form. Spread meringue evenly over hot filling, sealing edges to sides of dish. Bake until meringue is golden, 12-15 minutes. Cool on a wire rack for 1 hour. Refrigerate at least 3 hours before serving. Refrigerate leftovers.

1 serving: 293 cal., 7g fat (3g sat. fat), 58mg chol., 121mg sod., 53g carb. (38g sugars, 2g fiber), 5g pro.

TEST KITCHEN TIP

This Southern banana pudding is a perfect make-ahead treat. It lasts for about 4 days when stored in the fridge. Our Test Kitchen experts think banana pudding is best served cold, but go with your personal preference. To make it even creamier, serve the pudding with a dollop of whipped cream.

SOUTHERN BANANA PUDDING

CINNAMON NUT BARS

Classic bar meets good-for-you ingredients in this updated recipe. If you have the patience, store these in a tin for a day to allow the flavors to meld...they taste even better that way.
—Heidi Lindsey, Prairie du Sac, WI

PREP: 20 min.
BAKE: 15 min. + cooling
MAKES: 2 dozen

- ½ cup whole wheat flour
- ½ cup all-purpose flour
- ½ cup sugar
- 1½ tsp. ground cinnamon
- 1¼ tsp. baking powder
- ¼ tsp. baking soda
- 1 large egg, room temperature, beaten
- ⅓ cup canola oil
- ¼ cup unsweetened applesauce
- ¼ cup honey
- 1 cup chopped walnuts

ICING
- 1 cup confectioners' sugar
- 2 Tbsp. butter, melted
- 1 tsp. vanilla extract
- 1 Tbsp. water
- 2 Tbsp. honey

1. Preheat oven to 350°. In a large bowl, combine flours, sugar, cinnamon, baking powder and baking soda. In another bowl, combine the egg, oil, applesauce and honey. Stir into the dry ingredients just until moistened. Fold in the walnuts.
2. Spread batter into a 13x9-in. baking pan coated with cooking spray. Bake until a toothpick inserted in the center comes out clean, 15-20 minutes.
3. Combine icing ingredients; spread over warm bars. Cool completely before cutting into individual squares.
1 bar: 142 cal., 7g fat (1g sat. fat), 11mg chol., 44mg sod., 18g carb. (13g sugars, 1g fiber), 2g pro.

**STRAWBERRY PRETZEL
DESSERT**

STRAWBERRY PRETZEL DESSERT

A salty pretzel crust nicely contrasts with the cream cheese and gelatin layers in this classic potluck dessert.
—Aldene Belch, Flint, MI

PREP: 20 min.
BAKE: 10 min. + chilling
MAKES: 16 servings

- 2 cups crushed pretzels (about 8 oz.)
- ¾ cup butter, melted
- 3 Tbsp. sugar

FILLING
- 2 cups whipped topping
- 1 pkg. (8 oz.) cream cheese, softened
- 1 cup sugar

TOPPING
- 2 pkg. (3 oz. each) strawberry gelatin
- 2 cups boiling water
- 2 pkg. (16 oz. each) frozen sweetened sliced strawberries, thawed
  Optional: Additional whipped topping and pretzels

1. In a bowl, combine pretzels, butter and sugar. Press into an ungreased 13x9-in. baking dish. Bake at 350° for 10 minutes. Cool on a wire rack.

2. For filling, in a small bowl, beat whipped topping, cream cheese and sugar until smooth. Spread over pretzel crust. Refrigerate until chilled.

3. For topping, dissolve gelatin in boiling water in a large bowl. Stir in sweetened strawberries; chill until partially set. Carefully spoon over filling. Chill until firm, 4-6 hours. Cut into squares; if desired, serve with additional whipped topping and pretzels.

1 piece: 295 cal., 15g fat (10g sat. fat), 39mg chol., 305mg sod., 38g carb. (27g sugars, 1g fiber), 3g pro.

GINGER CREME SANDWICH COOKIES

🅿️ GINGER CREME SANDWICH COOKIES

With a lemony filling, these spiced cookies go over big because they have old-fashioned appeal. Party guests will snatch them up.
—Carol Walston, Granbury, TX

PREP: 25 min. + chilling
BAKE: 10 min./batch + cooling
MAKES: about 2½ dozen

- ¾ cup shortening
- 1 cup packed light brown sugar
- 1 large egg
- ¼ cup molasses
- 2¼ cups all-purpose flour
- 3 tsp. ground ginger
- 2 tsp. baking soda
- 1 tsp. ground cinnamon
- ½ tsp. salt
- ¼ cup sugar

FILLING
- 3 oz. cream cheese, softened
- ⅓ cup butter, softened
- 2 tsp. lemon extract
- 2 cups confectioners' sugar
- 1 tsp. vanilla extract

1. Cream the shortening and brown sugar until light and fluffy, 5-7 minutes. Beat in egg and molasses. In another bowl, whisk flour, ginger, baking soda, cinnamon and salt; gradually beat into creamed mixture. Refrigerate dough, covered, overnight.

2. Preheat oven to 375°. Shape dough into 1-in. balls; roll in granulated sugar. Place 2 in. apart on ungreased baking sheets. Flatten with a fork, forming a crisscross pattern. Bake until set (do not overbake), 8-10 minutes. Remove to wire racks to cool.

3. Meanwhile, combine filling ingredients until smooth. Spread over bottoms of half of the cookies; cover with remaining cookies. Refrigerate.

1 sandwich cookie: 184 cal., 8g fat (3g sat. fat), 14mg chol., 154mg sod., 26g carb. (19g sugars, 0 fiber), 1g pro.

(PM) CLASSIC TRES LECHES CAKE

A classic in Mexican kitchens, this rich cake gets its name from the three types of milk used to create its moist, tender texture. You can make this cake a day or two in advance, with the exception of the topping. In fact, letting the cake sit overnight is ideal—it will allow the milk to fully saturate the cake for that just-right texture.
—Taste of Home *Test Kitchen*

PREP: 45 min.
BAKE: 20 min. + chilling
MAKES: 10 servings

- 4 large eggs, separated, room temperature
- ⅔ cup sugar, divided
- ⅔ cup cake flour
  Dash salt
- ¾ cup heavy whipping cream
- ¾ cup evaporated milk
- ¾ cup sweetened condensed milk
- 2 tsp. vanilla extract
- ¼ tsp. rum extract

TOPPING
- 1¼ cups heavy whipping cream
- 3 Tbsp. sugar
  Optional: Dulce de leche or sliced fresh strawberries

1. Place the egg whites in a large bowl. Line the bottom of a 9-in. springform pan with parchment; grease the paper.

2. Meanwhile, preheat oven to 350°. In another large bowl, beat egg yolks until slightly thickened. Gradually add ⅓ cup sugar, beating on high speed until thick and lemon-colored. Fold in flour, a third at a time.

3. Add salt to egg whites; with clean beaters, beat on medium until soft peaks form. Gradually add the remaining ⅓ cup sugar, 1 Tbsp. at a time, beating on high after each addition until sugar is dissolved. Continue beating until soft glossy peaks form. Fold a third of the whites into batter, then fold in remaining whites. Gently spread into prepared pan.

4. Bake until the top springs back when lightly touched, roughly 20-25 minutes. Cool 10 minutes before removing from pan to a wire rack to cool completely.

5. Place on a rimmed serving plate. Poke holes in top with a skewer. In a small bowl, mix the whipping cream, evaporated milk, sweetened condensed milk and extracts; brush or pour slowly over cake. Refrigerate, covered, for at least 2 hours.

6. For topping, beat cream until it begins to thicken. Add sugar; beat until peaks form. Spread over top of cake. If desired, top cake with dulce de leche or strawberries just before serving.

1 piece: 392 cal., 23g fat (14g sat. fat), 142mg chol., 104mg sod., 40g carb. (33g sugars, 0 fiber), 8g pro.

CLASSIC TRES LECHES CAKE

GINGERBREAD FRUITCAKE COOKIES

GINGERBREAD FRUITCAKE COOKIES

Here's a recipe that combines two Christmastime classics—gingerbread and fruitcake—into one astounding favorite. I spread on a simple glaze of confectioners' sugar and orange juice.
—Jamie Jones, Madison, GA

PREP: 20 min.
BAKE: 10 min./batch + cooling
MAKES: 3 dozen

- 1 pkg. (14½ oz.) gingerbread cake/cookie mix
- ¼ cup butter, melted
- ¼ cup water
- 1 container (8 oz.) chopped mixed candied fruit
- ½ cup chopped pecans
- ½ cup raisins
- 1¼ cups confectioners' sugar
- 1 to 2 Tbsp. orange juice

1. Preheat oven to 350°. In a large bowl, mix cookie mix, melted butter and water to form a soft dough. Stir in the candied fruit, pecans and raisins. Drop dough by tablespoonfuls 2 in. apart onto ungreased baking sheets.
2. Bake until set, 8-10 minutes. Cool on pans 1 minute. Remove cookies from pans to wire racks to cool completely.
3. In a bowl, mix confectioners' sugar and enough orange juice to reach desired consistency. Spread or drizzle over cookies. Let stand until set.
1 cookie: 111 cal., 4g fat (1g sat. fat), 3mg chol., 91mg sod., 19g carb. (15g sugars, 1g fiber), 1g pro.

TO MAKE AHEAD

The dough for these cookies can be made ahead. Wrap and store in the refrigerator for up to 2 days.

TURTLE ICE CREAM SAUCE

Making this decadent caramel-fudge sauce is a family affair—my kids love to unwrap the caramels! The sauce can be made ahead and frozen.
—Marci Cullen, Milton, WI

PREP: 10 min.
COOK: 15 min. + cooling
MAKES: 9 cups

- 2 **cups butter, cubed**
- 2 **cans (12 oz. each) evaporated milk**
- 2 **cups sugar**
- ⅓ **cup dark corn syrup**
- ⅛ **tsp. salt**
- 2 **cups semisweet chocolate chips**
- 1 **pkg. (14 oz.) caramels**
- 1 **tsp. vanilla extract**

1. In a Dutch oven, combine the first 7 ingredients. Cook, stirring constantly, over medium-low heat until the caramels are melted and mixture is smooth (do not boil). Reduce heat to low.
2. With an electric hand mixer on medium speed, beat in vanilla; continue beating for 5 minutes. Beat on high for 2 minutes. Remove from the heat and cool for 30 minutes (sauce will thicken as it cools). Pour into glass or plastic food storage containers; refrigerate. Serve warm or cold.
2 Tbsp.: 83 cal., 3g fat (1g sat. fat), 4mg chol., 30mg sod., 15g carb. (14g sugars, 0 fiber), 1g pro.

WHITE CHOCOLATE POUND CAKE WITH CHOCOLATE SAUCE

WHITE CHOCOLATE POUND CAKE WITH CHOCOLATE SAUCE

As good as this homemade pound cake is on its own, it hits new heights when draped with a warm chocolate-orange sauce. Every bite is pure heaven!
—Mary Ann Lee, Clifton Park, NY

PREP: 35 min.
BAKE: 1 hour + cooling
MAKES: 16 servings

- 4 oz. white baking chocolate, chopped
- ½ cup water
- 1 cup butter, softened
- 1½ cups sugar
- 4 large eggs
- 2 tsp. vanilla extract
- 3 cups all-purpose flour
- 1 tsp. baking soda
- ½ tsp. salt
- 1 cup buttermilk

CHOCOLATE ORANGE SAUCE
- ⅔ cup heavy whipping cream
- ½ cup sugar
- 4 oz. semisweet chocolate, chopped
- 4 Tbsp. butter, divided
- 1 Tbsp. grated orange zest
- 1 Tbsp. orange juice
- 2 tsp. vanilla extract

1. In a small saucepan, combine the white chocolate and water; cook and stir over low heat until melted. Remove from the heat; cool slightly.

2. In a large bowl, cream butter and sugar until light and fluffy, about 5 minutes. Beat in white chocolate mixture. Add eggs, 1 at a time, beating well after each addition. Beat in vanilla. Combine flour, baking soda and salt; add to the creamed mixture alternately with buttermilk, beating well after each addition.

3. Transfer to a greased and floured 10-in. fluted tube pan. Bake at 350° until a toothpick inserted in center comes out clean, 60-65 minutes. Cool for 10 minutes before removing the cake from the pan to a wire rack to cool completely.

4. Meanwhile, in a small heavy saucepan, combine the cream, sugar, semisweet chocolate and 2 Tbsp. butter over medium heat until mixture comes to a boil, stirring constantly. Cook until sauce thickens slightly, stirring constantly, 4-5 minutes longer.

5. Remove from the heat. Stir in the orange zest, orange juice, vanilla and remaining butter. Serve warm with cake.

1 piece with 4½ tsp. sauce: 448 cal., 24g fat (15g sat. fat), 97mg chol., 322mg sod., 53g carb. (34g sugars, 1g fiber), 6g pro.

TO MAKE AHEAD
Cake and chocolate sauce can be prepared a day in advance. Cover and refrigerate sauce. Store cake in a resealable bag or airtight container at room temperature. Reheat sauce over low heat when ready to serve.

CRANBERRY
CHOCOLATE CHIP PECAN PIE

BANANA SPLIT ICEBOX CAKE

One day a friend showed me how to make a traditional icebox cake with just cream and graham crackers. I make it extra special with the fruit. Now everyone at your potluck can have a banana split with no fuss!
—Shelly Flye, Albion, ME

PREP: 30 min. + chilling
MAKES: 10 servings

- 1 carton (16 oz.) frozen whipped topping, thawed
- 1 cup sour cream
- 1 pkg. (3.4 oz.) instant vanilla pudding mix
- 1 can (8 oz.) crushed pineapple, drained
- 24 whole graham crackers
- 2 medium bananas, sliced
  Toppings: Chocolate syrup, halved fresh strawberries and additional banana slices

1. In a large bowl, mix whipped topping, sour cream and pudding mix until blended; fold in crushed pineapple. Cut a small hole in the tip of a pastry bag. Transfer the pudding mixture to bag.
2. On a flat serving plate, arrange 4 crackers in a rectangle. Pipe about 1 cup pudding mixture over crackers; top with about ¼ cup banana slices. Repeat layers 5 times. Refrigerate layers, covered, overnight.
3. Just before serving, top with chocolate syrup, strawberries and additional banana slices.
1 piece: 405 cal., 15g fat (11g sat. fat), 16mg chol., 372mg sod., 60g carb. (30g sugars, 2g fiber), 4g pro.

CRANBERRY CHOCOLATE CHIP PECAN PIE

I've been using this rich pecan pie recipe for 30 years, changing it up when the mood strikes. We love it any way I make it! It's awesome baked a day ahead, too.
—Joan Hallford, North Richland Hills, TX

PREP: 20 min. • **BAKE:** 40 min.
MAKES: 8 servings

- 1 sheet refrigerated pie pastry
- 4 large eggs
- 1 cup dark corn syrup
- ⅔ cup sugar
- ¼ cup butter, melted
- ¾ tsp. ground cinnamon
- ¼ tsp. ground nutmeg
- 1½ cups fresh or frozen cranberries, thawed, chopped
- 1 cup miniature semisweet chocolate chips
- 1 cup pecan halves

1. Preheat oven to 375°. Unroll pastry sheet into a 9-in. pie plate; flute edge. Refrigerate while preparing filling. Whisk together eggs, corn syrup, sugar, melted butter, cinnamon and nutmeg. Sprinkle cranberries and chocolate chips onto bottom of crust; top with the egg mixture. Arrange pecans over filling.
2. Bake on a lower oven rack until crust is golden brown and filling is puffed, 40-50 minutes. Cool on a wire rack. Refrigerate leftovers.
1 piece: 576 cal., 30g fat (12g sat. fat), 113mg chol., 239mg sod., 78g carb. (62g sugars, 3g fiber), 6g pro.

COCONUT, LIME & PISTACHIO COOKIES

Perfect for freezing, these cookies look like Christmas but taste like summer.
—Barbara Crusan, Pass Christian, MS

PREP: 30 min. • **BAKE:** 10 min./batch
MAKES: about 5½ dozen

- 1 cup shortening
- 1½ cups sugar
- 2 large eggs, room temperature
- 4 tsp. lime juice
- 1¼ cups all-purpose flour
- 1 pkg. (3.4 oz.) instant coconut cream pudding mix
- 1½ tsp. baking soda
- ½ tsp. baking powder
- 1 cup pistachios, chopped
- 1 cup dried cranberries
- 1 large egg white, room temperature
- 1 cup sweetened shredded coconut
- 1½ tsp. grated lime zest

1. Preheat oven to 375°. In a bowl, cream shortening and sugar until light and fluffy. Beat in eggs and lime juice. In another bowl, whisk flour, pudding mix, baking soda and baking powder; gradually beat into creamed mixture. Stir in pistachios and dried cranberries. With clean beaters, beat the egg white on medium speed until thick and foamy; stir in coconut.
2. Drop the dough by rounded tablespoonfuls 2 in. apart onto ungreased baking sheets. Flatten slightly with bottom of a glass dipped in sugar. Top with coconut mixture. Bake until until edges begin to brown, 10-12 minutes. Remove from pans to wire racks to cool. Sprinkle with lime zest. Store in airtight containers.
1 cookie: 82 cal., 4g fat (1g sat. fat), 5mg chol., 59mg sod., 10g carb. (8g sugars, 0 fiber), 1g pro.

COCONUT, LIME & PISTACHIO COOKIES

CHOCOLATE CARAMEL
HAZELNUT PIE

CHOCOLATE CARAMEL HAZELNUT PIE

I love chocolate, caramel and hazelnuts, so I came up with a dessert recipe that has all three. If you don't have a food processor, place crust ingredients in a zip-top freezer bag and smash with a rolling pin.
—Debbie Anderson, Mount Angel, OR

PREP: 25 min. + chilling
MAKES: 8 servings

- 1½ cups salted caramel pretzel pieces
- 12 Lorna Doone shortbread cookies
- ¼ cup sugar
- 6 Tbsp. butter, melted
- 5 Tbsp. caramel topping, divided

FILLING
- 1 pkg. (8 oz.) cream cheese, softened
- ½ cup Nutella
- 1 jar (7 oz.) marshmallow creme
- 1 carton (8 oz.) frozen whipped topping, thawed
- 1 cup miniature marshmallows
- 1 Snickers candy bar (1.86 oz.), chopped

1. Place the pretzel pieces and cookies in a food processor; pulse until fine crumbs form. Add sugar and melted butter; pulse just until blended. Press onto bottom and up side of a 9-in. pie plate. Drizzle with 3 Tbsp. caramel topping. Freeze while preparing filling.
2. For the filling, beat the cream cheese and Nutella until smooth. Gradually beat in marshmallow creme. Gently fold in whipped topping and marshmallows. Spoon into crust.
3. Refrigerate until set, 3-4 hours. Top with chopped candy and remaining 2 Tbsp. caramel topping before serving.
1 piece: 663 cal., 35g fat (19g sat. fat), 60mg chol., 327mg sod., 74g carb. (57g sugars, 1g fiber), 6g pro.

ⓅⓂ CREAM CHEESE ICE CREAM

This is the best homemade ice cream I've ever eaten. It tastes like cheesecake with a refreshing hint of lemon.
—Johnnie McLeod, Bastrop, LA

PREP: 20 min. + chilling
PROCESS: 20 min./batch + freezing
MAKES: 1½ qt.

- 2½ cups half-and-half cream
- 1 cup whole milk
- 1¼ cups sugar
- 2 large eggs, lightly beaten
- 12 oz. cream cheese, cubed
- 1 Tbsp. lemon juice
- 1 tsp. vanilla extract

1. In a large saucepan, heat the cream and milk to 175°; stir in sugar until dissolved. Whisk a small amount of hot mixture into the eggs. Return all to the pan, whisking constantly. Cook and stir over low heat until mixture reaches at least 160° and coats the back of a metal spoon.
2. Remove from the heat. Whisk in cream cheese until smooth. Cool quickly by placing pan in a bowl of ice water; stir for 2 minutes. Stir in lemon juice and vanilla. Press plastic wrap onto surface of custard. Refrigerate for several hours or overnight.
3. Fill cylinder of ice cream freezer two-thirds full; freeze according to manufacturer's directions. Refrigerate remaining mixture until ready to freeze. Transfer to a freezer container; freeze ice cream for 2-4 hours before serving.
½ cup: 273 cal., 16g fat (10g sat. fat), 87mg chol., 135mg sod., 25g carb. (25g sugars, 0 fiber), 5g pro.

CREAM CHEESE
ICE CREAM

TEST KITCHEN TIP
Serve this rich, creamy ice cream drizzled with hot fudge sauce or any kind of fruity dessert topping such as rhubarb-strawberry sauce. Any jam, gently warmed in the microwave and spooned over the cheesecake ice cream, would also be delicious. For extra flair, serve with a graham cracker tucked into the side of the dish.

FROSTED CHOCOLATE CHIP CHEESECAKE

Heavenly is a good description for this luscious dessert, conveniently made a day ahead.
—Arlene Butler, Ogden, UT

PREP: 40 min.
BAKE: 55 min. + chilling
MAKES: 12 servings

2 cups chocolate wafer crumbs
6 Tbsp. butter, melted

FILLING

3 pkg. (8 oz. each) cream cheese, softened
1 cup sugar
1 tsp. vanilla extract
3 large egg, room temperature, lightly beaten
1 cup miniature semisweet chocolate chips
1 milk chocolate candy bar (4 oz.), chopped
2 cups whipped topping
¼ cup sliced almonds, toasted

1. Preheat oven to 325°. Combine wafer crumbs and butter. Press crumb mixture onto the bottom and 1½ in. up the side of a greased 9-in. springform pan. Chill the crust until set, about 15 minutes.

2. In a large bowl, beat the cream cheese, sugar and vanilla until smooth. Add eggs; beat on low speed just until combined. Stir in chocolate chips. Pour into crust.

3. Place pan on a baking sheet. Bake until center is almost set, 55-60 minutes. Cool on a wire rack 10 minutes. Carefully run a knife around the edge of the pan to loosen; cool 1 hour longer. Cover and refrigerate overnight.

4. For frosting, in a microwave-safe bowl, melt chocolate candy bar; stir until smooth. Cool to room temperature. Gradually stir in whipped topping. Frost top of cheesecake; garnish with the almonds. Refrigerate leftovers.

1 piece: 442 cal., 26g fat (15g sat. fat), 92mg chol., 247mg sod., 48g carb. (31g sugars, 2g fiber), 6g pro.

WHY YOU'LL LOVE IT...

"I've been making this cheesecake for years, with and without the frosting. It is amazing every time! Love it, love it!"
—CARSYN, TASTEOFHOME.COM

FROSTED CHOCOLATE CHIP CHEESECAKE

SHORTBREAD
LEMON BARS

PEANUT BUTTER
& JELLY PIE

PM SHORTBREAD LEMON BARS

I've put together two family cookbooks over the years, and this recipe ranks among my favorites. The special lemon bars have a yummy shortbread crust and a refreshing citrus flavor. I make this for guests because I know the treats will be a hit with everyone.
—Margaret Peterson, Forest City, IA

PREP: 25 min.
BAKE: 25 min. + chilling
MAKES: 3 dozen

1½ cups all-purpose flour
½ cup confectioners' sugar
1 tsp. grated lemon zest
1 tsp. grated orange zest
¾ cup cold butter, cubed

FILLING
4 large eggs, room temperature
2 cups sugar
⅓ cup lemon juice
¼ cup all-purpose flour
2 tsp. grated lemon zest
2 tsp. grated orange zest
1 tsp. baking powder

TOPPING
2 cups sour cream
⅓ cup sugar
½ tsp. vanilla extract

1. Preheat oven to 350°. In a food processor, combine the flour, confectioners' sugar and lemon and orange zest. Add the butter; cover and process until mixture forms a ball.
2. Pat the crust into a greased 13x9-in. baking pan. Bake until set and the edges are lightly browned, 12-14 minutes.
3. In a large bowl, combine all the filling ingredients. Pour over hot crust. Bake until set and lightly browned, 14-16 minutes. In a small bowl, combine topping ingredients. Spread over filling.
4. Bake until the topping is set, 7-9 minutes longer. Cool on a wire rack. Refrigerate overnight. Cut into bars just before serving. Store in the refrigerator.
1 bar: 172 cal., 9g fat (5g sat. fat), 51mg chol., 70mg sod., 20g carb. (15g sugars, 0 fiber), 2g pro.

PM PEANUT BUTTER & JELLY PIE

A chocolate crumb crust is topped with a rich peanut butter layer, then strawberry preserves and whipped cream. The tasty peanut butter and jelly pie is sure to appeal to the young—and the young at heart.
—Vikki Rebholz, West Chester, OH

PREP: 10 min. + chilling
MAKES: 8 servings

- 1 pkg. (8 oz.) cream cheese, softened
- ½ cup confectioners' sugar
- ⅓ cup peanut butter
- 1 graham cracker or chocolate crumb crust (9 in.)
- ½ cup strawberry preserves
- 2 cups whipped topping
  Chopped salted peanuts, optional

In a large bowl, beat the cream cheese, sugar and peanut butter until smooth. Spoon into crust. Top with preserves and whipped topping. Cover and refrigerate for 4 hours or overnight.

1 piece: 397 cal., 24g fat (11g sat. fat), 29mg chol., 256mg sod., 42g carb. (36g sugars, 1g fiber), 5g pro.

TEST KITCHEN TIP

Use your microwave to soften cream cheese quickly. Remove the cream cheese brick from the wrapper and place it on a microwave-safe plate. Microwave the cream cheese in 5-second intervals, turning the cheese over on the plate each time. It should be completely softened in about 20 seconds total.

PEACH
BAVARIAN

Ⓟ PEACH BAVARIAN

Fruit molds are my specialty. This one, with its refreshing peach taste, makes a colorful salad or dessert.
—Adeline Piscitelli, Sayreville, NJ

PREP: 15 min. + chilling
MAKES: 8 servings

- 1 can (15¼ oz.) sliced peaches
- 2 pkg. (3 oz. each) peach or apricot gelatin
- ½ cup sugar
- 2 cups boiling water
- 1 tsp. almond extract
- 1 carton (8 oz.) frozen whipped topping, thawed
  Additional sliced peaches, optional

1. Drain the peaches, reserving ⅔ cup juice. Chop peaches into small pieces.
2. In a large bowl, dissolve gelatin and sugar in boiling water. Stir in reserved juice. Chill until slightly thickened. Stir extract into whipped topping; gently fold into gelatin mixture. Fold in peaches.
3. Pour into an oiled 6-cup mold. Chill overnight.
4. Unmold onto a serving platter; garnish with additional peaches if desired.
1 serving: 249 cal., 5g fat (5g sat. fat), 0 chol., 53mg sod., 47g carb. (47g sugars, 0 fiber), 2g pro.

HOMEMADE ICE CREAM SANDWICHES

Ⓟ HOMEMADE ICE CREAM SANDWICHES

I inherited my love of cooking from my mother, a former home economics teacher. She sent me this recipe so we can make our own homemade ice cream sandwiches. We love them.
—Kea Fisher, Bridger, MT

PREP: 25 min. + freezing
BAKE: 10 min. + cooling
MAKES: 16 servings

- 1 pkg. chocolate cake mix (regular size)
- ¼ cup shortening
- ¼ cup butter, softened
- 1 large egg
- 1 Tbsp. water
- 1 tsp. vanilla extract
- ½ gallon ice cream

1. In a large bowl, combine the cake mix, shortening, butter, egg, water and vanilla until well blended. Divide batter into 4 equal parts.
2. Between waxed paper, roll 1 part into a 10x6-in. rectangle. Remove top piece of waxed paper and invert the dough onto an ungreased baking sheet. Remove second piece of waxed paper. Score the dough into 8 pieces, each 3x2½ in. Repeat with remaining dough.
3. Bake at 350° until puffed, 8-10 minutes. Immediately cut along the scored lines and prick holes in each piece with a fork. Cool on wire racks.
4. Cut ice cream into 16 slices, each 3x2½x1 in. Place ice cream slice between 2 chocolate cookies; wrap in waxed paper or another wrap. Freeze on a baking sheet overnight. May be frozen for up to 2 months.
1 sandwich: 315 cal., 15g fat (8g sat. fat), 48mg chol., 321mg sod., 42g carb. (28g sugars, 1g fiber), 4g pro.

🅿️ RAINBOW COOKIES

I bake these cookies two weeks ahead. That gives the treats enough time to mellow, leaving them moist and full of sweet almond flavor!
—Mary Ann Lee, Clifton Park, NY

PREP: 50 min. + chilling
BAKE: 10 min./batch + cooling
MAKES: about 8 dozen

- 1 can (8 oz.) almond paste
- 1 cup butter, softened
- 1 cup sugar
- 4 large eggs, separated, room temperature
- 2 cups all-purpose flour
- 6 to 8 drops red food coloring
- 6 to 8 drops green food coloring
- ¼ cup seedless red raspberry jam
- ¼ cup apricot preserves
- 1 cup semisweet chocolate chips

1. Grease bottoms of 3 identical 13x9-in. baking pans (or reuse one pan 3 times). Line pans with waxed paper; grease the paper.
2. Place almond paste in a large bowl; break up with a fork. Cream with butter, sugar and egg yolks until light and fluffy, 5-7 minutes. Stir in flour. In another bowl, beat egg whites until soft peaks form. Fold into the dough, mixing until thoroughly blended.
3. Divide the dough into 3 equal portions (about 1⅓ cups each). Color 1 portion with red food coloring and 1 with green; leave the remaining portion uncolored. Spread each portion into the prepared pans. Bake at 350° until edges are light golden brown, 10-12 minutes.
4. Invert onto wire racks; remove waxed paper. Place another wire rack on top and turn over. Cool completely.

5. Place the green layer on a large piece of plastic wrap. Spread evenly with raspberry jam. Top with the uncolored layer and spread with apricot jam. Top with the pink layer. Bring the plastic wrap over layers. Slide onto a baking sheet and place a cutting board or a heavy, flat pan on top to compress the layers. Refrigerate overnight.
6. The next day, melt chocolate in a microwave; stir until smooth. Spread over top layer; allow to harden. With a sharp knife, trim edges. Cut into ½-in. strips across the width; then cut each strip into 4-5 pieces. Store the cookies in airtight containers.
1 cookie: 61 cal., 3g fat (2g sat. fat), 13mg chol., 19mg sod., 7g carb. (5g sugars, 0 fiber), 1g pro.

RAINBOW COOKIES

CHOCOLATE MARSHMALLOW PEANUT BUTTER SQUARES

I combined a couple of recipes to create these crunchy, chocolaty bars. They're so decadent, they could pass for fudge!
—Dawn Lowenstein, Huntingdon Valley, PA

PREP: 15 min.
COOK: 5 min. + chilling
MAKES: 5 dozen

- 1   can (14 oz.) sweetened condensed milk
- 1   pkg. (11 oz.) peanut butter and milk chocolate chips
- ½   cup milk chocolate chips
- ½   cup creamy peanut butter
- 1   tsp. vanilla extract
- 1½ cups miniature marshmallows
- 1   cup broken miniature pretzels
- 1   cup Rice Krispies

1. Place the first 5 ingredients in a large heavy saucepan; cook and stir over low heat until the mixture is smooth and blended, about 5 minutes (mixture will be very thick). Remove from heat; stir in the remaining ingredients. Spread mixture into a greased 13x9-in. pan.
2. Refrigerate, covered, until firm, about 4 hours. Cut into squares. Store in an airtight container in the refrigerator.
1 square: 85 cal., 4g fat (2g sat. fat), 3mg chol., 50mg sod., 12g carb. (8g sugars, 0 fiber), 1g pro.

TEST KITCHEN TIP

Lining your pan with greased foil with the ends extending up the sides makes it simple to remove the candy and cut it without scratching your pan.

CHOCOLATE MARSHMALLOW PEANUT BUTTER SQUARES

PAGE 234

PAGE 229

PAGE 238

Bonus—Cook Once, Eat Twice

Get a head start on the rest of the week while creating tonight's dinner!
These recipes help you budget your time and money wisely with planned
leftovers, double-yield casseroles and more.

PAGE 230

PAGE 233

🍲 BUTTER & HERB TURKEY

My kids love turkey for dinner, and this easy recipe lets me make it whenever I want. No special occasion required! The meat is so tender it comes right off the bone.
—Rochelle Popovic, South Bend, IN

PREP: 10 min. • **COOK:** 5 hours
MAKES: 12 servings (3 cups gravy)

- 1 bone-in turkey breast (6 to 7 lbs.)
- 2 Tbsp. butter, softened
- ½ tsp. dried rosemary, crushed
- ½ tsp. dried thyme
- ¼ tsp. garlic powder
- ¼ tsp. pepper
- 1 can (14½ oz.) chicken broth
- 3 Tbsp. cornstarch
- 2 Tbsp. cold water

1. Rub turkey with butter. Combine the rosemary, thyme, garlic powder and pepper; sprinkle over turkey. Place in a 6-qt. slow cooker. Pour broth over the top. Cover and cook on low until tender, 5-6 hours.

2. Remove turkey to a serving platter; keep warm. Skim the fat from cooking juices; transfer juices to a small saucepan. Bring to a boil. Combine cornstarch and water until smooth. Gradually stir into the pan. Bring to a boil; cook and stir until thickened, about 2 minutes. Serve with turkey.

5 oz. cooked turkey with ¼ gravy: 339 cal., 14g fat (5g sat. fat), 128mg chol., 266mg sod., 2g carb. (0 sugars, 0 fiber), 48g pro.

FOR MEAL 2: Cube enough leftover turkey to equal 2 cups; save to use in Thanksgiving's Not Over Enchilada Soup, opposite page.

2 CUPS

ONE OF THE BEST THINGS ABOUT A TURKEY DINNER IS FRESH SOUP MADE WITH THE LEFTOVERS!

THANKSGIVING'S NOT OVER YET ENCHILADA SOUP

Pumpkin adds a unique richness to this warm soup. You certainly can include Thanksgiving leftovers, but it's a good recipe to turn to anytime you have extra turkey.
—Denise Pounds, Hutchinson, KS

PREP: 20 min. • **COOK:** 20 min.
MAKES: 8 servings (3 qt.)

- 1 large sweet red pepper, finely chopped
- 1 medium onion, chopped
- 1 celery rib, chopped
- 1 Tbsp. olive oil
- 2 cans (14½ oz. each) reduced-sodium chicken broth
- 1 can (28 oz.) green enchilada sauce
- 1 can (15 oz.) pumpkin
- 1½ cups frozen corn
- 2 cans (4 oz. each) chopped green chiles
- 2 Tbsp. ranch salad dressing mix
- 2 cups cubed cooked turkey
  Optional: Crumbled queso fresco, shredded cheddar cheese, crushed tortilla chips, cubed avocado and minced fresh cilantro

In a Dutch oven, saute the red pepper, onion and celery in oil until crisp-tender. Add the broth, enchilada sauce, pumpkin, corn, chiles and dressing mix. Bring to a boil. Reduce heat; cover and simmer until vegetables are tender, 10-12 minutes. Stir in turkey and heat through. Garnish individual servings with toppings of your choice.

1½ cups: 209 cal., 6g fat (1g sat. fat), 27mg chol., 1451mg sod., 24g carb. (6g sugars, 4g fiber), 16g pro.

GREAT-GRANDMA'S ITALIAN MEATBALLS

A classic Italian dish isn't complete without homemade meatballs. This recipe can be used in other dishes, too.
—Audrey Colantino, Winchester, MA

PREP: 30 min. • **BAKE:** 20 min.
MAKES: 8 servings

- 2 tsp. olive oil
- 1 medium onion, chopped
- 3 garlic cloves, minced
- ¾ cup seasoned bread crumbs
- ½ cup grated Parmesan cheese
- 2 large eggs, lightly beaten
- 1 tsp. each dried basil, oregano and parsley flakes
- ¾ tsp. salt
- 1 lb. lean ground turkey
- 1 lb. lean ground beef (90% lean)
  Optional: Hot cooked pasta and pasta sauce

1. In a small skillet, heat oil over medium-high heat. Add onion; cook and stir until tender, 3-4 minutes. Add garlic; cook 1 minute longer. Cool slightly.
2. Combine bread crumbs, cheese, eggs, seasonings and onion mixture. Add turkey and beef; mix lightly but thoroughly. Shape into 1½-in. balls.
3. Place meatballs on a rack coated with cooking spray in a 15x10x1-in. baking pan. Bake at 375° until lightly browned and cooked through, 18-22 minutes. If desired, serve with pasta and pasta sauce.

About 7 meatballs: 271 cal., 13g fat (5g sat. fat), 125mg chol., 569mg sod., 10g carb. (1g sugars, 1g fiber), 27g pro. **Diabetic exchanges:** 4 lean meat, 1 fat, ½ starch.
FOR MEAL 2: Save about 20-25 meatballs for Three-Cheese Meatball Mostaccioli, opposite page.

FREEZE OPTION

Consider preparing meatballs in bulk to save on prep time. You can make several batches of meatballs, bake them and then freeze until needed. Bake meatballs according to recipe and allow to cool. Then arrange meatballs in a single layer on a baking sheet and freeze until firm. Place meatballs in freezer bags or freezer-friendly containers and store up to 3 months. When you want to use them, take out of the freezer a day ahead and allow to thaw overnight in refrigerator.

THREE-CHEESE MEATBALL MOSTACCIOLI

When my husband travels, I make a special dinner for my kids to keep their minds off missing Daddy. This tasty mostaccioli is meatball magic.
—Jennifer Gilbert, Brighton, MI

PREP: 15 min. • **BAKE:** 35 min.
MAKES: 10 servings

- 1   pkg. (16 oz.) mostaccioli
- 2   large eggs, lightly beaten
- 1   carton (15 oz.) part-skim ricotta cheese
- 1   lb. ground beef
- 1   medium onion, chopped
- 1   Tbsp. brown sugar
- 1   Tbsp. Italian seasoning
- 1   tsp. garlic powder
- ¼   tsp. pepper
- 2   jars (24 oz. each) pasta sauce with meat
- ½   cup grated Romano cheese
- 1   pkg. (12 oz.) frozen fully cooked Italian meatballs, thawed
- ¾   cup shaved Parmesan cheese
  Optional: Torn fresh basil or fresh oregano leaves

1. Preheat oven to 350°. Cook mostaccioli according to package directions for al dente; drain. Meanwhile, in a small bowl, mix eggs and ricotta cheese.

2. In a 6-qt. stockpot, cook beef and onion until beef is no longer pink, 6-8 minutes, breaking up beef into crumbles; drain.

Stir in the brown sugar and seasonings. Add pasta sauce and mostaccioli; toss to combine.

3. Transfer half the pasta mixture to a greased 13x9-in. baking dish. Layer with ricotta mixture and the remaining pasta mixture; sprinkle with Romano cheese. Top with the meatballs and Parmesan cheese.

4. Bake, uncovered, until heated through, 35-40 minutes. Top with basil or oregano if desired.

1⅓ cups: 541 cal., 23g fat (11g sat. fat), 105mg chol., 1335mg sod., 55g carb. (13g sugars, 5g fiber), 34g pro.

12 OZ.

HOMEMADE MEATBALLS CAN REPLACE BAGGED MEATBALLS FROM THE FREEZER SECTION.

PM BOURBON-SPICED GLAZED HAM

This amazing bourbon-spiked ham makes a wonderful main course for a holiday feast or Sunday dinner. Leftovers make delicious sandwiches.
—Karen Sublett-Young, Princeton, IN

PREP: 20 min. + marinating
BAKE: 3 hours
MAKES: 16 servings

1	cup packed brown sugar
1	cup orange juice
1	cup bourbon
1½	tsp. ground cloves
7	to 9 lbs. fully cooked bone-in ham

1. In a large bowl, whisk the first 4 ingredients. Add ham; turn to coat. Cover and refrigerate 8 hours or overnight, turning occasionally.

2. Preheat oven to 325°. Remove ham from marinade and place on a rack in a roasting pan; reserve remaining marinade, placing it in the refrigerator until ready to baste.

3. Using a sharp knife, score surface of ham with ¼-in.-deep cuts in a diamond pattern. Bake, covered, 2 hours.

4. Baste with about half the reserved marinade. Bake ham, uncovered, basting ham twice more during the first half hour, until a thermometer reads 140°, 1-1½ hours longer.

4 oz. cooked ham: 182 cal., 5g fat (2g sat. fat), 87mg chol., 1043mg sod., 4g carb. (3g sugars, 0 fiber), 29g pro.

FOR MEAL 2: Cube 1½ cups of cooked ham and save it to use in Ham & Broccoli Cornbread, opposite page.

HAM & BROCCOLI CORNBREAD

Leftovers haunt me. Often nobody wants to eat them, and I hate to see them go to waste. A cornbread casserole is an excellent way to leverage many combinations of leftover meat and veggies into exciting new meals that everyone will love.
—Fay Moreland, Wichita Falls,

PREP: 15 min.
BAKE: 35 min. + standing
MAKES: 12 servings

- 5 Tbsp. butter, divided
- 2 large eggs, room temperature
- 1 cup 2% milk
- ½ cup sour cream
  Pinch cayenne pepper
- 2 pkg. (8½ oz. each) cornbread/ muffin mix
- 2 cups chopped fresh broccoli
- 1½ cups shredded sharp cheddar cheese
- 1½ cups cubed fully cooked ham
- 3 green onions, thinly sliced

1. Preheat oven to 375°. Place 3 Tbsp. butter in a 12-in. cast-iron skillet; place pan in oven until butter is melted, 3-5 minutes. Carefully tilt pan to coat bottom and side with butter.
2. Melt remaining 2 Tbsp. butter. In a large bowl, whisk together eggs, milk, sour cream, cayenne pepper and melted butter until blended. Add muffin mixes; stir just until moistened. Fold in the remaining ingredients. Carefully pour into hot pan.
3. Bake until top is golden brown and a toothpick inserted in center comes out clean, 35-40 minutes. Let cornbread stand 15 minutes before serving.
1 piece: 338 cal., 18g fat (9g sat. fat), 73mg chol., 700mg sod., 31g carb. (10g sugars, 3g fiber), 12g pro.

1½ CUPS

LEFTOVERS FROM SUNDAY DINNER MAKE A GREAT WEEKNIGHT SKILLET MEAL.

PM GRILLED BUTTERMILK CHICKEN

I created this recipe years ago after one of our farmers market customers, a chef, shared the idea of marinating chicken in buttermilk. The chicken is easy to prepare and always turns out moist and delicious! I bruise the thyme sprigs by twisting them before adding them to the buttermilk mixture; this releases the oils in the leaves and flavors the chicken better.
—Sue Gronholz, Beaver Dam, WI

PREP: 10 min. + marinating
GRILL: 10 min. • **MAKES:** 12 servings

- 1½ **cups buttermilk**
- 4 **fresh thyme sprigs**
- 4 **garlic cloves, halved**
- ½ **tsp. salt**
- 12 **boneless skinless chicken breast halves (about 4½ lbs.)**

1. Place the buttermilk, thyme, garlic and salt in a large bowl or shallow dish. Add chicken and turn to coat. Refrigerate for 8 hours or overnight, turning occasionally.
2. Drain chicken, discarding the marinade. Grill, covered, over medium heat until a thermometer reads 165°, 5-7 minutes per side.

1 chicken breast half: 189 cal., 4g fat (1g sat. fat), 95mg chol., 168mg sod., 1g carb. (1g sugars, 0 fiber), 35g pro. **Diabetic exchanges:** 5 lean meat.

FOR MEAL 2: Save 4 cups of diced chicken (about 4 breast halves) to use in Chicken & Rice Casserole, opposite page.

HOW TO LOVE CHICKEN LEFTOVERS

- If you know you'll be using leftover grilled chicken within 3-4 days, dice it after cooling and store in an airtight container in the fridge. Then you can just toss it into stir-fries, salads and pastas on the fly.

- Grilled chicken also freezes beautifully. Let it cool and then freeze it in airtight containers for up to 6 months. To use, partially thaw chicken in the refrigerator overnight. It will tastes like it just came off the grill after it's thawed.

CHICKEN & RICE CASSEROLE

Everyone loves this casserole because it's a tasty combination of hearty and crunchy ingredients mixed in a creamy sauce. It's a time-tested classic.
—Myrtle Matthews, Marietta, GA

PREP: 15 min. • **BAKE:** 1 hour
MAKES: 12 servings

- 4 cups cooked white rice or a combination of wild and white rice
- 4 cups diced cooked chicken
- ½ cup slivered almonds
- 1 small onion, chopped
- 1 can (8 oz.) sliced water chestnuts, drained
- 1 pkg. (10 oz.) frozen peas, thawed
- ¾ cup chopped celery
- 1 can (10¾ oz.) condensed cream of celery soup, undiluted
- 1 can (10¾ oz.) condensed cream of chicken soup, undiluted
- 1 cup mayonnaise
- 2 tsp. lemon juice
- 1 tsp. salt
- 2 cups crushed potato chips Paprika

1. Preheat oven to 350°. In a greased 13x9-in. baking dish, combine the first 7 ingredients. In a large bowl, combine soups, mayonnaise, lemon juice and salt. Pour over the chicken mixture and toss to coat.
2. Sprinkle with potato chips and paprika. Bake until heated through, about 1 hour.
1 cup: 439 cal., 26g fat (5g sat. fat), 51mg chol., 804mg sod., 31g carb. (3g sugars, 3g fiber), 19g pro.

4 CUPS FOLLOW A NIGHT GRILLING OUT WITH A COZY CASSEROLE.

PM FLAVORFUL MARINATED PORK LOIN

Glazed with a mouthwatering marinade, this entree is relatively low in fat but still juicy and tender.
—Paula Young, Tiffin, OH

PREP: 20 min. + marinating
BAKE: 1 hour + standing
MAKES: 12 servings

- 1   cup orange juice
- ¾   cup apricot preserves
- 2   Tbsp. plus ¼ cup sherry or vegetable broth, divided
- 3   Tbsp. lemon juice
- 2   Tbsp. olive oil
- 1   Tbsp. curry powder
- 1   Tbsp. Worcestershire sauce
- 1   tsp. dried thyme
- ½   tsp. pepper
- 1   boneless pork loin roast (3 lbs.)
- 1   Tbsp. cornstarch

1. In a small bowl, combine the orange juice, preserves, 2 Tbsp. sherry, lemon juice, oil, curry, Worcestershire sauce, thyme and pepper. Pour ¾ cup of the marinade into a large dish; add the pork. Turn to coat; cover and refrigerate overnight, turning occasionally. Set aside 1 cup of remaining marinade for sauce; cover and refrigerate. Cover and refrigerate the rest of the marinade to use for basting.
2. Drain pork, discarding marinade in dish; place pork on a rack in a shallow roasting pan. Bake, uncovered, at 350° until a thermometer reads 145°, 1-1¼ hours; baste occasionally with the reserved marinade. Transfer to a serving platter. Let stand 10 minutes before slicing.
3. In a small saucepan, combine cornstarch with remaining ¼ cup sherry and 1 cup marinade. Bring to a boil; cook and stir until thickened, about 2 minutes. Serve with roast.

3 oz. cooked pork with about 2 Tbsp. gravy: 229 cal., 8g fat (3g sat. fat), 55mg chol., 51mg sod., 15g carb. (8g sugars, 0 fiber), 22g pro. **Diabetic exchanges:** 3 lean meat, 1 starch, ½ fat.
FOR MEAL 2: Save 1¾ cups of cubed pork for Pork Spanish Rice, opposite page.

PORK SPANISH RICE

My family wasn't fond of pork roast until I used it in this yummy casserole.
—Betty Unrau, MacGregor, MB

PREP: 20 min. • **BAKE:** 20 min.
MAKES: 4 servings

- 1 medium green pepper, chopped
- 1 small onion, chopped
- 2 Tbsp. butter
- 1 can (14½ oz.) diced tomatoes, drained
- 1 cup chicken broth
- ½ tsp. salt
- ¼ tsp. pepper
- 1¾ cups cubed cooked pork
- 1 cup uncooked instant rice
  Optional: Lime wedges and minced cilantro

1. Preheat oven to 350°. In a large skillet, saute green pepper and onion in butter until tender. Stir in the tomatoes, broth, salt and pepper. Bring to a boil; stir in pork and rice.
2. Transfer to a greased 2-qt. baking dish. Bake, covered, until rice is tender and the liquid is absorbed, 20-25 minutes. Stir before serving. If desired, serve with lime wedges and top with minced cilantro.

1 cup: 304 cal., 12g fat (6g sat. fat), 71mg chol., 756mg sod., 29g carb. (5g sugars, 3g fiber), 21g pro.
Diabetic exchanges: 3 lean meat, 2 starch, 1½ fat.

1¾ CUPS

USE A TRADITIONAL PORK ROAST TO MAKE A ZESTY SPANISH-STYLE CASSEROLE

HOMEMADE MARINARA SAUCE

This quick and easy homemade marinara sauce is my kids' favorite. It works fantastic with spaghetti, and my kids love it in meatball subs, too.
—Cara Bjornlie, Detroit Lakes, MN

TAKES: 30 min. • **MAKES:** 7 cups

- 1 Tbsp. olive oil
- 1 small onion, chopped
- 2 garlic cloves, minced
- 2 cans (28 oz. each) Italian crushed tomatoes
- 1 Tbsp. Italian seasoning
- 1 to 2 Tbsp. sugar
- ½ tsp. salt
- ½ tsp. pepper

In a large saucepan, heat oil over medium heat. Add onion; cook and stir until softened, 3-4 minutes. Add garlic; cook 1 minute longer. Add tomatoes, Italian seasoning, salt, pepper and sugar; bring to a boil. Reduce heat; simmer, covered, for 10 minutes.

About ¾ cup: 91 cal., 2g fat (0 sat. fat), 0 chol., 489mg sod., 12g carb. (8g sugars, 3g fiber), 3g pro.
Diabetic exchanges: 2 vegetable, ½ fat.

TURN THIS MARINARA INTO 2 EASY ENTREES.

ITALIAN CHICKEN STEW

My husband enjoys preparing this satisfying stew because it's so easy to make. With warm Italian bread, it's a winner on a cold day.
—Jo Calizzi, Vandergrift, PA

TAKES: 20 min.
MAKES: 4 servings

- 1 lb. boneless skinless chicken breasts, cubed
- 4 medium potatoes, peeled and cut into ¼-in. cubes
- 1 medium sweet red pepper, chopped
- 2 garlic cloves, minced
- 1 to 2 Tbsp. olive oil
- 1 jar (24 oz.) meatless spaghetti sauce
- 1¾ cups frozen cut green beans
- 1 tsp. dried basil
- ¼ to ½ tsp. salt
- ¼ tsp. crushed red pepper flakes
  Pepper to taste

In a Dutch oven, cook the chicken, potatoes, red pepper and garlic in oil until chicken is no longer pink and vegetables are tender. Stir in the remaining ingredients; cook and stir until heated through.

1½ cups: 475 cal., 13g fat (3g sat. fat), 63mg chol., 995mg sod., 62g carb. (0 sugars, 11g fiber), 31g pro.
Diabetic exchanges: 4 starch, 3 lean meat, 1 fat.

2½ CUPS HOMEMADE PASTA SAUCE ALSO MAKES A TERRIFIC STEW BASE.

CHEESY MEATBALL SLIDERS

These sliders are a fun way to serve up meatballs at your party without using a slow cooker. Made on mini Hawaiian rolls, they have a hint of sweetness to balance out all the great Italian seasonings.
—Taste of Home *Test Kitchen*

PREP: 1 hour • **BAKE:** 30 min.
MAKES: 12 servings

- 2 **lbs. lean ground beef (90% lean)**
- 1 **cup Italian-style bread crumbs**
- 3 **Tbsp. prepared pesto**
- 1 **large egg, lightly beaten**
- 1 **jar (24 oz.) pasta sauce**
- 1 **pkg. (18 oz.) Hawaiian sweet rolls**
- 12 **slices part-skim mozzarella cheese**
- ½ **tsp. dried oregano**
- ¼ **cup melted butter**
- 1 **Tbsp. olive oil**
- 3 **garlic cloves, minced**
- 1 **tsp. Italian seasoning**
- ½ **tsp. crushed red pepper flakes**
- 2 **Tbsp. grated Parmesan cheese**
- 1 **cup shredded part-skim mozzarella cheese or shredded Italian cheese blend**
  Minced fresh basil

1. Preheat oven to 350°. Combine ground beef, bread crumbs, pesto and egg; mix lightly. Shape into 12 meatballs; place on a greased rack in a 15x10x1-in. baking pan. Bake until browned and a thermometer reads 160°, about 35 minutes. Toss meatballs with sauce; set aside.

2. Meanwhile, without separating rolls, cut horizontally in half; arrange bottom halves in a greased 13x9-in. baking dish. Place half the cheese slices over roll bottoms; sprinkle with the oregano. Add the meatballs and sauce. Top with remaining cheese slices and bun tops.

3. Combine butter, olive oil, garlic, Italian seasoning and red pepper flakes; brush over buns. Bake, covered, for 20 minutes.

4. Uncover; sprinkle with the Parmesan and shredded mozzarella. Bake, uncovered, until the cheese is melted, 10-15 minutes longer. Sprinkle with basil before serving.

1 slider: 514 cal., 25g fat (12g sat. fat), 120mg chol., 856mg sod., 39g carb. (15g sugars, 3g fiber), 33g pro.

2½ CUPS

HOMEMADE MARINARA PLUS GREAT-GRANDMA'S ITALIAN MEATBALLS (PG. 230) MAKE THESE ULTRA-QUICK.

SEASONED TACO MEAT

I got this recipe from the restaurant where I work. Everyone in town loves the blend of different seasonings, and now the secret is out!
—Denise Mumm, Dixon, IA

PREP: 10 min. • **COOK:** 35 min.
MAKES: 6½ cups

> 3 **lbs. ground beef**
> 2 **large onions, chopped**
> 2 **cups water**
> 5 **Tbsp. chili powder**
> 2 **tsp. salt**
> 1 **tsp. ground cumin**
> ¾ **tsp. garlic powder**
> ¼ to ½ **tsp. crushed red pepper flakes**
> **Optional: Taco shells, lettuce, tomato, avocado, grated cheese, salsa**

1. In a large cast-iron skillet or Dutch oven, cook beef and onion over medium heat until meat is no longer pink; drain. Add water and seasonings. Bring to a boil. Reduce heat; simmer, uncovered, until the water is evaporated, about 15 minutes.
2. Serve in taco shells with optional toppings, or as desired (see "Tasty Ways to Use Taco Meat," left).
¼ cup: 113 cal., 7g fat (3g sat. fat), 35mg chol., 277mg sod., 2g carb. (1g sugars, 1g fiber), 10g pro.
FOR MEAL 2: Save 2 cups of the seasoned meat to make Taco Pizza Squares, opposite page.

TASTY WAYS TO USE TACO MEAT

- Mix it into scrambled eggs and top with diced tomatoes, chopped onion and avocado.
- Scoop it onto a baked potato with a dollop of sour cream, salsa and chopped green onion.
- Spoon it over nachos, along with cheddar cheese, shredded lettuce, sliced jalapeno and sour cream.
- Stir it into mac and cheese with green chiles and diced tomatoes.

TACO PIZZA SQUARES

Everyone will come running the minute you take this fun twist on pizza out of the oven. I top a convenient refrigerated pizza dough with leftover taco meat, tomatoes and cheese, bringing a full-flavored fiesta to the table. Try it with salsa on the side.
—Sarah Vovos, Middleton, WI

TAKES: 25 min.
MAKES: 10 servings

- 1 tube (13.8 oz.) refrigerated pizza crust
- 1 can (8 oz.) pizza sauce
- 2 cups seasoned taco meat
- 2 medium tomatoes, seeded and chopped
- 2 cups shredded mozzarella cheese
  Optional: Shredded lettuce and sour cream

Preheat oven to 400°. Unroll pizza dough and place in a 15x10x1-in. baking pan. Spread with pizza sauce; sprinkle with the taco meat, tomatoes and cheese. Bake until crust is golden brown, 15-20 minutes. Top with shredded lettuce and sour cream if desired.

1 piece: 259 cal., 11g fat (5g sat. fat), 40mg chol., 660mg sod., 23g carb. (4g sugars, 2g fiber), 17g pro.

2 CUPS

TACO NIGHT TURNS INTO A PIZZA PARTY WHEN YOU USE UP THOSE LEFTOVERS.

❄ 🍲 SPICY SHREDDED CHICKEN

I love Mexican food but not the high calorie count that often comes with it. This easy dish is healthy, delicious and a crowd favorite! I like to serve the chicken with warm tortillas, rice, beans and salsa.
—Heather Walker, Scottsdale, AZ

PREP: 40 min. • **COOK:** 4¼ hours
MAKES: 8 servings

2 Tbsp. olive oil
1 lb. boneless skinless chicken thighs
1 lb. boneless skinless chicken breasts
3 cups reduced-sodium chicken broth, divided
6 green onions, chopped
1 medium green pepper, chopped
2 Tbsp. ground cumin
1 Tbsp. garlic powder
1 Tbsp. chili powder
1 Tbsp. paprika
1 tsp. cayenne pepper
½ tsp. salt
¼ tsp. pepper
1 plum tomato, chopped

1. In a large skillet, heat oil over medium-high heat. Brown chicken in batches. Transfer to a 3- or 4-qt. slow cooker. Add 1 cup broth to pan. Cook, stirring to loosen browned bits from pan.
2. Add onions and green pepper; cook and stir until vegetables are tender, 3-5 minutes. Stir in seasonings; cook 1-2 minutes. Add tomato and the remaining 2 cups broth; pour over chicken. Cook, covered, on low until the chicken is tender, 4-5 hours.
3. Remove chicken from slow cooker. When cool enough to handle, shred meat with 2 forks; return to slow cooker. Cook, covered, on low until heated through, 15-20 minutes longer. Serve with a slotted spoon.

¾ cup: 202 cal., 10g fat (2g sat. fat), 69mg chol., 436mg sod., 5g carb. (2g sugars, 2g fiber), 24g pro. **Diabetic exchanges:** 3 lean meat, 1 fat.

FOR MEAL 2: Save 2 cups of the shredded cooked chicken for Chicken Chiles Rellenos Strata, opposite page.

┌─ **FREEZE OPTION** ─────────

Freeze cooled chicken mixture in freezer containers. To use, partially thaw in refrigerator overnight. Heat through in a saucepan, stirring occasionally. Add a little reduced-sodium broth or water if necessary.

TRANSFORM LEFTOVER CHICKEN INTO A HEARTY BRUNCH OR A HANDY WEEKNIGHT MEAL.

PM CHICKEN CHILES RELLENOS STRATA

This versatile bake can be made as an entree, a brunch option or a potluck dish. It's one of the easiest meals to assemble on a busy weeknight.
—Kallee Krong-McCreery, Escondido, CA

PREP: 20 min. + chilling
BAKE: 35 min. + standing
MAKES: 10 servings

- 6 cups cubed French bread (about 6 oz.)
- 2 cans (4 oz. each) chopped green chiles
- 2 cups shredded Monterey Jack cheese
- 2 cups shredded cooked chicken
- 12 large eggs
- 1½ cups 2% milk
- 2 tsp. baking powder
- 1 tsp. garlic salt
- 1 cup shredded cheddar cheese
  Salsa

1. In a greased 13x9-in. baking dish, layer half of each of the following: bread cubes, chiles, Monterey Jack cheese and chicken. Repeat layers.
2. In a large bowl, whisk eggs, milk, baking powder and garlic salt until blended. Pour over layers. Sprinkle with cheddar cheese. Cover dish and refrigerate overnight.
3. Preheat oven to 350°. Remove strata from refrigerator while oven heats. Bake, uncovered, until puffed and golden at the edges, 35-40 minutes. Let stand for 10 minutes before serving. Serve with salsa.
1 piece: 338 cal., 20g fat (9g sat. fat), 282mg chol., 820mg sod., 13g carb. (3g sugars, 1g fiber), 27g pro.

COMPANY POT ROAST

The aroma of this roast slowly cooking gives the home a cozy feeling, even on the chilliest winter days.
—Anita Osborne, Thomasburg, ON

PREP: 20 min. • **BAKE:** 2¾ hours
MAKES: 6 servings

- 1 boneless beef chuck roast (3 to 4 lbs.)
- 2 Tbsp. olive oil
- 1 cup sherry or beef broth
- ½ cup reduced-sodium soy sauce
- ¼ cup sugar
- 2 tsp. beef bouillon granules
- 1 cinnamon stick (3 in.)
- 8 medium carrots, cut into 2-in. pieces
- 6 medium potatoes, peeled and cut into 1½-in. pieces
- 1 medium onion, sliced
- 2 Tbsp. cornstarch
- 2 Tbsp. cold water

1. Brown roast in oil in a Dutch oven on all sides; drain. Combine the sherry, soy sauce, sugar, bouillon and cinnamon stick; pour over roast.

2. Bake, covered, at 325° until meat and vegetables are tender, 2¾ to 3¼ hours. Add the carrots, potatoes and onion during the last 30 minutes of cooking.

3. Remove roast and vegetables to a serving platter; keep warm. Combine cornstarch and water until smooth. Stir into pan. Bring to a boil; cook and stir until thickened, about 2 minutes. Serve with roast and vegetables.

6 oz. cooked meat with 2 cups vegetables and ¼ cup gravy: 713 cal., 26g fat (9g sat. fat), 148mg chol., 1437mg sod., 56g carb. (17g sugars, 5g fiber), 49g pro.

FOR MEAL 2: Save 2 cups cooked beef for Takeout Beef Fried Rice, opposite page.

TAKEOUT BEEF FRIED RICE

Transform leftover cooked beef into a quick dinner for six. You can use chuck roast or flank steak.

—Taste of Home *Test Kitchen*

TAKES: 30 min.
MAKES: 6 servings

- 1 Tbsp. plus 1 tsp. canola oil, divided
- 3 large eggs
- 1 can (11 oz.) mandarin oranges
- 2 medium sweet red peppers, chopped
- 1 cup fresh sugar snap peas, trimmed
- 1 small onion, thinly sliced
- 3 garlic cloves, minced
- ½ tsp. crushed red pepper flakes
- 4 cups cold cooked rice
- 2 cups cooked beef, sliced across grain into bite-sized pieces
- 1 cup beef broth
- ¼ cup reduced-sodium soy sauce
- ½ tsp. salt
- ¼ tsp. ground ginger

1. In a large skillet, heat 1 Tbsp. oil over medium-high heat. Whisk eggs until blended; pour into hot skillet. The mixture should set immediately at its edge. As eggs set, push cooked egg toward center, letting uncooked portions flow underneath. When eggs are thickened and no liquid egg remains, remove to a cutting board and chop. Meanwhile, drain oranges, reserving 2 Tbsp. juice.

2. In same skillet, heat remaining 1 tsp. oil over medium-high heat. Add peppers, sugar snap peas and onion; cook and stir until crisp-tender, 1-2 minutes. Add garlic and pepper flakes; cook 1 minute longer. Add remaining ingredients and reserved juice; heat through. Gently stir in eggs and drained oranges.

1⅓ cups: 367 cal., 9g fat (2g sat. fat), 136mg chol., 793mg sod., 45g carb. (11g sugars, 3g fiber), 26g pro. **Diabetic exchanges:** 3 starch, 3 lean meat, 1 fat.

2 CUPS

A TENDER, SLOW-BAKED ROAST MAKES A DELICIOUS HOMEMADE VERSION OF A CARRY-OUT CLASSIC.

🌙 THE BEST PIZZA DOUGH

This easy dough is the key to making extraordinary pizza and calzones. You can use all-purpose flour, but if you live near an Italian market or can purchase double-zero flour online, it will take your crust to the next level.
—Josh Rink, Milwaukee, WI

PREP: 30 min. + chilling
MAKES: 2 crusts (8 servings each)

- 1¼ cups warm water (110° to 115°)
- 2 tsp. sugar, divided
- 1 pkg. (¼ oz.) active dry yeast
- 3½ to 4 cups all-purpose or 00 flour
- 1 tsp. sea salt
- 1 tsp. each dried basil, oregano and marjoram, optional
- ⅓ cup vegetable or olive oil

1. In a small bowl, mix warm water and 1 tsp. sugar; add yeast and whisk until dissolved. Let stand until bubbles form on surface. In a large bowl, whisk 3 cups flour, salt, remaining 1 tsp. sugar and, if desired, dried herbs. Make a well in center; add yeast mixture and oil. Stir until smooth. Add enough remaining flour to form a soft dough.

2. Turn dough onto a floured surface; knead, adding flour to surface as needed until no longer sticky and dough is smooth and elastic, 6-8 minutes. Place in a large greased bowl; turn once to grease top. Cover and let rise in a warm place for 30 minutes; transfer to refrigerator and chill overnight.

3. Allow dough to come to room temperature, about 30 minutes, before rolling.

1 piece: 144 cal., 5g fat (1g sat. fat), 0 chol., 121mg sod., 22g carb. (1g sugars, 1g fiber), 3g pro.

❄ THE BEST SAUSAGE PIZZAS

What makes this recipe unique is the slow overnight fermentation of the dough. The flour has time to hydrate and relax, which makes the dough so much easier to roll out!
—Josh Rink, Milwaukee, WI

PREP: 30 min. • **BAKE:** 15 min.
MAKES: 2 pizzas (8 slices each)

- 1 batch The Best Pizza Dough
- 1 lb. bulk Italian sausage
- 1 cup pizza sauce
- 4 cups shredded part-skim mozzarella cheese
- 1 medium red onion, sliced
- 1 medium green pepper, chopped
- 2 cups sliced fresh mushrooms
  Optional: Grated Parmesan cheese, crushed red pepper flakes and fresh oregano leaves

1. Divide dough in half. With greased fingers, pat each half onto an ungreased 12-in. pizza pan. Prick dough thoroughly with a fork. Bake at 400° until lightly browned, 10-12 minutes. Meanwhile, in a large skillet, cook the sausage over medium heat until no longer pink; drain.

2. Spread pizza sauce over crusts. Top with cheese, onion, green pepper, mushrooms and sausage. Bake at 400° until golden brown and cheese is bubbling, 12-15 minutes. If desired, top with grated Parmesan cheese, crushed red pepper flakes and fresh oregano leaves.

1 piece: 344 cal., 20g fat (7g sat. fat), 41mg chol., 651mg sod., 26g carb. (2g sugars, 1g fiber), 15g pro.

SUPER CALZONES

A friend gave this recipe to me at my wedding shower. I realized then and there that I'd better learn how to cook! My husband loves these handheld pizzas.
—Laronda Warrick, Parker, KS

PREP: 30 min. • **BAKE:** 20 min.
MAKES: 4 servings

- ½ lb. ground beef
- 2 Tbsp. finely chopped onion
- 2 Tbsp. finely chopped green pepper
- 1 garlic clove, minced
- 1 can (15 oz.) tomato sauce
- 1 tsp. Italian seasoning
- 1 tube (13.8 oz.) refrigerated pizza crust
- 3 oz. cream cheese, softened
- 1 cup shredded part-skim mozzarella cheese
- 1 can (4 oz.) mushroom stems and pieces, drained
- 1 can (2¼ oz.) sliced ripe olives, drained

1. Preheat oven to 400°. In a large skillet, cook beef, onion, green pepper and garlic over medium heat, breaking beef into crumbles until no longer pink, 5-7 minutes. Drain and set aside.

2. In a small saucepan, bring the tomato sauce and Italian seasoning to a boil. Reduce heat; cover and simmer for 5 minutes. Stir ½ cup into the meat mixture; keep remaining sauce warm.

3. Unroll pizza crust onto a floured surface. Roll into a 12-in. square; cut into quarters. Spread cream cheese over each to within ½ in. of edges. Top with meat mixture. Sprinkle with mozzarella cheese, mushrooms and olives.

4. Fold dough over filling, forming a triangle; press edges with a fork to seal. Place on a greased baking sheet.

5. Bake until golden brown, 20-25 minutes. Serve with the remaining sauce.

1 calzone: 541 cal., 24g fat (11g sat. fat), 67mg chol., 1552mg sod., 58g carb. (10g sugars, 4g fiber), 28g pro.

TEST KITCHEN TIP

Homemade pizza dough can be kept in the refrigerator for up to 5 days or frozen for up to 3 months. It can be used in place of commercial refrigerated or frozen dough in most recipes, so it's convenient to have on hand. To use, let it come to room temperature (if frozen, thaw it in the fridge overnight first), then roll it out.

1 CRUST HOMEMADE PIZZA DOUGH IN THE FRIDGE OR FREEZER MAKES CALZONES A SNAP!

BONUS—COOK ONCE, EAT TWICE **247**

🍲 MEXICAN PORK

The first time I made this dish, it was a hit with everyone in my family, both young and old. Serve with black beans and white rice, or use as meat for tacos, enchiladas or tamales!
—Amy Vazquez, Brandon, MS

PREP: 20 min. • **COOK:** 8 hours
MAKES: 18 servings

- 1 bone-in pork shoulder roast (4 to 5 lbs.)
- 1 can (28 oz.) enchilada sauce
- 1 large green pepper, chopped
- 1 medium onion, finely chopped
- 2 garlic cloves, minced
- ¼ cup minced fresh cilantro
- 1 Tbsp. lime juice
- 1½ tsp. grated lime zest
  Flour tortillas (8 in.), optional
  Toppings of your choice

1. Cut roast in half; place in a 4- or 5-qt. slow cooker. Top with enchilada sauce, green pepper, onion and garlic. Cook, covered, on low until meat is tender, 8-10 hours.
2. Remove roast; cool slightly. Skim fat from cooking juices. Remove meat from bone; discard bone. Shred pork with 2 forks and return to slow cooker.
3. Stir in the cilantro, lime juice and lime zest; heat through. Using a slotted spoon, serve on tortillas, if desired, with toppings of your choice.

½ cup pork: 162 cal., 9g fat (3g sat. fat), 51mg chol., 280mg sod., 4g carb. (1g sugars, 1g fiber), 17g pro.
FOR MEAL 2: Save 2 cups shredded meat for Chunky Chipotle Chili, opposite page.

✳ CHUNKY CHIPOTLE PORK CHILI

Perfect for using leftover pork roast, this tasty, easy recipe can be made ahead and reheated. It's even better the second day.
—*Peter Halferty, Corpus Christi, TX*

PREP: 15 min. • **COOK:** 20 min.
MAKES: 4 servings

- 1 medium green pepper, chopped
- 1 small onion, chopped
- 1 chipotle pepper in adobo sauce, finely chopped
- 1 Tbsp. canola oil
- 3 garlic cloves, minced
- 1 can (16 oz.) red beans, rinsed and drained
- 1 cup beef broth
- ½ cup salsa
- 2 tsp. ground cumin
- 2 tsp. chili powder
- 2 cups shredded cooked pork
- ¼ cup sour cream
  Sliced jalapeno pepper, optional

1. In a large saucepan, saute the green pepper, onion and chipotle pepper in oil until tender. Add garlic; cook 1 minute longer.
2. Add the beans, broth, salsa, cumin and chili powder. Bring to a boil. Reduce heat; simmer, uncovered, until thickened, about 10 minutes. Add pork; heat through. Serve with sour cream and, if desired, jalapeno slices.

1 cup: 340 cal., 14g fat (4g sat. fat), 73mg chol., 834mg sod., 24g carb. (3g sugars, 7g fiber), 27g pro.

FREEZE OPTION

Cool chili and transfer to freezer containers. Freeze up to 3 months. To use, thaw in the refrigerator. Transfer to a large saucepan to heat through; add water to thin if desired. Serve with sour cream.

2 CUPS
START WITH TACOS OR ENCHILADAS, FOLLOW WITH A ZESTY SOUTHWESTERN CHILI

❅ CHEESE-STUFFED SHELLS

When I was living in California, I loved a rich cheesy pasta dish at a neighborhood Italian restaurant. I got the recipe, made a few changes to it and now I think it's even better!
—Lori Mecca, Grants Pass, OR

PREP: 35 min. **BAKE:** 50 min.
MAKES: 12 servings (2 casseroles)

- 1 lb. bulk Italian sausage
- 1 large onion, chopped
- 1 pkg. (10 oz.) frozen chopped spinach, thawed and squeezed dry
- 1 pkg. (8 oz.) cream cheese, cubed
- 1 large egg, lightly beaten
- 2 cups shredded part-skim mozzarella cheese, divided
- 2 cups shredded cheddar cheese
- 1 cup 4% cottage cheese
- 1 cup grated Parmesan cheese
- ¼ tsp. salt
- ¼ tsp. pepper
- ⅛ tsp. ground cinnamon, optional
- 24 jumbo pasta shells, cooked and drained

SAUCE
- 1 can (29 oz.) tomato sauce
- 1 Tbsp. dried minced onion
- 1½ tsp. dried basil
- 1½ tsp. dried parsley flakes
- 2 garlic cloves, minced
- 1 tsp. sugar
- 1 tsp. dried oregano
- ½ tsp. salt
- ¼ tsp. pepper

1. In a large skillet, cook sausage and onion over medium heat until meat is no longer pink; drain. Transfer to a large bowl. Stir in spinach, cream cheese and egg. Add 1 cup mozzarella cheese, the cheddar cheese, cottage cheese, Parmesan cheese, salt, pepper and, if desired, cinnamon.
2. Stuff pasta shells with sausage mixture. Arrange in 2 shallow 2-qt. or 11x7-in. baking dishes coated with cooking spray. Combine sauce ingredients; spoon over shells.
3. Cover and bake at 350° for 45 minutes. Uncover; sprinkle with remaining mozzarella. Bake until bubbly and cheese is melted, 5-10 minutes longer. Let stand 5 minutes before serving.
2 stuffed shells: 397 cal., 23g fat (14g sat. fat), 94mg chol., 1097mg sod., 24g carb. (5g sugars, 2g fiber), 24g pro.

> ┌ **FREEZE OPTION** ─────
>
> Cool unbaked casseroles; cover and freeze. To use, partially thaw in refrigerator overnight. Remove from refrigerator 30 minutes before baking. Cover casserole with foil; bake at 350° for 50 minutes. Uncover; bake until heated through and a thermometer inserted in center reads 165°. 15-20 minutes longer.

❄ 2-FOR-1 CHICKEN TETRAZZINI

A good friend shared a version of this recipe with me 35 years ago. I pay it forward by taking the second casserole to friends when they are unable to cook.
—Helen McPhee, Savoy, IL

PREP: 30 min. • **BAKE:** 20 min.
MAKES: 2 casseroles
(4 servings each)

- 1   pkg. (12 oz.) spaghetti
- ⅓ cup butter, cubed
- ⅓ cup all-purpose flour
- ¾ tsp. salt
- ¼ tsp. white pepper
- 1   can (14½ oz.) chicken broth
- 1½ cups half-and-half cream
- 1   cup heavy whipping cream
- 4   cups cubed cooked chicken
- 3   cans (4 oz. each) mushroom stems and pieces, drained
- 1   jar (4 oz.) sliced pimientos, drained
- ½ cup grated Parmesan cheese

1. Cook spaghetti according to package directions. In a Dutch oven, melt butter. Stir in the flour, salt and pepper until smooth. Gradually add the broth, half-and-half and whipping cream. Bring to a boil; cook and stir until thickened, about 2 minutes.
2. Remove from the heat. Stir in the chicken, mushrooms and pimientos. Drain spaghetti; add to the chicken mixture and toss to coat.
3. Transfer to 2 greased 11x7-in. baking dishes. Sprinkle with cheese. Cover and freeze 1 casserole for up to 2 months. Bake the second casserole, uncovered, at 350° until heated through, 20-25 minutes.
1 cup: 576 cal., 30g fat (17g sat. fat), 144mg chol., 814mg sod., 41g carb. (4g sugars, 2g fiber), 31g pro.

FREEZE OPTION

To use frozen casserole Thaw in the refrigerator overnight. Cover and bake at 350° for 30 minutes. Uncover; bake until heated through. 15-20 minutes longer. Stir before serving.

❄ SIMPLE SHEPHERD'S PIE

This classic recipe makes one pie to eat right away and one batch of meat mixture to freeze for another day. Just pull out the frozen beef any time you have some leftover mashed potatoes.
—Paula Zsiray, Logan, UT

PREP: 10 min. • **BAKE:** 30 min.
MAKES: 2 casseroles
(4 servings each)

- 2 lbs. ground beef
- 2 cans (12 oz. each) home-style beef gravy
- 2 cups frozen corn
- 2 cups frozen peas and carrots
- 2 tsp. dried minced onion

ADDITIONAL INGREDIENTS (FOR EACH CASSEROLE)
- 2 to 3 cups mashed potatoes
- 2 Tbsp. butter, melted
  Paprika

1. In a Dutch oven, cook beef over medium heat until no longer pink, breaking beef into crumbles, 6-8 minutes; drain. Add the gravy, vegetables and onion. Spoon half into a greased 2-qt. baking dish or 4 oven-safe 2-cup dishes.
Top with mashed potatoes. Drizzle with butter and sprinkle with paprika.
2. Bake, uncovered, at 350° until heated through, 30-35 minutes.
3. Place the remaining beef mixture in a freezer container and freeze for up to 3 months.
1 cup: 380 cal., 20g fat (8g sat. fat), 80mg chol., 776mg sod., 24g carb. (1g sugars, 3g fiber), 27g pro.

FREEZE OPTION

To prepare frozen casserole: Thaw in the refrigerator overnight. Transfer to a greased 2-qt. baking dish. Top with mashed potatoes, butter and paprika; bake as directed.

❄ CHICKEN & CHEESE NOODLE BAKE

This is the meal my daughters and I often make for new parents when they come home from the hospital. Recently I served this for our Wednesday night church supper and was asked for the recipe by many people. The cheeses truly make the dish!
—Fancheon Resler, Albion, IN

PREP: 20 min. • **BAKE:** 25 min.
MAKES: 2 casseroles
(6 servings each)

- 1 **pkg. (16 oz.) spaghetti, broken**
- 2 **medium onions, chopped**
- 1 **medium green pepper, chopped**
- 1 **medium sweet red pepper, chopped**
- ½ **cup butter, cubed**
- 6 **Tbsp. all-purpose flour**
- 2 **cups 2% milk**
- 4 **cups cubed cooked chicken**
- 1 **can (10¾ oz.) condensed cream of chicken and mushroom soup, undiluted**
- 1 **can (10¾ oz.) condensed cream of mushroom soup, undiluted**
- 1 **cup sour cream**
- ½ **tsp. celery salt**
- ½ **tsp. pepper**
- 2 **cups shredded part-skim mozzarella cheese**
- 1 **cup shredded cheddar cheese**

1. Preheat oven to 350°. Cook spaghetti according to the package directions.

2. Meanwhile, in a Dutch oven, saute onions and peppers in butter until tender. Stir in flour until blended; gradually add milk. Bring to a boil; cook and stir until thickened, about 2 minutes. Stir in chicken, soups, sour cream, celery salt and pepper.

3. Drain spaghetti; add to sauce mixture and toss to coat. Transfer to 2 greased 11x7-in. baking dishes. Sprinkle with cheeses. Bake, covered, 20 minutes. Uncover and bake until bubbly, 5-10 minutes longer.

1 cup: 509 cal., 24g fat (13g sat. fat), 102mg chol., 691mg sod., 42g carb. (7g sugars, 3g fiber), 29g pro.

FREEZE OPTION

Cover and freeze unbaked casseroles up to 3 months. To use, partially thaw in refrigerator overnight. Remove from refrigerator 30 minutes before baking. Preheat oven to 350°. Cover casserole with foil; bake as directed, increasing covered time to 40 minutes or until heated through and a thermometer inserted in the center reads 165°. Uncover; bake casserole until bubbly, 5-10 minutes longer.

Index

Index (continued)